HOWE'S
TRANSCENDENTAL
TOYBOX
PRESENTS

UNOFFICIAL AND UNAUTHORISED

BLAKE'S 7
THE MERCHANDISE GUIDE

UNOFFICIAL AND UNAUTHORISED

BLAKE'S 7
THE MERCHANDISE GUIDE

MARK B OLIVER

First published in the UK in 2012 by
Telos Publishing Ltd
17 Pendre Avenue, Prestatyn, Denbighshire, LL19 9SH, UK
www.telos.co.uk

Telos Publishing Ltd values feedback. Please e-mail us with any comments you may have
about this book to: feedback@telos.co.uk

ISBN: 978-1-84583-059-5 (paperback)

Internal design, typesetting and layout by Arnold T Blumberg.

Printed in England by Berforts Group Ltd

British Library Cataloguing in Publication Data.
A catalogue record for this book is available from the British Library.

CONTENTS

To
Terry, David, Chris and Vere

IT is a testament to Terry Nation's ingenuity, and the dedication, skill and sheer talent of all involved in the production of *Blake's 7* that the series is so fondly remembered today. The number of people and organisations that have gone out of their way to assist with this guide is frankly astonishing, all of whom seem to remember the series with great affection.

So in alphabetical order my heartfelt thanks go out to: 10th Planet Events, John Ainsworth, Neil Alsop, Tony Attwood, John Archdeacon, The BBC Written Archive, Todd Beilby, Keith Barnfather, Trevor Baxendale, Phil Bhullar, Chris Boucher, Wakefield Carter, John Cartmell, Daniel Cohen, Comet Miniatures Ltd., Sue Cowley, Kevin Jon Davies, Patrick Devanney, Fabulous Films Ltd, Barry Ford, Diane Gies, Jason Haigh-Ellery, Gary Holland, Russ Jenkins, Just Entertainment Ltd, Derek Hambly, Andy Hopkinson, Jean Hopkinson, Trevor Hoyle, Andrew Kearley, Ian Kennedy, Rob Kirby, Julian Knott, Kevin Kobos, Richard Leon, Shaqui Le Vesconte, Alistair Lock, Damian May, Una McCormack, Fiona Moore, Joel Nation, Kate Nation, Simon Peters of Roadshow Entertainment NZ, Michael Reccia, David Richardson, John Roulston-Bates, Jim Sangster, *Sci-fi & Fantasy Modeller*, Sci-Fi South Collectors, Paul Scoones, Frank Setchfield – Badge Collectors Circle, Warwick Sharpin, The Stamp Centre, Alan Stevens, Lewis Tarrant, Pam Tarrant, Janneke ten Dam, Mark J Thompson, Paul Vyse, Richard Walker and Matt West.

While all have provided invaluable assistance, special thanks must go to Andrew Pixley without whom the section on Audio Themes would be tragically poor, and who seems to proofread faster than I can breathe. He is truly a splendid fellow and I couldn't be more grateful for his considerable help, encouragement and knowledge.

Gary Russell suggested that my pet project could be published, so if you enjoy this guide, your thanks must go to him. If you dislike it, then that would be my fault entirely.

Chris Tarrant is a man with an impressive *Blake's 7* collection, who invited me into his home one Saturday afternoon, so I could take photos galore. I was previously unaware that it was his wife's 40th birthday that day and a party in her honour was due to start a few hours later. The couple hadn't wanted to let me down knowing I was only in the country a few days.

David VanRiper has taken the most inept of my photographs complete with dishwashers, cats and dogs in the background and turned them into the masterpieces printed on these pages.

Andrew Williams has both a remarkable memory and terrific *Blake's 7* collection. It is a wonder of this modern age that I can owe so much to a man I have never met and who lives on the opposite side of the world. He has provided everything from proofreading services and interesting snippets of information to photographs of long since forgotten merchandise.

Despite all this help, any errors contained within are but my own, which will annoy me much more than you when pointed out. I hope that is small consolation for any mistakes or omissions you might find.

ABOUT THE GUIDE

It all started out so simply, a pet project to update the two or three page merchandise guides for the BBC television series *Blake's 7* that appeared in a few cult magazines in the 1980's. That couldn't take long now could it? After all, there were just a few books and annuals and the videos of course... Ah the optimism and folly of youth.

This book is the result of many hours scouring the internet, begging both friends and strangers to go into the darkest recesses of their attics in search of that 'final' item I was missing, and thousands of miles of globe-trotting to take photographs so that each and every item could be presented in glorious colour.

CRITERIA

So what's included? This guide is an attempt to fully catalogue all professionally produced *Blake's 7* merchandise, both licensed

and unlicensed, released on or before 31 December 2011. The advent of desktop publishing moved fanzines away from grainy black and white photocopies, into shiny, professional quality magazines. Of course fan produced items aren't limited to the written word, with fan ingenuity filling merchandising gaps. A visit to a *Blake's 7* convention led to a virtual Aladdin's cave with *Blake's 7* clocks, teddy bears, umbrellas and wall mirrors to name but a few. Several extremely talented artists produced everything from ACEOs (Artist Cards Editions and Original), to limited edition prints.

Professionally made prop replicas have been commissioned over the years, with some being made available through Horizon – The *Blake's 7* Appreciation Society and others direct from the model maker. These replicas fall outside the scope of this guide.

The aim of the guide, is to catalogue those items that were available to buy by the general public, not members of fandom (of which in case it wasn't clear already, I have been since the series first aired on BBC1). Like most rules, I have taken liberties on occasion including items that fall outside of these criteria (stand up *The Horizon Blake's 7 Technical Manual*) because to not include them would be a disservice to both the reader and the people behind these projects.

I apologise in advance if I didn't bend this rule often enough, but hopefully there will be much for even the most ardent fan to discover.

ABBREVIATIONS

These are included to decrease word count, increase readability and to explain such things as 'LPs' to those born after 1986.

Audio
C: Cassette.
CD: Compact Disk. If followed by a number in parentheses it indicates the number of disks.
EP: Extended Playing Record.
LP: Long Playing Record.
7": Seven inch single record.
12": Twelve inch single record.

Books
h/b: Hardback.
p/b: Paperback.
ISBN: International Standard Book Number. The ISBN system allocates all published books with a thirteen digit number (prior to 1 January 2007, a ten digit number).
ISSN: International Standard Serial Number. Both the ISBN and ISSN numbering systems are used for books in a series and with annuals or biennials. The ISBN identifies the individual book in a series or a specific year for an annual or biennial. The ISSN identifies the ongoing series, or the ongoing annual or biennial serial.

Other
DWM: A magazine devoted to the BBC television show *Doctor Who*. Initially entitled *Doctor Who Weekly* it subsequently changed its named to *Doctor Who Monthly* upon assuming a monthly publication schedule

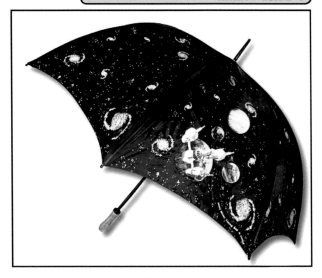

with effect from issue 44. Its name changed once more to *Doctor Who Magazine* when it commenced publication every four weeks.

RRP: Original recommended retail price.

Video
Betamax: A home video cassette recording format.
DVD: Digital Versatile Disk. If followed by a number in parentheses it indicates the number of disks.
DVD-R: A recordable DVD that cannot be rewritten.
VHS: Video Home System is a home video cassette recording format.

RARITY GUIDE

Blake's 7 produced a wide array of merchandise but only a limited amount was produced during the show's original terrestrial broadcast in the United Kingdom. In the days before the internet and before *Blake's 7 Magazine* that accompanied season 4, the availability of merchandise for consumers to purchase was a subject of chance. While the Corgi *Liberator* models were widely available across the country, the Jotastar and Blue Box items were less widely distributed and are rarer as a result.

This guide, in addition to the original retail price will, where possible, indicate the rarity of an item, in a near mint condition. Generally this means that all packaging is intact and crease free, any 'blister' packs have not yellowed with age or split, all print items are flat and crease free and without missing or damaged pages, all metallic items are not subject to rust or other corrosion, badges are scratch free, all mechanisms work and clothing is unworn and should not be faded. As an example a good condition white Corgi *Liberator* toy could sell for £2 to £10. In its original undamaged blister pack however, it will likely sell in the £30 to £80 range.

As the market for *Blake's 7* items is somewhat limited, with the rarer items only coming up for sale very infrequently, this guide does not seek to determine the current market value of an item. Similar items on various internet auction sites can sell at large price differentials. Accordingly this guide will grade each item as follows:

🗩 Freely available.
🗩 🗩 Limited availability in near mint condition.
🗩 🗩 🗩 Rare.
🗩 🗩 🗩 🗩 Extremely rare in near mint condition.
🗩 🗩 🗩 🗩 🗩 Extremely rare, with or without packaging.

CONSISTENCY

The logo seen on screen for the first three seasons and indeed the revised logo for the fourth season referred to *Blakes 7* without an apostrophe. While grammatically incorrect

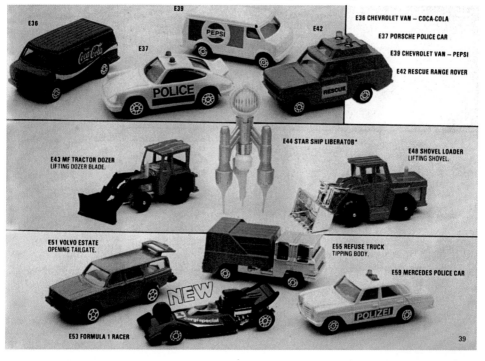

E36 CHEVROLET VAN – COCA-COLA
E37 PORSCHE POLICE CAR
E39 CHEVROLET VAN – PEPSI
E42 RESCUE RANGE ROVER
E43 MF TRACTOR DOZER LIFTING DOZER BLADE.
E44 STAR SHIP LIBERATOR*
E48 SHOVEL LOADER LIFTING SHOVEL.
E51 VOLVO ESTATE OPENING TAILGATE.
E53 FORMULA 1 RACER
E55 REFUSE TRUCK TIPPING BODY.
E59 MERCEDES POLICE CAR

this has been taken as the name of the series. This creates a problem when referring to merchandise as while most licensed product will display the series logo, when in print format, the show is commonly referred to as *Blake's 7*. As an example, Trevor Hoyle's second novelization has the series logo on the front cover (so no apostrophe) and the subtitle *Project Avalon*. On the spine however the book is titled *Blake's 7 Project Avalon*.

For consistency, this guide will include the apostrophe and the series and associated merchandise will be referenced as *Blake's 7*.

The production code for the first series of *Blake's 7* was 'Season A' with the alphabetical code continuing through seasons B and C, with the final season being season D. Merchandise however, when referring to a particular season of *Blake's 7*, refers to seasons 1 through 4. While technically incorrect, this guide will refer to each season numerically rather than alphabetically.

INTRODUCTION

Terry Nation created *Blake's 7* in 1975 having already found considerable success as a comedy writer and script writer for action adventure series and most notably for creating the Daleks for *Doctor Who*. It was through the Daleks that Nation was first introduced to the importance of merchandising, something that while commonplace in television and film today, was little thought of back in the 1960s.

By his mid-twenties Nation, who was born in 1930, found himself working on radio scripts for some of the biggest names in comedy such as Frankie Howerd, Terry Scott and Eric Sykes. In 1961, the hugely popular comedian Tony Hancock severed his relationship with his long term writers Ray Galton and Alan Simpson (who would shortly after create *Steptoe and Son*) and moved from the BBC to ATV. Terry Nation was commissioned to write alongside Godfrey Harrison for the new ATV television series and for Hancock's stage show. During this time, Nation contributed three scripts to the ABC science fiction anthology series *Out of this World*, which was broadcast in 1962. This drew him to the attention of David Whitaker who was the script editor for the new BBC television series *Doctor Who*. Nation declined to write for the science fiction series and continued to work on the Hancock scripts. In 1963, Hancock and Nation ended their working relationship after Hancock continually failed to use Nation's material. Economic necessity made Nation reappraise his rejection of Whitaker's offer

and he accepted a commission to write a seven part story, which would be the second *Doctor Who* serial to be transmitted.

The first of the seven scripts comprising the *Doctor Who* story, 'The Dead Planet', was transmitted on 21 December 1963 and the cliff-hanger ending saw the character of Barbara Wright terrified at the sight of something almost entirely off-screen with just a plunger arm being visible to viewers. The following Saturday, the Daleks, with their electronic voices and now legendary design by Raymond P Cusick, both terrified and enthralled the audience and Dalekmania was born. Children across the nation were gripped by Dalek fever; cries of 'Exterminate' could be heard in every playground, parents sought to make costumes for their offspring and Verity Lambert, the producer of *Doctor Who*, quickly commissioned Nation to write another Dalek story, despite their apparent demise at the conclusion of their debut.

The demand for Dalek merchandise was insatiable and the product range extensive. Items produced included pencils, writing pads, pottery, toy guns, PVC costumes, transfers, snow globes, candy, annuals and of course numerous toy Daleks. As Nation's agent, Beryl Vertue, had astutely negotiated that he retain jointly with the BBC the copyright to the likeness and characters of the Daleks; both the corporation and Nation benefited greatly from the merchandising boom. The height of Dalekmania was probably reached in the summer of 1965, concurrent with the transmission of Nation's third Dalek story, entitled 'The Chase'.

Following the transmission of his fourth Dalek story 'The Daleks' Master Plan' which was co-written with Dennis Spooner, the now much-in-demand Nation concentrated instead on (unsuccessfully) launching the Daleks in the United States and writing scripts for shows such as *The Avengers*, *The*

Persuaders!, *Department S* and *The Saint*. Subsequent *Doctor Who* Dalek stories were written by David Whitaker and with the 1967 serial 'The Evil of the Daleks' Whitaker wrote what was intended to be the final appearance of the Daleks in *Doctor Who*. In 1972 however, Nation gave permission for the Daleks to reappear in the *Doctor Who* story 'Day of the Daleks' and in 1973 Nation agreed to write the six part serial 'Planet of the Daleks', returning to pen two more Dalek serials in 1974 and 1975.

This renewed Nation's contact with the BBC, and, aware that there wouldn't be a second series of *The Persuaders!*, led Nation to pitch two potential series to Andrew Osborn, the Head of Series at the BBC; *Beyond Omega* and *The Incredible Dr Baldick*.

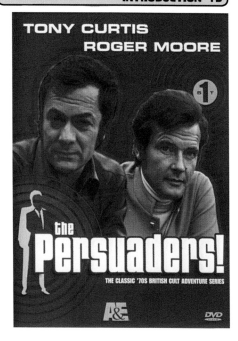

TONY CURTIS
ROGER MOORE

the Persuaders!

THE CLASSIC '70S BRITISH CULT ADVENTURE SERIES

The first concerned the struggle for survival in a post-apocalyptic world, the second was a 'Victorian Gothic Suspense' series. Both pilots were commissioned for the second season of *Drama Playhouse*, which the BBC used to gauge audience reaction and so was a potential launching pad for a full series. The three-part first season of *Drama Playhouse* resulted in full season orders of both *The Regiment* and the hugely successful *The Onedin Line*.

Unable to deliver both scripts in the required timeframe, it was agreed with Osborn that Nation would drop *Beyond Omega* and instead concentrate on what would become *The Incredible Robert Baldick*. The producer of *Drama Playhouse* was Anthony Coburn and Robert Hardy played the title character. During production, a series commission seemed likely and a production team was assembled. The intended transmission date of 23 August 1972 would kick off the second season of *Drama Playhouse*. Unexpected legal difficulties arose over the use of the title character's name (Robert Baldick was a friend of Nation's and Baldick's death in April led to his son objecting to the use of his father's name), resulting in the production being moved to the third transmission slot on 6 September 1972, with the pilot for *Sutherland's Law* moving forward to fill the vacant gap.

The Black September massacre on 5 September 1972 at the Munich Olympics resulted in *The Incredible Robert Baldick* being removed from the schedules. It was eventually transmitted on 2 October 1972. A series was never commissioned, instead *Sutherland's Law* would run for five seasons.

Nation and Coburn enjoyed a good working relationship during production of *The Incredible Robert Baldick* and in May 1972 the pair discussed the *Beyond Omega* outline. At Coburn's suggestion Nation wrote scripts and character outlines for a

The remnants of humanity struggle for survival in a post-technological world: a haunting, prophetic novel of the near future.

SURVIVORS

TERRY NATION

FUTURA

proposed series on which Coburn would act as producer. The scripts and character outlines were delivered to Osborn in late 1973. Osborn commissioned a thirteen part series but appointed Terrence Dudley as producer not Coburn. The renamed series became *Survivors*, and told the story of a group of people who had survived a biological disaster that devastates the planet's population.

While heavily involved in the first of its three seasons, Nation found himself at odds with Dudley on the future direction of the show and left to concentrate on other work. The first episode of *Survivors* was transmitted in April 1975 and shortly after Nation attended a meeting at the BBC to discuss ideas for future programmes. Also in attendance was Ronnie Marsh, Head of Drama Series, who was particularly taken

with one of Nation's ideas, documenting the idea as a 'Cracking Boys Own/kidult sci-fi. A space-western adventure. A modern swashbuckler'. Nation was commissioned to write a pilot episode for *Blake's 7*, as the show was now called, on 11 September 1975, and this was delivered in April 1976. The second episode was commissioned on 4 June 1976 with four more scripts commissioned in November 1976. The intention was for Nation to write all thirteen scripts that would make up the first season (which would end on a cliff-hanger) and the first episode of the second season, with an option to write further scripts after that.

With six scripts commissioned by the end of November 1976, and prior to a full production team being in place, initial discussions about merchandising were held. Dalekmania had taken both the BBC and Nation by surprise in the sixties and this time both wanted to be prepared. The nature of the show meant that Nation would be able to incorporate new gadgets, ships, and space weaponry into virtually every episode that he was to write and so create a large number of products to be licensed. An example of this was the Federation security robot which Nation included in the scripts for 'Time Squad' and 'Seek-Locate-Destroy'. Despite being included in promotional photographs (taken during the location filming for 'Bounty') an unimaginative design and the difficulty of using the prop on location hampered the robot's appearance in the series and it was quietly dropped.

THE MERCHANDISE

At the start of June 1977, prior to any principal shooting taking place, the BBC issued a five page press release to announce the series and to act as an incentive to merchandisers to purchase licences. Mention is made of the fact that Nation created the Daleks and that 'the special aim of the series is to provide family viewing and it is designed to appeal to a very large audience in a wide age group'. It further stated that 'toy manufacturers, publishers and product advertisers have already responded to the series with great enthusiasm and a huge range of merchandise is planned for release to coincide with the programme's launch'. After fully describing the series and the seven characters that comprised *Blake's 7*, the release described the flexibility of the format, with the genesis of this section clearly being the meeting held in the preceding December. 'A very essential feature of the series will be the specially designed equipment. Starting with the space ship itself and going through weapons; hand guns; laser swords; communicators; teleport bracelets; utility belts (a power pack fixed to a belt from which numerous gadgets can be operated); survival kits; locators and so on. New equipment will appear in almost every episode of the series'. It further elaborated '[on] board the *Liberator* is a teleport section, a flight deck and a space laboratory. Surface vehicles are stored on board. There are space capsules for limited space travel. In short, there is no limit to the product range that can be genuinely attributed to *Blake's 7*.

Initial interest from merchandisers was impressive and numerous options were purchased to produce items related to the show, with both Videomaster and Palitoy signing agreements as early as March 1977.

The Videomaster option was for a video shooting game, while Palitoy sought to produce 'figures, board game, talking vehicle, painting sets, play suit and accessories such as guns and communicators'.

Thomas Salter signed a licence on 15 June 1977 for Space Station kits, Poster Art kits, Moon Creepers and Mission kits.

By this time, commencement of principal photography was still several months away (it began on 29 September 1977 with the location work for the episode 'Time Squad') and manufacturers had yet to receive the visual reference material that they would need to develop their product lines. This led to Palitoy writing to the BBC on 14 July 1977 as it had decided not to proceed with the clothing and accessories for children 'as this is easily the longest lead in time in terms of development'. Palitoy proposed splitting the licence with its sister company, Denys Fisher who would develop the figure range and boxed board game, with Palitoy pursuing the painting sets and talking vehicles.

In August, Roger Hancock instructed the BBC to write to those firms that had been issued licences to give them a deadline of 9 September for return of signed copies and payment of advances. Those letters were to stress that none of the negotiations were subject to visuals or casting details being available and the letters were sent as requested.

On 6 September 1977 Roger Hancock telephoned A D J Hanson of BBC Enterprises and stated that he and Terry Nation would stick to their guns on this issue. They were unconcerned even if everyone dropped out as they believed that when the series appeared on screen there would be a queue for licences.

Internal BBC correspondence shows that Mr Hanson was less optimistic when, later that day, he wrote to R Williams, Head of BBC Merchandising, informing him that 'other companies have made enquiries following the mailshot but all wish to see something before committing themselves, preferably an episode. It seems to me therefore that, in spite of all the big talk earlier in the year, we are back to normal on this and should arrange a launch when there is something to show except for those that have paid or might do so in the meantime'.

Discussions continued with merchandisers but some, such as Videomaster, decided not to proceed. Denys Fisher meanwhile was now interested (in addition to a board game and figures) in plastic vehicles, plastic construction kits, painting sets, the Federation Dome, transporter bracelets, a spaceship hanger and a map reader.

In November 1977, the BBC reiterated its belief to licensees that the Birmingham Toy Fair that was to begin on 14 January 1978 was vital to the merchandising effort. With the series set to debut less than two weeks earlier (on 2 January 1978) *Blake's 7* would be enjoying a high public profile through the duration of the fair. The BBC hoped that all of the licensees would join in the effort to maximise publicity.

Lyons Maid, uninvolved with the upcoming toy fair as they produced consumables, signed an option on 10 November 1977 to produce 'ice confectionary including iced lollies' for twelve months from 1978.

On the same day, Denys Fisher wrote to BBC Enterprises to inform them that at this point in time they would not be proceeding with *Blake's 7* products for 1978. This was because there was 'no way in which we can have any form of product available in proto-type stage for the Toy Fair which opens in Birmingham on January 14th and bearing in mind lead times for tooling and production it is very unlikely that we would have any products available for distribution prior to July 1978'. Their Director of Marketing, Christopher Tailby, did however further state that 'if we were to receive all of the visual references we require, I think that we would be likely to reconsider our decision. However I must emphasise that these references would be required immediately'.

Communication Vectors signed a licence on 3 February 1978 to produce metal badges, with Jotastar Limited buying a licence on 3 May 1978 for 'the Laser gun, the Federation gun and the Federation helmet'.

Letraset showed interest in early 1978, and signed an option for rub down transfers featuring the space vehicles from the series together with the character likenesses of Blake, Jenna, Avon, Cally, Vila and Gan on 7 June 1978.

Meanwhile the prevailing economic climate continued to deteriorate. The UK

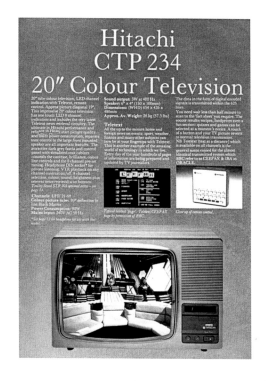

economy had been in decline since the late 1960's resulting in a break down between successive governments and the trade unions. By 1973-1974 the continued economic deterioration and the oil crisis of 1973 led to a three day week. Despite some relative calm in the ensuing years by 1978, relationships had soured to such an extent that trade unions repeatedly went on strike seeking higher pay for members while the government sought to maintain a pay freeze to control spiralling inflation. This was later dubbed 'The Winter of Discontent'.

In the space of a month, three of the primary merchandisers withdrew; Lyons Maid on 22 August, Letraset on 13 September and Thomas Salter on 21 September 1978. By this time Denys Fisher was only pursuing the board game which was ultimately withdrawn due to a poor reception from both children and retailers.

This reduced the number of licensees to a handful; Blue Boy Toys (spaceships), Communication Vectors (badges), Jotastar (Federation and *Liberator* guns), Palitoy (die cast vehicles), Sphere Books (novelisations), and World Distributors (annuals).

SERIES IMPACT

Blake's 7 ran for four seasons and fifty-two episodes, concluding in December 1981 during which time it had entered the general public awareness well beyond what its (impressive) viewing figures would suggest. Radio DJ Terry Wogan's near constant comments on his radio show, Hitachi using images from the series in print advertisements for television sets, the producers of the *Battle Beyond the Stars* film specifically referencing the series in its UK

£1.50

COMET
MINIATURES

46-48 LAVENDER HILL LONDON SW11 5RH
Tel: 0171-228 3702 (day) 0181-200 6126 (eve)

MODEL & TOY
CATALOGUE
AUTUMN/WINTER 1995/1996

poster campaign, and the letters read out on the BBC's *Points of View* programme helped raise the show's profile. Even television critic Clive James' less than flattering comments in his column in the *Observer*, some of which can be found in his book *Glued to the Box* (1983, Jonathan Cape, ISBN: 0 224 020668) increased public awareness of the series.

This in turn led to the series being referenced in the unlikeliest of merchandise. The English comic *Jackpot* printed a 'Jake's Seven' comic strip, in a series that also included such gems as 'The Incredible Sulk' and 'Angel's Charlies'. With perhaps the most subtle being the incorporation of the series into a cookbook with the 'Flake 7 Rocket' recipe found in *Cadbury's Novelty Cookbook* by Patricia Dunbar (1983, Hamlyn, ISBN: 0 600 32322 6).

Blake's 7 aired in the United States in the mid 1980's and developed a cult following. Merchandise was produced in an attempt to satisfy the demand of the American market and the release of the entire series on VHS in the early 1990's led to yet further interest in the series and merchandise growth which continues to this day. Metrostar Media is currently (as of end 2011) marketing *Blake's 7* to potential licensees and new products are planned for release.

AUDIO

The series theme is the most prolific piece of merchandise to have been made available, having been released in a variety of forms over twenty times.

The success of the first series prompted Nation's agent Roger Hancock on 24 February 1978 to write to Alan Bilyard of BBC Records to remind him of an earlier conversation in which they had discussed the possibility of a spoken word LP based on the series. This could have been either a new story (like the Argo release in July 1976 of *Doctor Who and the Pescatons*, LP ZSW 564) or as a reworked version of a televised episode.

Bilyard responded that despite the good ratings and the commissioning of the series for a second season, he was not willing to commit to the idea at the time, as drama records tended to sell in limited qualities. He did however suggest they reconsider at a later date. While nothing came of the *Blake's 7* proposal, the following year BBC Records released Terry Nation's *Doctor Who* serial, 'Genesis of the Daleks'(1979, BBC Records, REH 364 (LP) and ZCR 364 (C)).

In 1991 trance music group The Orb, who had released groundbreaking singles in the preceding years and were championed by DJ John Peel, released their first album, *The Orb's Adventures Beyond the Ultraworld*

to critical acclaim. The reference to 'Ultraworld' is no coincidence. One of the tracks is entitled 'A Huge Ever Growing Pulsating Brain That Rules from the Centre of the Ultraworld', a clear reference to the season 3 episode. The exact same title was given to a sound effect from the episode that was released by BBC Records in 1981 on the LP *Science-Fiction Sound Effects No.26 – Sci-Fi Sound Effects*.

Arjen Anthony Lucassen's Star One released the album *Space Metal* (2002, Inside Out Music, ISBN: 5 052205 021323) which he states was based on films that took place entirely in space. Despite the reference to films, the ninth track, 'Intergalactic Space Crusaders', is clearly referencing *Blake's 7*, as the lyrics state: 'Seven Fighters, Navigators, Intergalactic Space Crusaders, Federation, Dictators, No Scruples, Lethal Traitors, Outriders, Invaders, Intergalactic Space Invaders, Domination, Liberation, Fighting to Survive'.

AUDIO, BOOKS

ABO-001 *Blake's 7: The Way Back*

Compact Disc (3): 180 minutes

Publisher: BBC Audiobooks (9 April 2009);

AudioGo: MP3 Download (2010)

ISBN: CD: 978 1 4084 0987 9;

MP3 Download: 978 1 4084 0922 0

RRP: CD: £15.65; MP3 Download: £10.99

Other Editions: *Blake's 7 – A Novel* by Trevor Hoyle

Gareth Thomas reads the first half of Trevor Hoyle's original novel covering the television episodes 'The Way Back' and 'Space Fall'. Original music and effects composed and performed by Simon E Power for Meon Productions. Text and biographies of Trevor Hoyle and Gareth Thomas were written by Andrew Pixley.

ABO-002 *Blake's 7: Cygnus Alpha*

Compact Disc (3): 200 minutes

Publisher: BBC Audiobooks (9 April 2009);

AudioGo: MP3 Download (2010)

ISBN: 978 1 4084 0988 6;

MP3 Download: 978 1 4084 0923 7

RRP: CD: £15.65; MP3 Download: £10.99

Other Editions: *Blake's 7 – A Novel* by Trevor Hoyle

Paul Darrow reads the second half of Trevor Hoyle's original novel covering the television episodes 'Cygnus Alpha' and 'Time Squad'. Original music and effects composed and performed by Simon E Power for Meon Productions. Text and biographies of Trevor Hoyle and Paul Darrow were written by Andrew Pixley.

AUDIO, DRAMAS – ORIGINAL SERIES

ADO-001 *Blake's 7 – The Sevenfold Crown* by Barry Letts

Audio Tape (2): 110 minutes approximately

Publisher: BBC Radio Collection (5 January 1998)

ISBN: 0 563 38200 7

RRP: £8.99

Other Editions: CD (*The Radio Adventures,*

THE WAY BACK
FROM THE NOVELLISATION BY TREVOR HOYLE READ BY GARETH THOMAS

ABO-001

CYGNUS ALPHA
FROM THE NOVELISATION BY TREVOR HOYLE READ BY PAUL DARROW

ABO-002

Radio Collection BBC

THE SEVENFOLD CROWN
A BBC RADIO 4 FULL-CAST DRAMATISATION
OF THE CULT SCI-FI SPACE-ADVENTURE

ADO-001

with *The Syndeton Experiment* (4 October 2004), ISBN: 0 563 52586 X)

An original full cast dramatisation. *The Sevenfold Crown* is set between the season 4 episodes 'Stardrive' and 'Animals' and was broadcast on Radio 4 on 17 January 1998. The original actors returned with the exception of Josette Simon (Dayna) and Glynis Barber (Soolin) with their roles being recast with Angela Bruce and Paula Wilcox respectively.

THE SYNDETON EXPERIMENT

A BBC RADIO 4 FULL-CAST DRAMATISATION

ADO-002

THE RADIO ADVENTURES

ADO-003

ADO-002 *Blake's 7 – The Syndeton Experiment* by Barry Letts

Compact Disc: 60 minutes

Publisher: BBC Radio Collection (5 April 1999)

ISBN: 0 563 55871 77

RRP: £7.99

Other Editions: CD (The Radio Adventures, with *The Sevenfold Crown* (4 October 2004), ISBN: 0 563 52586 X)

An original full cast dramatisation with the same cast as *The Sevenfold Crown*. It was broadcast on BBC Radio 4 on 10 April 1999.

ADO-003 *Blake's 7 – The Radio Adventures* by Barry Letts

Compact Disc (2): 170 minutes

Publisher: BBC Audiobooks (4 October 2004);

AudioGo: MP3 Download (2010)

ISBN: 0 563 52586 X

RRP: CD: £7.99; MP3 Download: £13.14

Other Editions: CD (*The Radio Adventures*, with *The Sevenfold Crown* (4 October 2004), ISBN: 0 563 52586 X)

This CD boxset was released to tie-in with *Blake's 7* being made available on DVD for the first time, and the packaging echoes that of the DVD releases. It was re-released in 2010 as an MP3 download by AudioGo.

AUDIO, DRAMAS – RE-IMAGINED SERIES

In 2007, three episodes of a recast series were produced for audio, and subsequently broadcast on BBC7. The new series roughly followed the events of the first season but there were significant departures such as the non-inclusion of Cally.

Commencing in 2008, a series of audio dramas were released each centring on the life of a main character prior to the initial episode. The first season comprised stories relating to Vila, Gan, Travis, Avon, Cally and Jenna. A second series was announced that would include the 'early years' of Zen, Servalan, Blake, Tarrant and Soolin. To date only the Zen orientated drama has been released.

ADR-001 *Blake's 7, Episode 1: Rebel* by Ben Aaronovitch

Compact Disc: 70 minutes approximately

Publisher: B7 Media in association with Sci-Fi Channel (UK) (4 July 2007); MP3 Download (28 July 2010)

ISBN: 978 1 906577 01 8

RRP: CD: £9.99; MP3 Download: £4.95

Other Editions: In a box set with *Episode 2: Traitor* and *Episode 3: Liberator* (September 2007,

ISBN: 978 1 906577 04 9

Broadcast: 22 December 2007 (BBC7)

A reimagining of *Blake's 7* with a new cast and starring Derek Riddell, Colin Salmon and Daniella Nardini. Originally broadcast in May 2007 as 12 x 5 minute

episodes on the Sci-Fi Channel UK website, it loosely
follows the introductory storyline of season 1. Cover
designed by David E Carey.

ADR-002 *Blake's 7, Episode 2: Traitor* by
Marc Platt
Compact Disc: 70 minutes approximately
Publisher: B7 Media in association with Sci-Fi Channel
(UK) (6 August 2007); MP3 Download (28 July 2010)
ISBN: 978 1 906577 02 5
RRP: CD: £9.99; MP3 Download: £4.95
Other Editions: In a box set with *Episode 1: Rebel*
and *Episode 3: Liberator* (September 2007,
ISBN: 978 1 906577 04 9)
Broadcast: 29 December 2007 (BBC7)

Originally broadcast in June 2007 as 12 x 5 minute episodes
on the Sci-Fi Channel UK website. Blake aboard the
Liberator with a crew must ascertain who his friends and
who his enemies are. Cover designed by David E Carey.

ADR-003 *Blake's 7, Episode 3: Liberator* by
James Swallow
Compact Disc (2): 60 minutes approximately
plus 40 minutes of bonus features
Publisher: B7 Media in association with Sci-Fi Channel
(UK) 3 September 2007); MP3 Download (28 July 2010)
ISBN: 978 1 906577 03 2
RRP: CD: £9.99; MP3 Download: £4.95
Other Editions: In a box set with *Episode 1: Rebel*
and *Episode 2: Traitor* (September 2007,
ISBN: 978 1 906577 04 9)
Broadcast: 3 January 2008 (BBC7)

Originally broadcast in July 2007 as 12 x 5 minute
episodes on the Sci-Fi Channel UK website. The
Federation's grip is tightening and the crew of the
Liberator has nowhere to hide. Bonus Features: *Blake's
7: A Rebellion Reborn* documentary, Sci-Fi channel mini-
documentaries, extended theme tune, wallpapers,
blooper reel. Cover designed by David E Carey.

ADR-001

ADR-002

ADR-003

ADR-004

ADR-005

ADR-006

ADR-004 *Blake's 7: Rebel / Traitor / Liberator* **Box Set**

Compact Disc (4): 225 minutes approximately

Publisher: B7 Media (12 May 2008);

MP3 Download (29 July 2010)

ISBN: 978 1 906577 04 9

RRP: CD: £34.99; MP3: £9.95

Other Editions: Each episode previously released individually. It includes the bonus features featured on the *Liberator* release.

ADR-005 *Blake's 7: The Early Years: When Vila Met Gan* **by Ben Aaronovitch**

Compact Disc: 50 minutes approximately

Publisher: B7 Media (16 June 2008);

MP3 Download (28 July 2010)

ISBN: 978 1 906577 05 6

RRP: CD: £9.99; MP3 Download: £4.95

Other Editions: None known but the broadcast edition is a re-cut version.

Broadcast: 4 June 2010 (BBC7)

The Early Years is a series of prequel stories that establishes the life of the crew, Travis and Servalan, prior to their meeting Blake. The title of *When Vila Met Gan* is self-explanatory and for the first time since the series conclusion on television, Michael Keating recreates the role of Vila. Cover designed by Lee Thompson.

ADR-006 *Blake's 7: The Early Years: Avon / Travis: Point of No Return / Eye of the Machine* **by James Swallow and Ben Aaronovitch**

Compact Disc (2): 70 minutes approximately

Publisher: B7 Media (24 November 2008);

MP3 Download (28 July 2010)

ISBN: 978 1906577 06 3

RRP: CD: £14.98;

MP3 Download: £3.95 for each of the two stories

Other Editions: Also available in a box set

Broadcast: *Eye of the Machine* – 31 May 2010 (BBC7)

Two individual background stories for Avon and Travis, both set prior to the first televised episode. Cover designed by Lee Thompson.

ADR-007 *Blake's 7: The Early Years: Cally: Blood & Earth / Flag & Flame* by Ben Aaronovitch and Marc Platt

Compact Disc: 60 minutes approximately

Publisher: B7 Media (24 August 2009);

MP3 Download (28 July 2010)

ISBN: 978 1906577 07 0

RRP: CD £9.56; MP3 Download: £5.95 for each story

Other Editions: Also available in a box set

Broadcast: *Blood & Earth* – 1 June 2010 (BBC7)

Jan Chappell returns to *Blake's 7* for the first time since the fourth season television episode 'Rescue' but this time as one of Cally's clone sisters. Cover designed by Lee Thompson.

ADR-008 *Blake's 7: The Early Years: Jenna: The Dust Run / The Trial* by Simon Guerrier

Compact Disc: 70 minutes approximately

Publisher: B7 Media (30 November 2009);

MP3 Download (16 March 2010)

ISBN: 978 1906577 08 7

RRP: CD £10.99; MP3 Download: £3.95 per story

Other Editions: Also available in a box set

Broadcast: *The Dust Run* – 2 June 2010 (BBC7); *The Trial* – 3 June 2010 (BBC7)

Two linked background stories for the character of Jenna prior to her meeting Blake. Cover designed by Lee Thompson.

ADR-009 *Blake's 7: The Early Years* Box Set

Compact Disc: 250 minutes approximately

Publisher: B7 Media (7 December 2009)

ADR-007

ADR-008

ADR-009

ISBN: 978 1906577 10 0

RRP: £37.49

Other Editions: Also available as individual releases.

Contains the previous released 'early years' stories for Gan, Vila, Avon, Travis, Cally and Jenna. Cover designed by Lee Thompson.

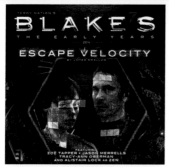

ADR-010

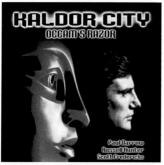

ADS-001

ADS-002

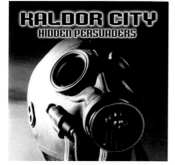

ADS-003

ADR-010 *Blake's 7: The Early Years: Zen: Escape Velocity* by James Swallow
Compact Disc: 60 minutes approximately
Publisher: B7 Media (26 April 2010);
MP3 Download: (26 April 2010)
ISBN: 978 1906577 09 4
RRP: CD: £10.99; MP3 Download: £7.95

The System accesses Zen's memory files to ascertain how DSV2's main computer became Zen of the *Liberator*. Cover designed by Lee Thompson.

(AUDIO, DRAMAS – SPIN-OFFS)

ADS-001 *Kaldor City 1: Occam's Razor* by **Alan Stevens and Jim Smith**
Compact Disc: 60 minutes approximately
Publisher: Magic Bullet (2001)
RRP: £10.99 Ref: KC001

The *Kaldor City* series continues the storyline of the BBC *Doctor Who* novel *Corpse Marker* (a sequel to *Doctor Who* story 'The Robots of Death') by Chris Boucher. Scott Fredericks, reprises his *Blake's 7* role of Carnell the psychostrategist from the season 2 episode 'Weapon', by the same author. Paul Darrow plays Kaston Iago and Russell Hunter, resumes his role of Uvanov from 'The Robots of Death'. *Occam's Razor* also features Brian Croucher, Peter Miles, Peter Tuddenham, and Patricia Merrick.

ADS-002 *Kaldor City 2: Death's Head* by **Chris Boucher**
Compact Disc: 55 minutes approximately
Publisher: Magic Bullet (2002)
RRP: £10.99 Ref: KC002

The discovery of shady dealings at a desert research station leads Operations Supervisor Rull into a twisted maze of ambition, carnal desire, injustice and assassination attempts. At the hub of this web of intrigue seems to be the enigmatic psychostrategist Carnell.

ADS-003 *Kaldor City 3: Hidden Persuaders* by **Jim Smith and Fiona Moore**

Compact Disc: 60 minutes approximately

Publisher: Magic Bullet (2003)

RRP: £10.99 Ref: KC003

Terrorism is on the increase and, amidst media frenzy, hostages are being taken. The Church of Taren Capel is fighting back and nobody in Kaldor City is safe.

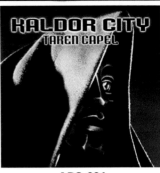

ADS-004

ADS-004 *Kaldor City 4: Taren Capel* by: **Alan Stevens**

Compact Disc: 60 minutes approximately

Publisher: Magic Bullet (2003)

RRP: £10.99 Ref: KC004

A long-vanished prophet reappears; a plot is uncovered hinting at corruption among the Founding Families and even the robots on which the city depends might hold secrets that no one dares imagine. Carnell pits himself against an unseen adversary in a deadly game.

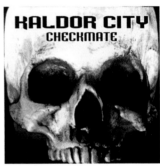

ADS-005

ADS-005 *Kaldor City 5: Checkmate* by **Alan Stevens**

Compact Disc: 60 minutes approximately

Publisher: Magic Bullet (October 2003)

RRP: £10.99 Ref: KC005

Taren Capel's legacy is unleashed, and death stalks the streets. As Uvanov fights for his career and his life, Paullus contacts a force which could be the salvation of the people of Kaldor, or their destruction.

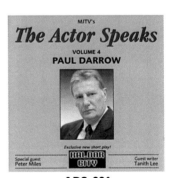

ADS-006

ADS-006 *Kaldor City: The Prisoner* by **Alan Stevens and Fiona Moore**

Compact Disc: 20 minutes approximately

Publisher: Magic Bullet in a co-production with MJTV (2004)

RRP: £10.99

A play featuring Paul Darrow and Peter Miles reprising their *Kaldor City* roles. It was released on the CD *The Actor Speaks: Paul Darrow*, produced by MJTV. The play features an interrogation between Kaston Iago and Firstmaster Landerchild.

ADS-007

Together Again - Blake's Back

TOGETHER AGAIN - ACTION!

Together Again - Elements

AIN-001 Vols 1, 3, 5

ADS-007 *Kaldor City 6: Storm Mine* by Daniel O'Mahony

Compact Disc: 60 minutes approximately
Publisher: Magic Bullet (December 2004)
RRP: £10.99 Ref: KC006

Eighteen months after her final confrontation with Kaston Iago, Blayes awakes to find Kaldor City in quarantine and herself on a Storm Mine in the Blind Heart Desert.

AUDIO, INTERVIEWS

AIN-001 *The Together Again* Series

Publisher: Sheelagh Wells
Format: Cassette Tape
Duration: 60 minutes (except volume 7; 80 minutes) approximately
RRP: £8.25 each

A series of interviews with cast and crew offering a look at life behind the cameras of *Blake's 7*.

Volume 1: 'Blake's Back' (Summer 1995), Volume 2: 'Liberated' (Autumn 1996), Volume 3: 'Action' (Spring 1977), Volume 4: 'Kingmaker' (Autumn 1997), Volume 5: 'Elements' (Spring 1998), Volume 6, 'Solstice' (20th March 1999), Volume 7; 'Seven' (Spring 2000).

AIN-002 *Jacqueline Pearce in Conversation*

Publisher: Maximum Power
Date: 1997
Format: Cassette Tape
Duration: 60 minutes approximately
RRP: £5.00

Recorded over three separate sessions, Jacqueline Pearce watched clips from the series with John Ainsworth recording her responses. The cover was designed by Paul Vyse.

AIN-003 *The Actor Speaks*

A series of CDs, released over five volumes, with each focusing 'on the diverse talents of one much loved actor'. Three of the five volumes featured actors from *Blake's 7*, while volumes 2 and 5 featured Elisabeth Sladen and Louise Jameson from *Doctor Who* respectively. The releases were published by MJTV. RRP: £9.99 each. 🖉 🖉

Jacqueline Pearce *in conversation*
1: Servalan

AIN-002

AIN-003a *Volume 1: Gareth Thomas with Nicholas Courtney (2000)*

The volume includes two interviews with Thomas and two monologues, 'Ruined Garden' and 'Benedictine' both of which were written by Thomas and performed by Nicholas Courtney. Thomas performs the monologue 'Is this My Life' and the volume concludes with 'Jake's Heaven' an advert for a *Blake's 7* pastiche.

MJTV's
The Actor Speaks
VOLUME 1 - GARETH THOMAS

with special guest Nicholas Courtney

AIN-003a

AIN-003b *Volume 3: Jacqueline Pearce with Tanith Lee (2003)*

The CD includes interviews with Pearce and excerpts from other productions ('Ghostlands', 'Written Off' and 'Soldiers of Love'). Pearce reads the poem 'Keep Me in Mind' and performs the monologue 'Eyes Down' and the Tanith Lee penned 'His Brother's Keeper'. Rear cover illustration by Brian Gorman.

MJTV's
The Actor Speaks
VOLUME 3
JACQUELINE PEARCE

with special guest writer
Tanith Lee

AIN-003b

AIN-003c *Volume 4: Paul Darrow with Peter Miles and Tanith Lee (2004)*

The penultimate CD in the series includes four interviews with Darrow. Darrow performs three monologues; 'Sunset in the City' by Tanith Lee, and 'The Unwelcome Visitor' and 'The Woman in My Dreams'. The volume also contains 'Kaldor City – The Prisoner' a duologue from the 'Kaldor City' universe with Darrow as Kaston Iago and Peter Miles as Landerchild.

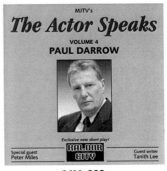

MJTV's
The Actor Speaks
VOLUME 4
PAUL DARROW

Exclusive new short play!
HALDOR CITY
Special guest Peter Miles
Guest writer Tanith Lee

AIN-003c

ASH-001

AUDIO, SHEET MUSIC

ASH-001 *Blake's 7* **Theme**
Manufacturer: Chappell & Co Ltd. (1978)
RRP: £0.75
Ref: 1-0-50160 F

A four page manuscript of the series theme in an A4
booklet. The black and white front cover depicted the
Liberator below the series logo.

ASO-001

AUDIO, SOUND EFFECTS

ASO-001 *BBC Radiophonic Workshop 21*
Manufacturer: BBC Records (1979)
Record Number: REC 354
Other Editions: Cassette (ZCM 354)

A celebration of 21 years of the BBC Radiophonic
Workshop. Track 4 on Side 2 'Mysterioso' by Richard
Yeoman-Clarke is an atmospheric background track for
the *Liberator* (1'08"). This track was rereleased on *BBC
Radiophonic Workshop: A Retrospective*.

ASO-002

ASO-002 *Science-Fiction Sound Effects No.26
– Sci-Fi Sound Effects*
Manufacturer: BBC Records (1981)
Record Number: REC 420
Other Editions: Cassette (ZCM 420); Released in CD
format as *Essential Science Fiction Sound Effects Volume 1*
(BBC Enterprises (1991), ISBN: 5 011755 084721)

This record comprised sound effects from
The Hitchhiker's Guide to the Galaxy (the radio
dramatisation), *Doctor Who* (season 18), *Blake's 7* and
Earthsearch (the radio dramatisation). The cover was of
the *Liberator* orbiting a planet.

The album compilation was by William Grierson
with recordings by Dick Mills, Elizabeth Parker, Lloyd
Silverthorne and Richard Yeoman-Clarke, many of
which are in monaural sound.

ASO-003

The *Blake's* 7 track listings were:

Series 4 Stereo Effects by Elizabeth Parker:

1. 'Dawn of Emptiness' (1'55")
2. 'Space bells of ceremonial room' (1'22")
3. '*Scorpio* spaceship lands' (0'35")
4. 'Dematerialisation' (0'09")
5. 'Rematerialisation' (0'06")
6. '*Scorpio* gun' (0'07")

Series 1-3 Mono Effects by Richard Yeoman-Clark and Elizabeth Parker

7. 'Orac switch on' (0'02")
8. 'Orac working' (0'31")
9. 'Orac switch off' (0'04")
10. '*Liberator* computer malfunction' (0'33")
11. '*Liberator* plasma bolt explosions' (0'10")
12. '*Liberator* laser' (0'25")
13. 'Federation ship laser explosions' (0'26")
14. '*Liberator* life capsule ready to be launched' (0'39")
15. '*Liberator* ship background' (1'35")
16. '*Liberator* guns x 3' (0'13")
17. 'Avon's communicator bracelet Transportation sounds' (0'09")
18. 'Disappearance' (0'11")
19. 'Reappearance' (0'11")
20. 'Mysterious "being" disappears in a flame' (0'05")
21. 'Alien gun' (0'06")
22. 'Appearance of the Ovoid (a stone surrounded in mystery and magic)' (0'35")
23. 'Heavy voltage force' (0'09")
24. 'Glow from a mysterious ghost who haunts the *Liberator*' (0'25")
25. 'The core, a huge evergrowing pulsating brain which rules from the centre of Ultraworld'(0'32")
26. 'Interior of Federation Patrol ship' (1'14")
27. 'Going through a Black Hole in the *Liberator*' (1'19")
28. 'Space centre medical unit hum' (0'43")
29. 'Machine monster with a black sense of humour! (who chases our heroes around, winking)' (0'37")
30. 'Break down of machine monster' (0'09")
31. 'Extra terrestrial heavenly choir' (1'24")

ASO-003 *Essential Science Fiction Sound Effects Vol. I*

Artist: Dick Mills, Richard Yeoman-Clark, Elizabeth Parker and Lloyd Silverthorne
Manufacturer: BBC Enterprises (1991);
AudioGo: MP3 Download (2011)
Record Number: BBCCD847
RRP: MP3 Download: £3.69

CD: 🔊 🔊 🔊   MP3: 🔊

This was a CD re-issue of *Sci-Fi Sound Effects No. 26* (REC 420). It comprised sound effects from *The Hitchhiker's Guide to the Galaxy* (the radio dramatisation; Tracks 1-15), *Doctor Who* (from season 18; tracks 16-30), *Blake's 7* season 4; Tracks 31-32), *Blake's 7* (seasons 1-3; tracks 37-61) and *Earthsearch* (from the radio dramatisation; tracks 62-81).

Season 4

31. 'Dawn of Emptiness' (1'55")
32. 'Space bells of ceremonial room' (1'22")
33. '*Scorpio* spaceship lands' (0'35")
34. 'Dematerialisation' (0'09")
35. 'Rematerialisation' (0'06")
36. '*Scorpio* gun' (0'07")

From Seasons 1 – 3

37. 'Orac switch on' (0'02")
38. 'Orac working' (0'31")
39. 'Orac switch off' (0'04")
40. '*Liberator* computer malfunction' (0'33")
41. '*Liberator* plasma bolt explosions' (0'10")
42. '*Liberator* laser' (0'25")
43. 'Federation ship laser explosions' (0'26")
44. '*Liberator* life capsule ready to be launched' (0'39")
45. '*Liberator* ship background' (1'35")
46. '*Liberator* guns x 3' (0'13")
47. 'Avon's communicator bracelet Transportation sounds' (0'09")
48. 'Disappearance' (0'11")
49. 'Reappearance' (0'11")
50. 'Mysterious "being" disappears in a flame' (0'05")

51. 'Alien gun' (0'06")
52. 'Appearance of the Ovoid (a stone surrounded in mystery and magic)' (0'35")
53. 'Heavy voltage force' (0'09")
54. 'Glow from a mysterious ghost who haunts the *Liberator*' (0'25")
55. 'The core, a huge evergrowing pulsating brain which rules from the centre of Ultraworld' (0'32")
56. 'Interior of Federation Patrol ship' (1'14")
57. 'Going through a Black Hole in the *Liberator*' (1'19")
58. 'Space centre medical unit hum' (0'43")
59. 'Machine monster with a black sense of humour! (who chases our heroes around, winking)' (0'37")
60. 'Break down of machine monster' (0'09")
61. 'Extra terrestrial heavenly choir' (1'24")

Dick Mills: Track 34
Elizabeth Parker: Tracks 31-33, 35-36, 41-44 and 50-61
Richard Yeoman-Clark: Tracks 37-40 and 45-49

ASO-004 BBC Radiophonic Workshop: A Retrospective

Manufacturer: The Grey Area of Mute Records (3 November 2008)
Compilation: Mark Ayres
ISBN: 5 099923 698826
RRP: £11.99

This two CD release is a compilation of music and sound effects produced by the BBC Radiophonic Workshop. Track 54 on the first disc, 'Mysterioso' (1'07"), was composed by Richard Yeoman-Clark in 1977 to create an atmospheric background to the *Liberator*. This track was previously released on *BBC Radiophonic Workshop 21*.

AUDIO, SOUNDTRACKS

AST-001 Blake's 7: Rebellion – Music from the Audio Adventures – Volume 1 by Alistair Lock

MP3 Download: 71 minutes approximately
Publisher: B7 Media (16 June 2010)
RRP: £3.95

This downloadable album contains fifteen individual scores from B7 Media's audio reboot of *Blake's 7*. The tracks in numerical order are 'Rebel', 'The Trial', 'The Derelict', 'Breaking Orbit', 'Cygnus Alpha', 'The Escape', 'Breakdown', 'The New Crew', 'Zen', 'Blake and Travis', 'The *Liberator*', 'The Nebula', 'Avon's Betrayal', 'The Trap', and 'Wipeout'.

AUDIO, THEMES

ATH-001 Blake's 7 / The Federation March

Manufacturer: BBC Records (5 January 1979); BBC Records & Tapes (US)
Distributor: PYE Records (UK); Gemcom Inc. (US)
Record Number: RESL 58 (UK); BBC 452 (US)
RRP: 90p
Other Editions: Plain cover

(UK). (US)

Under the direction of composer Dudley Simpson, the theme was recorded on Thursday 13 July 1978 at Studio MV 4, in Maida Vale, London by ten musicians (three trombonists, three French horn players, two trumpeters, one percussionist and an organist playing the Allen Organ). Simpson then overdubbed the tracks that afternoon on a Polymoog synthesizer (which was programmed by Richard Yeoman-Clark for Simpson). Both tracks were produced by Derek Goom.

It was released with a photographic cover of the *Liberator* and the series logo on both sides, this 7" single comprised the theme on side 'A' and 'The Federation March' on side 'B'.

This record was released in the United States in 1982 and distributed by Gemcom Inc. It was available with the same cover as in the UK (except the sleeve

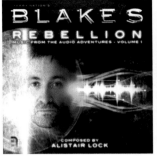

ASO-004　　　　　**AST-001**　　　　　**ATH-001 (UK)**

ATH-002

referred to 'BBC records & tapes' as opposed to simply 'BBC records'). An alternate cover with a colour photograph of the season 4 crew was purportedly released in the US, although no documentary evidence has confirmed this to date.

ATH-002 BBC Space Themes
Manufacturer: BBC Records (1978)

Record Number: REC 324

Other Editions: Plain cover; cassette (ZCR 324)

This LP was of theme tunes of BBC television and radio shows with a space theme. These included *Blake's 7* – from RESL 58 – *Apollo*, *Doctor Who*, *Quatermass*, *The Sky at Night*, *Star Trek* and *Journey into Space*. The cover was of the *Liberator* and smaller images of the TARDIS, the *USS Enterprise* and the Apollo capsule, in space.

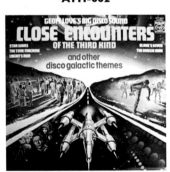

ATH-003 (LP)

ATH-003 Close Encounters of the Third Kind and other disco galactic themes
Artist: Geoff Love's Big Disco Sound

Manufacturer: EMI/Music For Pleasure (1978)

Record Number: MFP 50375

Other Editions: Cassette (TC MFP 50375)

This LP was a compilation of notable science fiction themes from film and television, including a cover version of the *Blake's 7* theme.

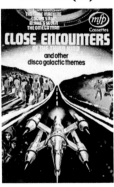

ATH-003 (Cassette)

ATH-004

ATH-004 *Sixteen Small Screen Greats*

Artist: Ronnie Hazlehurst and his Orchestra

Manufacturer: Polydor (1978)

Record Number: 2384.107

Other Editions: Cassette (3192.486)

This LP was a compilation of television themes, including a cover version of the *Blake's 7* theme.

ATH-005

ATH-005 *Blake's 7 Disco*

Manufacturer: BBC Records (1979)

Distributor: PYE Records

Record Number: BEEB 027

Conceived as a dance record, the 'A' side runs to 4'40" with 132 beats per minute. While Dudley Simpson is listed as the composer, the artist is 'Federation'. The 'B' side ('Disco Jimmy') was unrelated to *Blake's 7* and ran to 3'35" and had 134 beats per minute. While consideration was given to a 12" version, a photographic sleeve and coloured vinyl, only a standard 7" single with standard BBC sleeve was released.

ATH-006

ATH-006 *Themes For Super Heroes*

Artist: Geoff Love and his orchestra

Manufacturer: EMI/Music For Pleasure (1979)

Record Number: MFP 50439

Other Editions: Cassette (TC MFP 50439)

This LP was a compilation of notable science fiction themes from film and television, including the cover version of the *Blake's 7* theme included on *Close Encounters of the Third Kind* and other disco galactic themes.

ATH-007 *Top BBC TV Themes Vol. 2*

Manufacturer: BBC Records (1979)

Record Number: REC 365

Other Editions: Cassette

Blake's 7 – from RESL 58 – was merely one track on this vinyl LP. Others included *All Creatures Great and Small*, *Sexton Blake*, *Telford's Change* and *The Onedin Line*.

ATH-007

ATH-008 *Themes Ain't What They Used To Be* – Themes Machine

Manufacturer: BBC Records (1981)

Record Number: RESL 104

Single with medley of television themes including *Blake's 7*.

ATH-008

ATH-009 *Space Invaded: BBC Space Themes*

Manufacturer: BBC Records (1982)

Record Number: REC 442

Other Editions: Cassette (ZCR442)

Besides *Blake's 7* from RESL 58, tracks included *K9 & Company*, the Peter Howell arrangement of the *Doctor Who* theme and *Tomorrow's World*.

ATH-009

ATH-010 *20 BBC Drama Themes*

Artist: Dudley Simpson Orchestra

Manufacturer: BBC Records (1983)

Record Number: REH 464

Other Editions: Cassette (ZCR 464)

This LP was a compilation of notable BBC television themes, including the *Blake's 7* theme from RESL 58.

ATH-010

ATH-011

ATH-012 (Cassette)

ATH-012 (CD)

ATH-013

ATH-011 *An Hour of Superthemes*

Artist: Geoff Love and his Orchestra

Manufacturer: EMI/Music for Pleasure (1986)

Cassette Number: HR 41 8103 4

This cassette was a compilation of science-fiction and fantasy file and TV themes, including the cover version from *Close Encounters of the Third Kind and other disco galactic themes.*

ATH-012 *50 BBC Television Themes*

Artist: Various. Compilation by John D Derry

Manufacturer: Polygram (1986)

Record Number: ZCBBC 3006

Other Editions: Compact Disc (BBCCD 2020)

RRP: AU$19.99

This compilation of BBC television themes comprised three audio cassettes in one soft plastic rectangular box. The cover illustration (by Robert R McLarnon) was of Miss Marple's cottage from the popular BBC series starring Joan Hickson.

It was made in Australia, and only released in Australasia. The *Blake's 7* theme from RESL 58 appeared on cassette one, side two, track one.

In 1996 it was re-released on two compact discs with a different cover, and like the cassette release, was only available in Australasia. The *Blake's 7* theme was on disc one, at track number ten.

This was the theme's first release on compact disc and it would be another five years before it was released in the UK on the emerging format. The CD release was partially sponsored by the airline British Airways.

ATH-013 *Sci-Fi Themes*

Artist: London Theatre Orchestra

Manufacturer: Music Collection International Ltd. (1996)

CD number: EMPRCD 655

This CD was a compilation of 16 science fiction themes from film and television including the *Blake's 7* theme.

ATH-014 *The A to Z of British TV Themes*

Volume Three

Artist: Dudley Simpson Orchestra

Manufacturer: Play It Again (25 June 1996)

CD: PLAY 010

This CD was a compilation of British TV themes, including the *Blake's 7* theme from BBC RESL 58. There were two versions of the cover.

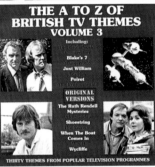

ATH-014 (both covers)

ATH-015 *The Cult Files*

Artist: Mark Ayres

Manufacturer: Silva Screen (October 1996)

CD: FILMXCD 184

This double CD was a compilation of science-fiction and fantasy TV and film themes, including a new cover version of the *Blake's 7* theme.

ATH-015

ATH-016 *The No. 1 Sci-Fi Album*

Artist: Various

Manufacturer: Polygram TV (17 March 1997)

CD Number: 553 360-2

This CD was a compilation of forty science fiction themes, including the *Blake's 7* theme played by Mark Ayres from FILMXCD 184

ATH-016

ATH-017

ATH-018

ATH-019

ATH-017 *Star Wars and Other Space Themes*

Artist: Geoff Love and His Orchestra

Manufacturer: EMI Music For Pleasure (1 June 1997)

CD: CDMFP 6395

This CD was a repackaging of two Geoff Love LPs, one being *Close Encounters of the Third Kind and other disco galactic themes.*

ATH-018 *Space Moods*

Artist: The Outer Limits

Manufacturer: Music Collection International Ltd. (16 February 1998)

CD Number: ETDCD 008

This CD was a compilation of twenty science fiction themes from film and television including the *Blake's 7* theme.

ATH-019 *The Cult Files Big Box*

Artist: Mark Ayres

Manufacturer: Silva Screen (5th June 2000)

CD Number: FILMX CD 343

This four CD set was a reissue of *The Cult Files* along with *The Cult Files Re-opened.*

ATH-020 *The Best of Cult Fiction*

Artist: Dudley Simpson Orchestra

Manufacturer: Virgin/EMI (23 February 2004)

CD Number: VTDCD 597

This double CD was a compilation of cult TV and film themes, including the *Blake's 7* theme from BBC RESL 58.

ATH-020

ATH-021

ATH-021 *The Best of Fantasy Themes*

Artist: Geoff Love and his Orchestra

Manufacturer: EMI Gold (14 February 2005)

CD Number: 5636792

This double CD set was a compilation of numerous fantasy TV and film themes, including the cover version of the *Blake's 7* theme from *Close Encounters and other disco galactic themes.*

ATH-022 *X-Treme Themes Sci-Fi Greats*

Artist: Phantasm

Manufacturer: Music Masters Ltd. (2006)

CD Number: SUN 2006

ATH-022

Featuring both movie and television themes by Phantasm, it contained twenty newly arranged tracks from *Star Wars* to *Quantum Leap*. The eleventh track was the *Blake's 7* theme.

ATH-023 *100 Greatest TV Themes – Vol. 2*

Artist: Mark Ayres

Manufacturer: Silva Screen (22 October 2007)

CD: SIL CD 1240

ATH-023

This four CD set was a compilation of numerous TV themes, including the cover version of the *Blake's 7* theme from *The Cult Files.*

ATH-024

ATH-024 *Cult TV Themes – Volume I*

Artist: Various

Manufacturer: Union Square Music (7 June 2009)

MP3 Download

RRP: £7.99 (album); £0.79 (*Blake's 7* theme only)

This downloadable album contains 25 tracks. The *Blake's 7* theme is track 19, and is the version by Mark Ayres previously released on *The Cult Files*.

AUDIO, UNLICENSED

AUN-001 *Travis: The Final Act* **by Alan Stevens**

Audio Cassette: 87 minutes approximately

Publisher: Magic Bullet (October 1992)

RRP: £5.75

A documentary exploring Travis's background, career and motives. It features interviews with Brian Croucher, Stephen Greif, Chris Boucher and David Maloney. It is narrated by Peter Miles who played Rontane in the season 2 episode 'Trial'.

AUN-001

AUN-002 *The Mark of Kane* **by Alan Stevens with David Tulley**

Audio Cassette: 47 minutes approximately

Publisher: Magic Bullet (1996)

RRP: £5.50

This cassette comprises two linked stories; 'War Crimes' (22'44) and 'Friendly Fire' (24'08) which feature Travis and Blake respectively. *The Mark of Kane* tells the story of Travis, the disgraced soldier, and Blake, the revolutionary leader, whose fates are linked through the disturbing quest of the bounty hunter Kane. It starred Brian Croucher as Travis and Gareth Thomas as Blake.

AUN-002

AUN-003 *The Logic of Empire* **by Alan Stevens and David Tulley**

Audio Cassette: 46 minutes approximately

Publisher: Magic Bullet (1997)

RRP: £7.50

This story starred Paul Darrow, Jacqueline Pearce, Gareth Thomas and Peter Tuddenham. Set several years after the final episode, 'Blake', it finds a post-Gauda Prime Avon answering a cry for help from an old friend.

AUN-003

BOOKS

During the original transmission of *Blake's 7*, very few books were published; three novels by Trevor Hoyle and three annuals. In the years that followed two original novels were released and fandom filled the literary gap with numerous short stories, novellas and full length books. These fan produced materials fall outside the scope of this guide.

On 4 July 2011, B7 Enterprises and Big Finish Productions announced a licensing deal that would see Big Finish release two hardback original novels each year commencing 31 May, 2012.

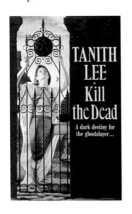

Blake's 7 made an indelible footprint on the history of television science-fiction and is covered in numerous factual books, some solely devoted to the series, others covering science fiction in general.

One other area worthy of note are novels that have been published professionally and while not directly related to *Blake's 7* may have been influenced by them in some way.

Perhaps the most well known example is *Kill the Dead* by Tanith Lee (1980, Legend Books, ISBN: 0 09 966360 0), who wrote the episodes 'Sarcophagus' and 'Sand'. The main protagonist is Parl Dro (whose name is similar to Paul Darrow's signature) a ghost slayer who bears a striking resemblance to Avon. His sidekick later in the book is pickpocket Myal Lemyal and of course the first time we see Vila in 'The Way Back' he steals Blake's watch from his wrist. The book is dedicated to 'Valentine' which is Paul Darrow's middle name. Lee herself insists that the characters are not based on the copyrighted characters of Avon and Vila.

The IDIC Epidemic is a *Star Trek* original novel by Jean Lorrah (1988, Pocket Books, ISBN: 0 6717 0768X). On pages 232 and 233

Spock watches Landing Party Seven arrive: '… six people drawn from engineering, computer sciences, medicine, economics, security and ship's stores. Kirk sometimes referred to this team as the "IDIC party", because their talents were so diversified, but the designation was actually one of the captain's jokes, for to hear them squabble you would think they could not agree on so much as who would stand on which transporter pad.

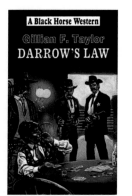

'Despite their disagreements, though, they were as efficient as any other team. They were directed by the engineer, Rogers, a portly man with curly brown hair. Running to the marine vehicle that landed just after them, they began to assemble it, the giant security officer holding the pieces together by sheer strength while the two women in the party bolted them into place.

'Meanwhile, the third man assembled the onboard computer with almost Vulcan concentration, while the last member of the team, a small, nondescript sort of man, always had the right tools ready to hand to those who needed them.'

The computer expert in the landing party is identified on page 251 as Chevron who was 'second only to Spock among the *Enterprise* crew at putting a computer through its paces'. Chevron was the alias used by Avon in the episode 'Powerplay'.

Star Trek: Deep Space Nine: The Siege by Peter David (1993, Pocket Books, ISBN: 0 671 87083 1) makes reference to 'Ayvon of the Seven' on pages 181 and 182.

'"One of the freedom fighters in Bajoran history was a man named Ayvon of the Seven," said Kira. "He had many famous sayings, and I think that paraphrasing one here would be appropriate: I'm not Starfleet, I'm not a coward, and I'm not going."'

In the episode 'Horizon', Avon tells Vila 'I'm not expendable, I'm not stupid and I'm not going.'

Barbara Paul has written several books that include a character by the name of Curt Holland that some saw as an Avon clone. While the author disagreed, she nonetheless entered into a spirited discussion with the proponents of the theory. While writing *Full Frontal Murder* (1997, Scribner, ISBN: 0 684 19716 2) the fourth book to feature the character, Paul found she had typed 'Avon' when she had meant to type 'Holland' and thereafter accepted that the character was based on Avon as played by Paul Darrow. The novel contains innumerable *Blake's 7* references: Albian, Bartolomew, Carnell, Dorian, Egrorian…

Darrow's Law by *Blake's 7* fan and professional writer Gillian Taylor (1999, Robert Hale, ISBN: 0 7090 6400 4) is a western concerning Sherriff Darrow and his seemingly ineffectual deputy

Hugh Keating. A sequel *Darrow's Word* followed (2001, Robert Hale, ISBN: 0 7090 6879 4).

The popular *Vampire Diaries* series of novels by L J Smith concern the characters of Stefan and Damon, who are brothers; one good, one bad. Initial reactions to the books included the assertion by some that these two characters were based on Blake and Avon. While this may be just a case of fanciful thinking, the fourth book in the series *The Dark Reunion* by L J Smith (1992, HarperCollins, ISBN: 0 06 106775 X) includes several famous lines of *Blake's 7* dialogue.

Doctor Who - *Prisoner of the Daleks* by Trevor Baxendale (2009, BBC Books, ISBN: 978-1-846-07641-1) has a character by the name of Cuttin' Edge. On pages 47 and 112 he talks about his upbringing on a tough planet called Gauda Prime - the name of Soolin's home planet and the location of the final episode 'Blake'. On page 48 Auros is described as the home planet of another character, Stella. Auros was the name of the planet where Travis was alleged to have massacred civilians in the season 1 episode 'Seek-Locate-Destroy'.

The Inform Designer's Manual

Graham Nelson

Fourth Edition 2001

In a different vein, *The Meaning of Liff* by Douglas Adams and John Lloyd (1983, Pan Books, ISBN: 0 330 289121 6) is a fictitious dictionary of words and their explanations. In the original edition, on page 29, 'Clackavoid' is defined as a: 'Technical BBC term for a page of dialogue from *Blake's Seven*.'

Later editions replaced the reference to the series with *Star Trek* (for the US market) and *Neighbours*.

There are numerous other potential examples but those given here are the most overt.

One of the more obscure places that *Blake's 7* references can be found is in *The Inform Designer's Manual* by Graham Nelson (1994, The Interactive Fiction Library, ISBN: 0 9713119 3 5). Inform is a computer language primarily designed for the development of games and puzzles. The author uses *Blake's 7* characters and planets in some of the guide's exercises such as simulating conversations with Avon and Zen. There are references to 'Destiny' (from the episode 'Mission to Destiny' and the planet 'Centauro' (presumably Centero from 'Seek-Locate-Destroy').

Special Sound: The Creation and Legacy of the BBC Radiophonic Workshop by Louis Niebur (2010, Oxford University Press, H/B ISBN: 978 0 19 536840 6, P/B ISBN: 978 0 19 536841 3) contains relatively few references to *Blake's 7* (pages 170, 185, and 200-201) but is nonetheless a fascinating insight into the BBC department that created the sound effects for the series.

BAN-001

BAN-002

BAN-002 (misprint)

BAN-003

BOOKS, ANNUALS

BAN-001 *Blake's 7 Annual 1979*

Hardback: 63 pages

Publisher: World Distributors (Manchester) Limited (August 1978)

SBN: 7235 0446 0

RRP: £1.50

Included the fictional stories, 'Crystal Gazing', 'Revenge of the Mutoes', 'The Body Stealers', 'The Box', 'The Sima Experiment' and 'Mother Ship'. Features included 'Meet the 7', 'Mid-Reader Zen', 'Alien Encounters', 'Dateline', 'Super Computer', 'Space Warp' and 'Blake's Wonders of the Universe'. The front cover was a montage of the series logo and season 1 photographs of the crew with the exception of Zen: Blake (from 'Cygnus Alpha'), Cally ('Time Squad'), Gan ('Cygnus Alpha') Avon and Vila ('Time Squad') and Jenna ('Space Fall'). The rear cover featured the logo, the *Liberator* and the same photograph of Blake as on the front cover. No writers or artists were credited, although Don Harley was responsible for 'The Body Stealers' and 'Mother Ship'.

World Distributors were granted a licence to produce the annual on 4 May 1977. Only the likenesses of the six crew members were licensed (as separate agreements had to be reached with the actors concerned) so neither Servalan nor Travis appeared. Lack of visual reference material hampered the production of the annual and lack of copy was also a substantive issue. Despite this by 19 June 1978, 43,000 copies had been sold, out of an initial print run of 50,000 which was then increased by a further 10,000 units. By 31 December 1978 out of 68,544 copies printed, 57,972 were sold at full price with the rest remaindered.

BAN-002 *Blake's 7 Annual 1980*

Hardback: 63 pages

Publisher: World Distributors (Manchester) Limited

under their World and Whitman imprint (August 1979)

SBN: 7235 6548 1

RRP: £1.75

Regular copy: Misprint:

Included the fictional stories, 'Planet of No Escape', 'Museum Piece', 'Sabotage!', 'A Task for Bondor' and 'Red for Danger'. Features included 'UFO', 'Space Calling... Are You Receiving Me?', 'Federation Test Sheet', 'Space Facts', 'Lumps of the Lunar Landscape', 'Cygnus the Swan Constellation', 'Calling all Cals', 'Blake's Space Scrapbook', 'A Numbered Spacecraft', 'Space Logbook', 'Planet of the Ashen Light', 'All Set for Take-Off', 'The Constellations' and 'Blake's Space Race'. The front cover was an illustration of the *Liberator* passing some planets with the series logo predominately displayed. The rear cover was the logo again, a publicity still of a Federation trooper and the *London* with docking tube extended (from 'Space Fall'). No writers or artists were credited, but Melvyn Powell drew the contents page, and possibly some of 'Museum Piece' and 'Red for Danger' – the style varies between being recognisably his, and possibly someone else.

The BBC issued the licence to publish the annual on 17 November 1978. The artwork was received by the BBC for review on the 13 March 1979. The BBC queried the inclusion of the characters of Servalan and Travis and enquired of World whether agreement had been reached with Jacqueline Pearce and Brian Croucher. It had not, so to make the pictures of these characters 'anonymous' Servalan was given long blonde hair and Travis's eye patch was removed and he was given a goatee.

Some copies of this annual were misprinted, with the content pages put into the cover upside down and back to front. These misprinted annuals are rare.

Of a print run of 46,764, 34,267 copies were sold with all other annuals being remaindered.

BAN-003 *Blake's 7 Annual 1981*

Hardback: 63 pages

Publisher: World Distributors (Manchester) Limited

under their World imprint (August 1980)

SBN: 7235 6593 7

RRP: £1.95

Included the stories 'Message from Nowhere', 'Double Decoy', 'The Island', 'Capsule: Part One: Silent Satellite', and 'Capsule: Part Two: Planetfall'. Features included 'Zen Facts', 'Peril from the Skies', 'Pluto's Planet', 'Pioneers of Space', 'An Alphabet of Space and Science', 'A Star Studded Quiz', 'Beware the Superchip!' and 'Stories of the Stars'. The front cover was a mixture of illustrations of the *Liberator*, a tower and a ship not seen in the series with a season 3 publicity photograph of the crew. The rear cover used a different season 3 publicity shot and different illustrations of the *Liberator* and another unknown ship. No writers or artists were credited, however Paul Green (who worked for World around this time) in his *Green's Guide To Annuals* refers to Melvyn Powell as being responsible for the art in this annual but variant styles may mean that others were involved also.

The licence to publish the final *Blake's 7* annual was issued on 21 May 1979. This time Servalan bore no resemblance to Jacqueline Pearce. For the first time, no major accounts picked up the title resulting in a much smaller print run of 26,329, with net sales of 20,681 – around a third of the 1979 annual.

The lack of major accounts picking up the third annual meant that despite being approached by the BBC to produce a fourth annual to coincide with season 4, World wrote to the BBC on 10 April 1980 to inform them that they did not wish to proceed as in all likelihood the 1981 annual would only just break even.

BAN-004 *Star Lord Annual 1982*

Hardback: 95 pages

Publisher: IPC Magazines Ltd. ('A Fleetway Annual')

(August 1981)

SBN: 85037 732 3

RRP: £2.25

Although not a *Blake's 7* annual, the front cover depicted the *Liberator* against a starscape and it included an eight page article; 'Big Thrills on the Small Screen: Fact and Figures About Your Favourite TV Programmes!' The article included an interview with series producer, David Maloney.

BOOKS, AUTOBIOGRAPHY

BAU-001 *Paul Darrow – You're Him, Aren't You? An Autobiography*

Hardcover: 192 pages

Publisher: Big Finish Productions Ltd (29 June 2006)

ISBN: 1 84435 236 6

RRP: £14.99

Paul Darrow's story of his life and career. It tells of his association with *Blake's 7* and his memories of Terry Nation, the cast and the crew. It also tells of his childhood, his time playing Elvis Presley and his wider career. The cover was designed by Stuart Manning and incorporated a photograph of Darrow as Avon from the fourth season.

BOOKS, FACTUAL

BFA-001 *Heroes of the Spaceways* by Bill Harry

Oversized Paperback: 127 pages

Publisher: Omnibus Press (November 1981)

ISBN: 0 86001 806 7

RRP: £3.95 (Omnibus Press) and US $9.95 (Quick Fox)

Other Editions: Quick Fox (November 1981;

ISBN 0 8256 39603)

A brief overview, and limited encyclopaedia of terms,

of science fiction movies and television shows including *Blake's 7* and *Doctor Who*. It was published simultaneously in the UK and the USA with Quick Fox securing the USA distribution rights. The cover illustration was by Mick Brownfield. The book was reviewed in issue 4 of *Blake's 7 – A Marvel Monthly*.

BFA-002 *Starlog TV Guidebook: TV Episode Guides, Volume 2: Science Fiction Adventure and Superheroes* compiled and written by David Hirsch, Gary Gerani, David Houston, Mike Cotter and Bill Clark

Paperback: 98 pages

Publisher: Starlog Press (January 1982)

ISBN: 0 931064 48 1

RRP: US $8.95

An episode guide for several science fiction television shows including the first three seasons of *Blake's 7*.

BFA-003 *Blake's 7: The Programme Guide* by Tony Attwood

Hardback: 192 pages

Publisher: W.H. Allen & Co. Ltd. (18 November 1982)

ISBN: 1 903889 54 5

RRP: h/b £5.95; p/b (1) £1.75; p/b (2) £4.99

Other Editions: Paperback (Target (16 June 1983), ISBN: 0 426 19449 7), Second Edition Paperback (Virgin (1 December 1994), ISBN: 0 426 19449 7)

Hardback: 🦅 🦅 🦅 🦅   Other Editions: 🦅 🦅

Tony Attwood approached Roger Hancock, Terry Nation's agent, to see if a *Blake's 7* programme guide might be possible as one had been successfully published for *Doctor Who*. Hancock was very keen on the project and it was him who pushed the project to fruition. Attwood had to agree contracts with all of the interested parties in the show as while Terry Nation owned the rights to the characters, concepts and scripts, the BBC and the writers of the other episodes also had rights in the material. The book eventually comprised an episode guide to each season,

BAN-004

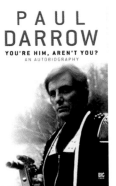

BAU-001

BFA-001

cast listings, writer details, encyclopaedia of terms and interviews with Vere Lorrimer, Chris Boucher, Paul Darrow, Michael Keating and Paul Tuddenham. The book also included thirteen black and white photographs spread over eight pages in the centre of the book. It was problematic finding shots from the first three seasons and eventually just four were from season 1 with the remainder being from season 4. The initial intent was to have the original series logo adorn the front cover, but producer Vere Lorrimer (who had no objection to this, provided that the season 4 logo also appeared somewhere) could not find a suitable image to be used.

BFA-002

The second edition was revised and updated and included a new merchandise guide (by Kevin Davies), a chapter on fan clubs (by Diane Gies, Jackie Ophir and Rob Emery) and a section on the novel *Afterlife* by Attwood and the proposed sequel *State of Mind*. It also corrected an error that was present in the first edition; in the episode summary, 'Headhunter' was originally listed as the fifth episode of the fourth season and 'Animals' the sixth, but the correct transmission order was the reverse. The cover was designed by Slatter-Anderson.

BFA-003

BFA-003 (2nd ed)

BFA-004

BFA-005

BFA-006

BFA-005 *The Encyclopedia of TV Science Fiction* **by Roger Fulton**

Paperback: 596 pages

Publisher: Boxtree Limited (1990)

ISBN: 1 85283 277 0

RRP: £17.95

Other Editions: A revised second edition (1995, Boxtree, ISBN: 1 85283 953 8), a revised third edition (November 1997, Boxtree, ISBN: 0 7522 1150 1).

As the title suggests this is an A-Z of television science fiction programmes from *A for Andromeda* to *Z for Zachariah*. Each entry consisted of a series overview, regular cast list, principal crew, transmission dates and an episode guide.

The *Blake's 7* entry runs to ten pages and provides an accurate overview of the series.

In addition to being updated in 1995 and 1997, a version was written for the US market; *The Sci-Fi Channel Encyclopedia of TV Science Fiction* by Roger Fulton and John Betancourt (1998, Aspect, ISBN: 0 446 67478 8). Some material from this US version found its way into the fourth and final UK version now entitled *TV Times Encyclopedia of TV Science Fiction* by Roger Fulton with additional material by John Betancourt (2000, Boxtree, ISBN: 0 7522 7167 9).

BFA-004 *Doctor Who Special Effects* **by Mat Irvine**

Hardback: 96 pages

Publisher: h/b: Hutchinson Children's Books Limited (22 August 1986)

ISBN: 0 09 167920 6

RRP: h/b £8.95; p/b £5.95

Other Editions: Oversize Paperback (Beaver Books, an imprint of Arrow Books Limited; ISBN: 0 09 942630 7)

Hardback: Paperback:

While predominantly concerned with the special effects on *Doctor Who*, Irvine references *Blake's 7* several times and there are some nice colour photographs from the series.

BFA-006 *The DWB Compendium*

Hardback: 134 pages

Publisher: DreamWatch Publishing (1993)

RRP: £16.99 h/b; £12.99 p/b

Other Editions: Oversize Paperback (ISBN: 0 9522307 0 4)

Hardback: Paperback:

Compiled and edited by Gary Leigh, this was a compendium of material from the first 100 issues of *DWB* magazine. *Blake's 7* related material included ratings and merchandise information. The hardback edition was a limited edition, bound in linen and embossed with gold and silver and came complete with a dust jacket.

BFA-007 *The Guinness Book of Classic British TV* **by Paul Cornell, Martin Day and Keith Topping**

Paperback: 444 pages
Publisher: Guinness Publishing (1993)
ISBN: 0 85112 543 3
RRP: £14.99

An encyclopedia style book covering British television drama from the mid fifties until the date of publication. The first entry in the chapter entitled 'BBC Telefantasy' is *Blake's 7* (page 298). The entry is three and a half pages long, with production credits and episode listings in the margins. The text is largely subjective.

BFA-008 *The DWB Interview File*

Hardback: 182 pages
Publisher: DreamWatch Publishing (1994)
ISBN: 0 9522307 1 4
RRP: £18.99 h/b; £14.99 p/b
Other Editions: Oversize Paperback
(ISBN: 0 9522307 1 2)
Hardback: 🕊 🕊 🕊 🕊 Paperback: 🕊 🕊

Compiled and edited by Gary Leigh this was a compendium of interviews from the first 100 issues of *DWB* magazine. *Blake's 7* related material included interviews with Ian Scoones, Gareth Thomas, Michael Keating, Jacqueline Pearce and Paul Darrow. The hardback edition was a limited edition, bound in linen and embossed with gold and silver and came complete with a dust jacket.

BFA-009 *The Making of Terry Nation's Blake's 7* **by Adrian Rigelsford**

Paperback: 95 pages
Publisher: Boxtree (30 June 1995)
ISBN: 0 7522 0891 8
RRP: £9.99

🕊 🕊

A general introduction to *Blake's 7* and a review of each season with numerous photographs.

BFA-007

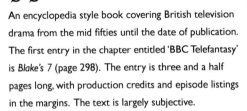

BFA-008

BFA-009

BFA-010

BFA-010 *Classic Sci-Fi and Fantasy Models Vol. I*

Paperback: 128 pages
Publisher: Strange Light Limited (1996)
ISBN: 0 9528820 0 0
RRP: £9.99

🕊 🕊 🕊

Compiled by M G Reccia this digest of material from *Sci-Fi and Fantasy Models* magazine reprints articles on making *Liberator* handguns and *Scorpio* bracelets (Kevin Davies) from issue 1 of the magazine and Martin Bowers covers the *Liberator*, Federation Pursuit Ships, the *Ortega*, the *FT7*, one of Servalan's ships and *Liberator* teleport bracelets in an extensively illustrated article that was originally printed in issue 7 of the magazine.

BFA-011

BFA-012 (hardcover)

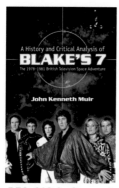

BFA-012 (softcover)

BFA-011 *Blake's 7: The Inside Story* **by Joe Nazzaro and Sheelagh Wells**
Paperback: 128 pages
Publisher: Virgin (17 April 1997)
ISBN: 0 7535 0044 2
RRP: £12.99

A detailed review of *Blake's 7* including the cast, location filming, special effects, costume and make-up, the fourth season and the final episode as well as an episode guide.

BFA-012 *A History and Critical Analysis of Blake's 7, the 1978-81 British Television Space Adventure* **by John Kenneth Muir**
Library Binding: 232 pages
Publisher: McFarland & Co Inc (31 August 1999)
ISBN: 0 786406 00 3
RRP: p/b £26.95
Other Editions: Revised second Edition Paperback
(ISBN: 0 786426 60 8, 15 May 2006)

The book details the origins and history of *Blake's 7*, an overview of each season and several essays. Many of the hardback copies were signed by the author. The front cover of the paperback edition was a BBC photograph of the season 2 crew taken from the episode 'Redemption', superimposed upon a background created by PhotoSpin.

BFA-013 *Liberation. The Unofficial and Unauthorised Guide to Blake's 7* **by Alan Stevens and Fiona Moore**
Hardback: 228 pages
Publisher: Telos Publishing Ltd; Deluxe Limited Signed Edition (25 September 2003)
ISBN: 1 903889 55 3
RRP: h/b £30; p/b £12.99; eBook £5.99
Other Editions: Paperback (ISBN: 1 903889 54 5), eBook for Kindle (27 April 2011)
Hardback: Paperback:

ebook:

The book contains a highly detailed critical analysis of every aspect of *Blake's 7*. This includes production problems and script alterations, to observations of the episodes, characters and sub-texts. The cover of the hardback edition was designed by David J Howe and incorporated an image by Nathan Skreslet. The cover for the paperback edition was illustrated and designed by Dariusz Jasiczak.

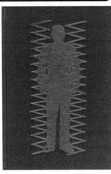

BFA-013 (softcover)   **BFA-013 (hardcover)**

**BFA-014 *The Television Series: Terry Nation*
by Jonathan Bignell and Andrew O'Day**

Hardcover: 230 pages

Publisher: Manchester University Press (2004)

ISBN: 0 7190 6546 1

RRP: £14.99

Other Editions: Paperback (ISBN: 0 7190 6547 X)

This book is an 'academic study of the science fiction television devised and written by Terry Nation'. The book was distributed in the USA by Palgrave and by UBC Press in Canada. Fifteen small black and white photographs taken from programmes written by Nation were printed on pages 110-112. Eight were from *Blake's 7*; a space battle from 'Duel', a pixilated image of Blake from the season 1 and 2 title sequence, drugged Federation citizens from 'The Way Back', the graveyard from 'Duel', Sinofar against a statute and Sinofar and Giroc (both from 'Duel') and finally a portrait of Servalan from 'Traitor'.

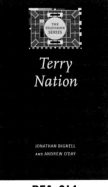

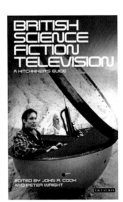

BFA-014   **BFA-015**

**BFA-015 *British Science Fiction Television:
A Hitchhikers Guide* edited by John R Cook
and Peter Wright**

Hardcover: 304 pages

Publisher: I B Tauris & Co Ltd (28 October 2005)

ISBN: 1 84511 047

RRP: h/b £47.50; p/b £17.99

Other Editions: Paperback (ISBN: 1 8451 1048X)

This book, by leading writers in television history and science fiction, offers a detailed survey of this popular television genre. It provides in depth assessments of shows as diverse as *Survivors* and *The Last Train* to *Thunderbirds* and *Doctor Who*. Chapter 9, 'Resist the Host – *Blake's 7* – a very British future' is written by Una McCormack and provides a unique and insightful analysis of the series. The cover image was a BBC photograph of a scene from the television adaptation of *Hitchhiker's Guide to the Galaxy* and the cover design was by Chris Bromley.

BFA-017

BFA-016

BFA-018

BFA-016 *Fantastic TV: 50 Years of Cult Fantasy and Science Fiction* by Steven Savile

Softcover: 272 pages

Publisher: Plexus (January 2010)

ISBN: 978 0 85965 420 3

RRP: £14.99

Steven Savile writes engaging essays on his favourite shows from the past 50 years. He splits them into diverse categories such as 'A New Kind of Hero' (*Wonder Woman, Ultraviolet, Angel, Lost,* and *Heroes*), 'They Came From Outer Space' (*V, The Tripods* and *Alien Nation*) and the first chapter, 'The Stars Our Destination' (*Lost in Space,* various *Star Trek*s, *Babylon 5, Firefly, Battlestar Galactica* and *Blake's 7*). The *Blake's 7* entry runs to six pages and includes a publicity shot of Dayna and Tarrant from 'Harvest of Kairos'. The essay focuses on 'dissent' being the primary creative driving force in the series.

BFA-017 BBC *VFX: The History of the BBC Visual Effects Department* **by Mat Irvine and Mike Tucker**

Hardback: 240 pages

Publisher: Aurum Press Ltd (8 November 2010)

ISBN: 978 1 84513 556 0

RRP: £30

A review of the history of the BBC Visual Effects Department which closed in 2003. The book's largest section is entitled 'Showcase' and details 50 'iconic FX programmes'. All four seasons of *Blake's 7* are covered in eight pages (pages 54 – 61) with numerous colour photos. The *Liberator* features prominently on the front cover and there is a full page colour photo of the ship on page 2.

BFA-018 *The Man Who Invented the Daleks: The Strange Worlds of Terry Nation* **by Alwyn W Turner**

Hardback: 356 pages

Publisher: Aurum Press Ltd (April 2011)

ISBN: 978 1 84513 609 3

RRP: £20

The Man Who Invented the Daleks is the first biography of Terry Nation and it contains substantial coverage of *Blake's 7*. Two (out of sixteen) chapters are devoted to the show and there is also significant further material in the sixteenth chapter, the book's introduction and the closing section.

A section of black and white photos in the book includes two *Blake's 7* shots; the first a publicity still of the second season crew (from the episode 'Redemption') and a photograph of Servalan and two mutoids ('Pressure Point'). Jacqueline Pearce as Servalan also appears on the back jacket in a colour photograph.

BOOKS, NOVELISATIONS

BNO-001 *Blake's 7: A Novel* **by Trevor Hoyle**

Paperback: 204 pages

Publisher: Sphere Books (December 1977)

ISBN: 0 7221 6321 5

RRP: p/b: 85p; h/b £4.50

Other Editions: Hardback (May 1978, Arthur Baker, ISBN: 0 213 16673 9).

Citadel Press Reprint. Two audio books, *The Way Back* (April 2009, BBC Audiobooks, ISBN: 978 1 4084 0987 9) and *Cygnus Alpha* (April 2009, BBC Audiobooks, ISBN: 978 1 4084 0988 6)

Hardback: 🏵 🏵 🏵 🏵 Other Editions: 🏵 🏵

Trevor Hoyle was commissioned by Nick Austin, the fiction editor at Sphere Books, to write this novelisation of the first four episodes. It was published in December 1977 shortly before the series began transmission. Trevor Hoyle wrote the book based on the four scripts, not copies of the completed episodes, which resulted in some of the descriptions differing from that seen in the transmitted programmes. The hardback edition is credited to both Trevor Hoyle and Terry Nation. The front cover of the hardback edition showcased a BBC photograph of the *Liberator* taken by Bob Komar with the series logo designed by Bob Blagden. While the inside flaps of the dust jacket contain a synopsis of the book and a very short biography of Trevor Hoyle, the back cover is completely unrelated to the book. It instead describes the book *Close Encounters of the Third Kind* by Steven Spielberg (1977, Sphere, ISBN: 0 8234 1850 2 h/b and 0 440 11433 0 p/k).

BNO-002 *Blake's 7: Project Avalon* **by Trevor Hoyle**

Paperback: 191 pages

Publisher: Arrow Books (22 January 1979)

ISBN: 0 09 919 340 X

RRP: First Cover: 95p; Second Cover £1.00

Other Editions: Paperback (with revised cover), Citadel Press Reprint

🏵 🏵

A novelisation of the season 1 episodes 'Seek-Locate-Destroy', 'Duel', 'Project Avalon', 'Deliverance' (in a heavily truncated form) and 'Orac' which was published to tie-in with the launch of the second season. Trevor Hoyle included the draft 'Deliverance' script in his manuscript in whole. The pages were either cut for one of two reasons. The completed episode deviated significantly from the draft script used by Hoyle (with there being insufficient time to rewrite prior to the publishing deadline) or the book was reduced in length due to cost factors by Arrow Books. Two editions were published in 1979, the first with a photograph of Blake on the cover and the second, after Gareth Thomas had left the series, with a redesigned cover including a photograph of three Federation Pursuit Ships. Both copies had the same ISBN.

BNO-001 (hardcover)

BNO-001 (softcover)

BNO-002

BNO-002 (2nd ed)

BNO-003

BNO-003 *Blake's 7: Scorpio Attack* by Trevor Hoyle

Paperback: 156 pages

Publisher: BBC Publications (30 September 1981)

ISBN: 0 563 20014 6

RRP: p/b £1.50; h/b £6.75

Other Editions: Hardback (September 1981, ISBN: 0 563 17978 3), Citadel Press Reprint Hardback: Other Editions:

A novelisation of the season 4 episodes 'Rescue', 'Traitor' and 'Stardrive'.

BNO-004

BNO-004 *Blake's 7: Their First Adventure*

Paperback: 204 pages

Publisher: Citadel Press (August 1988)

ISBN: 0 8065 1103 6

RRP: US $3.95

Other Eds: Paperback (Sphere), Hardback (Arthur Baker)

A US reprint of *Blake's 7 – A Novel*. The illustrated cover was by Norris Burroughs.

BNO-005 *Blake's 7: Project Avalon* by Trevor Hoyle

Paperback: 191 pages

Publisher: Citadel Press (August 1988)

ISBN: 0 8064 1102 8

RRP: US $3.95

Other Editions: Paperback (Arrow)

A US reprint with a cover by Norris Burroughs.

BNO-005

BNO-006

BNO-006 *Blake's 7: Scorpio Attack* by Trevor Hoyle

Paperback: 156 pages

Publisher: Citadel Press (August 1988)

ISBN: 0 8065 1082 X

RRP: US $3.50

Other Editions: Paperback (BBC), Hardback (BBC)

A US reprint with a cover by Norris Burroughs.

BOOKS, ORIGINAL NOVELS

BON-001 *Blake's 7: Afterlife* **by Tony Attwood**

Paperback: 209 pages

Publisher: Target Books (15 November 1984)

ISBN: 0 426 19924 3

RRP: £1.80

An original novel set after the events of the final

television episode.

BON-001

BON-002 *Avon: A Terrible Aspect* **by Paul Darrow**

Hardback: 189 pages

Publisher: Citadel Press (January 1989)

ISBN: 0 8065 1112 5

RRP: h/b US $18.95; p/b US $4.50

Other Editions: Paperback (Carol Paperbacks (1991),

ISBN: 0-8216-2503-9)

Hardback: Other Editions:

An original novel telling the story of Avon's early

years before he met Blake. The novel was released in

the US only. The cover design (both versions) was by

Morris Taub which incorporated the season 4 logo. The

hardcover jacket illustration was by Karen River.

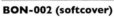

BON-002 (softcover)

BON-002 (hardcover)

BON-003 *Doctor Who: Corpse Marker* **by Chris Boucher**

Paperback: 282 pages

Publisher: BBC Worldwide (November 1999)

ISBN: 0 563 55575 0

RRP: £5.99

A *Doctor Who* book featuring the Fourth Doctor and

Leela. The concepts and characters derived from

the 1977 *Doctor Who* story 'The Robots of Death'.

The character of 'Carnell' from the *Blake's 7* episode

'Weapon' also features in the book. The characters of

Leela and Carnell were created by, and the episodes

'The Robot's of Death' and 'Weapon' were written by,

Blake's 7 script editor Chris Boucher. The book formed

the basis for the *Kaldor City* audio series.

BON-003

BTM-001

BOOKS, TECHNICAL MANUAL

BTM-001 *The Horizon Blake's 7 Technical Manual*

Manufacturer: Horizon, The Official *Blake's 7* Fan Club

Artist: Paul Holroyd

Date: October 1988 (Part 1), May 1990 (Part 2) and April 1992 (Part 3)

RRP: £4.50 (Part 1), £4.00 (Part 2) and £4.50 (Part 3)

Designed, drawn and written by Paul Holroyd, the technical manual consists of a highly detailed set of plans divided into four sections: The *Liberator*, *Scorpio* and Xenon Base, The Federation and Non-Federation (such as the Chase Craft). The manual was released in three parts, with a starter folder being included with the first instalment. A fourth release was planned but never produced.

CLOTHING ETC., ACCESSORIES

CAA-001 *Blake's 7 Cap*

Manufacturer: Not Known (1989)

A black baseball cap featuring the original series logo.

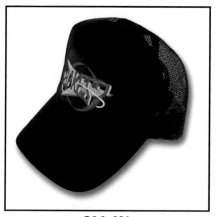

CAA-001

CAA-002 *Blake's 7 Cufflinks*

Manufacturer: Unknown (2006)

RRP: £6.95

Silver plated cufflinks depicting the original series logo.

CAA-002

CAA-003 *Blake's 7 Slogan Winter Cap*

Manufacturer: Auton (2010)

RRP: £10.99

Produced by 'Avon', the group behind the book *Auton: Shock and Awe*, two caps were made, both were 100% acrylic, and available in one size only. 'Well Now' was available in black only, while 'Confirmed' was available in black, red, blue and grey.

CAA-003

CLOTHING ETC., BADGES

CBA-001 The *Blake's* 7 Badge Set

Manufacturer: Communication Vectors (1978)

RRP: 40p or three badges for £1.00

Complete Set:

Individual Badges: 🎫 🎫 🎫

A licence was granted to Communication Vectors on 3 February 1978 for the production of metal badges from the series. Initial correspondence indicated that the badges would consist of the *Blake's* 7 logo, the *Liberator*, the *London*, Blake and Avon.

Thirteen lithographed (printed directly onto tin) badges are known to have been produced; three depicting publicity shots taken during the location filming of 'Bounty', the original series logo, the *Liberator*, a Federation Pursuit Ship, and two badges each for the characters of Avon, Blake, Cally and Jenna. While identical photographs were used, the name of the *Liberator* crewmember was included on the second badge, in the same font as on the *Liberator* badge.

Vila, Gan and the aforementioned *London* are conspicuous by their absence. While it is possible that these additional badges were produced, to date no paperwork or other material has surfaced to indicate they were.

To use the likeness of Michael Keating and David Jackson, Communication Vectors would have required separate agreements with the two actors, and it is possible this was never done. The *London* could simply have been replaced by the Federation Pursuit Ship which would appear in more episodes, and therefore be more marketable.

CBA-001

CBA-002

CBA-003

CBA-002 Illustrated *Blake's* 7 *Liberator* Badge

Manufacturer: Unknown (1978 – 1979)

RRP: 50p approximately

A 65mm badge that unlike the *Blake's* 7 Badge Set was not lithographed but a button badge print covered by acetate. It probably came from a sci-fi comic shop.

CBA-003 Enamel Pins (US)

Manufacturer: Not Known (1989)

🎫 🎫 🎫

There were two colour designs; one of the series logo and another of the *Liberator* on a starfield. These were produced in the US.

CBA-004

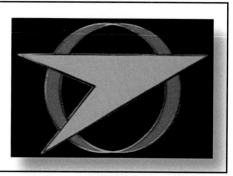

CBA-005

CPT-001

CPT-002

CBA-004 Metal Pin

Manufacturer: Not Known (c. 2000)

RRP: US $8.00

A metal pin of the series logo, approximately 2" long.

CBA-005 *Blake's 7* Federation Badge

Manufacturer: Termight Replicas (July 2010)

RRP: £6.95

A licensed 3cm x 4.5cm enamel Federation badge made from silver plated metal with four colours in hard enamel on the front.

CLOTHING ETC., PATCHES

CPT-001 Sew-on-Patch

Manufacturer: Quick & Fabulous Limited (1979)

Measuring approximately 5" x 3", it featured the series logo on a red background.

CPT-002 Sew-on-Patch (US)

Manufacturer: Not Known (1989)

RRP: US $7.00

Manufactured in the US, this was a cloth patch of approximately 4" x 3". It featured the series logo on a black background.

CPT-003 *Blake's 7* Embroidered Logo Patch (US)

Manufacturer: Not Known (2011)

RRP: US $6

Manufactured in the US, this was a cloth patch of approximately 4" x 2¾". It featured the series logo on a black background, and was stitched to a high standard.

CPT-004 *Blake's 7* Logo Multicolour Patch (US)

Manufacturer: Not Known (June 2011)

CPT-003

CPT-004

RRP: US $5

This was a nearly identical patch to that released earlier in year but of lesser quality.

CLOTHING ETC., SWEATSHIRTS

CSS-001 Season 4 Logo Sweatshirt

Manufacturer: Image Screencraft (1982)

RRP: £7.95

Image Screencraft initially obtained a licence from the BBC to produce *Doctor Who* related merchandise, with a 'hologram badge' arriving in 1980 to coincide with introduction of a new *Doctor Who* logo to the series. On 20 October 1981, the company was granted a licence to manufacture *Blake's 7* T-shirts and sweatshirts. A black sweatshirt with a pocket sized season 4 logo in blue and gold over the left breast was produced. It was available in small, medium and large in adult sizes only from Image Screencraft by mail order or through specialist retailers.

CSS-002 *Blake's 7* Sweatshirt

Manufacturer: Marcus Young Images (2009)

RRP: Sweatshirt: US $31.50; Hooded Sweatshirt: US $56.20

Marcus Young Images sold both standard and hooded sweatshirts that depicted designer Mark Young's montage design of the *Liberator* in the style of Constructivist Russian Art. Both styles were available in white or gray.

CSS-001

CSS-002

CSS-003

CSS-003 *Blake's 7* Slogan Sweatshirt

Manufacturer: Avon

RRP: Sweatshirt: £15.99; Hooded Sweatshirt: £19.99

Produced by 'Avon', the sweatshirt was available in black only with the Federation logo over the right breast in silver.

The hooded sweatshirt had the slogan 'Down and Safe' centred on the garment, and was available in numerous colours.

CLOTHING ETC., T-SHIRTS

CTS-001 Season 4 Logo T-Shirts

Manufacturer: Image Screencraft (1982)

RRP: £3.95

Three varieties were produced:

(1) A black t-shirt with a blue and gold pocket sized print of the season 4 logo;

(2) A black t-shirt with a blue and gold full size print of the season 4 logo; and

(3) A black t-shirt with a phosphorescent full size print of the season 4 logo.

These were available for both adults and children. The phosphorescent logo glowed green in the dark. Like the sweatshirt, the t-shirts were sold by mail order or through genre retailers. Produced in Romania, they comprised 83.4% cotton and 16.6% viscose. Underneath the logo on the left hand side were the words 'PRINTED BY IMAGE', and to the right '© CRESTA CONSULTANCY LTD 1981'.

CTS-001

CTS-002 *Blake's 7* Original Logo T-Shirts

Manufacturer: Platinum T's (Mid 1980's)

RRP: Unknown

This black t-shirt was manufactured in the United States in the mid 1980's. It featured the original series logo beneath which was an illustration of the *Liberator*.

CTS-002

CTS-003

CTS-003 *Blake's 7* **T-Shirt**

Manufacturer: Marcus Young Images (2009)

RRP: US $19.95 – US $49.45

Marcus Young Images sold t-shirts that depicted a montage design of the *Liberator* in the style of Constructivist Russian Art.

CTS-004 *Blake's 7* **Retro T-Shirt**

Manufacturer: T-Shirts-UK (2010)

RRP: £11.95

These white t-shirts were available in adult sizes small to XX large. Beneath the original logo were colour portrait drawings of the original crew members (minus Zen).

CTS-004

CTS-005

CTS-006

CTS-007

CTS-005 *Blake's 7* Slogan T-Shirt

Manufacturer: Auton (2010)

RRP: £11.99

Another 'Avon' product, the slogans were derived from the series with some being deliberately humorous. The slogans were: 'Well Now', 'Down and Safe', 'Ze Klute', 'Oh it Hurts, Pella', 'Jenna, Pull Them Up', and simply 'Confirmed'.

Available in numerous colours, the t-shirts could be ordered with the slogans appearing on generically cut t-shirts or t-shirts specifically designed for women. Sizes 3XL – 5XL were also available at the higher price of £16.99.

CTS-006 *Blake's 7* Liberator T-Shirt

Manufacturer: Gekko T-Shirts (2011)

RRP: £17.99

Manufactured in Portugal, this unlicensed t-shirt featured an original design comprising the *Liberator* and referencing 'DSV 2'. The design was screen printed onto a dark blue cotton t-shirt. It was available in small to extra, extra large.

CTS-007 *Blake's 7* T-Shirts by Push Merchandising

Manufacturer: Push (August 2011)

RRP: £15, with each additional t-shirt, ordered at the same time, £11

On 25 July 2011, B7 Enterprises announced a licensing deal with Push Merchandising to produce a series of retro t-shirts, based on *Blake's 7*. The following month seventeen t-shirts were available to order from Push Merchandising's website (www.shotdeadinthehead.com), with select specialist stores also expected to carry some, or all, of the line.

The t-shirts employ classic imagery from the series, such as the original logo, photographs of the *Liberator*, Federation Pursuit Ships, Servalan, Vila and a Federation Trooper. Quotable phrases are also used such as 'I'm not expendable, I'm not stupid and I'm not going'. There are original designs such as a 'The Federation Needs You!' reminiscent of the Lord Kitchener's famous recruiting poster used to boost enlistment to the English Armed Services in World War I. The t-shirts are available in many colours and sizes, are made for both men and women, and are 100% cotton.

COMPUTER ACCESSORIES, MOUSEMAT

CPA-001 Mousemat
Manufacturer: Stamp Souvenirs
& Sci-Fi Promotions (2002)
RRP: £4.99

A montage of *Blake's 7* images (series logo, the *Liberator*, Blake, Servalan, and a Federation Trooper). Assorted unlicensed mousemats have also been produced by a number of different organisations.

GAMES, COMPUTER

GCP-001 *Starship Command*
Manufacturer: Acornsoft (1983)
Author: Peter J M Irvin
Number: SLG22
RRP: £9.95 (tape); £6.50 (ROM Cart)
Compilation Releases: Acornsoft Hits 2
(Superior/Acornsoft, 1989, £9.95);
Pres Games Disc 5 (Pres, 1989, £9.95)

Although not officially associated with *Blake's 7*, presumably to avoid the necessity of a licence, the game borrows heavily from the series. The design of the initial unnamed starship under the player's command is clearly the *Liberator* and the terminology employed will be familiar to viewers of *Blake's 7*. The ship has energy banks, short and long-range scanners and has the capacity to launch escape capsules. The enemy ships, like Federation Pursuit Ships, fire plasma bolts. A German version was also released in 1984.

CPA-001

GCP-001

GCP-002

GCP-002 *Space Trader: Merchant Marine*

Manufacturer: Meridian4 (October 2008)

Developer: HermitWorks Entertainment Corporation

ISBN: 8 77949 00018 3

RRP: £24.99

Other Releases: Downloadable version also available.

A PC game where players are star traders in a future alternate universe. The aim is to make as much money in as short a time frame as possible. Although not a *Blake's 7* game, the image of the *Liberator* appears on the box artwork and in the game itself.

GAMES, JIGSAWS

GJI-001 Puzzler 240: The *Liberator*

Manufacturer: Hestair Puzzles (1979)

Code: 03202

A 240 piece puzzle that when completed is 10-3/8" x 15-1/8". The pieces were medium sized and the completed picture was a photograph of the *Liberator* in space.

GJI-001

GJI-002 Puzzler 240: Crew on Flight Deck with Blake

Manufacturer: Hestair Puzzles (1979)

Code: 03202

A 240 piece puzzle that when completed is 10-3/8" x 15-1/8". The pieces were medium sized and the completed picture was a photograph of the season 2 crew on the flight deck of the *Liberator* (from the episode 'Redemption'). Only Vila's left arm and torso are in the picture and Blake is barely visible to the right of the picture. A photograph of Blake (taken from the same episode) was superimposed into the bottom centre of the picture surrounded by an effect similar to that of the *Liberator* view screen.

GJI-002

HOUSEHOLD, CLOCKS

HCL-001 Alarm Clock

Manufacturer: Tianguan (1980)

This square Perspex alarm clock was made in China
and featured a photographic image of the *Liberator*. It
takes one AA battery.

HCL-002 Pocket Clock

Manufacturer: Tianguan (1980)

Made by the same manufacturer as the alarm clock,
this pocket watch opened like a fob watch. The display
was a season 2 publicity photograph of the *Liberator*
crew and it requires one AA battery.

HCL-001

HCL-002

MAGAZINES

Blake's 7 was a mainstream television series that was shown in numerous countries around
the globe. Consequently, it is neither possible nor particularly desirable to list all newspaper
and magazine editions in which the series is mentioned. The remit of this guide is to fully
catalogue all magazines that were exclusively related to *Blake's 7* and to summarise those
magazines in which a substantial article on the series was printed in English.

Interviews with the stars of the series that are unrelated to the programme itself (for
example, *Titbits* (May 5-12 1979), 'Girls Wouldn't Leave Me Alone All Night', an interview
with Paul Darrow and his wife) are excluded.
What is 'substantive' is a subjective term and
some readers may question the inclusion of
some pieces and the omission of others.

The guideline followed was simply

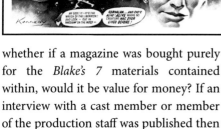

whether if a magazine was bought purely for the *Blake's 7* materials contained within, would it be value for money? If an interview with a cast member or member of the production staff was published then it qualifies for inclusion if *Blake's 7* forms a substantive part of the article. Such interviews are referenced by naming the interviewed person only for clarity. DVD and VHS reviews are not included as the norm.

MAGAZINES, BLAKE'S 7-A MARVEL MONTHLY

On 11 October 1979, Marvel Comics UK, Ltd. published issue 1 of *Doctor Who Weekly*. The *Doctor Who* title experienced growing pains and became a monthly magazine from issue 44 in September 1980.

By this time the final episode of season 3 of *Blake's 7* had been transmitted some months before (31 March 1980). Although it had been thought that 'Terminal' would be the final episode of *Blake's 7*, the series was unexpectedly renewed for a fourth season, reportedly by Bill Cotton, Head of BBC Television.

With the *Blake's 7* production office having been disbanded at the end of season 3, there was a longer than usual break between seasons as a new production team was assembled and contracts negotiated with cast members. The resultant delay meant that filming for season 4 commenced on 23 February 1981.

The relaunch of *DWM* as a monthly title had resulted in the magazine becoming a successful part of the Marvel Comics UK catalogue and Marvel UK thought a sister title, covering *Blake's 7* would also prove popular. A licence was signed with the BBC to produce *Blake's 7 – A Marvel Monthly* on 25 February 1981, just two days after principal filming had commenced on the fourth season. The licence was for two years from 1 October 1981. The agreement was for the use of the characters of Avon, Vila, Dayna, Tarrant, Soolin and Servalan. If Marvel were to use other characters it was the responsibility of Marvel to separately negotiate with the individual actors to use their likeness.

A team was hastily assembled by Marvel to ensure access to filming and to launch the title around the time of transmission of the first episode of the new season. Stewart Wells was appointed editor, art was by Bernard McGowan, Ian Kennedy drew the comic strip and Ken Armstrong was employed to follow the production of season 4 to take photographs. It is thought that Armstrong was the 'guiding force' behind the magazine and it was Armstrong that approached Kennedy to draw the comic strip. Armstrong was the only member of the team to remain throughout its run of 23 issues and two specials. He wrote many of the early comic strips and stories but went uncredited. From issue 15, Armstrong was credited as 'Consultant Editor'.

Armstrong employed two cameras, one to take the black and white photographs and another to take colour photographs. With the exception of a few colour photographs that adorned the covers of the magazine or were included as pull out posters, *Blake's 7 Monthly* (as the magazine became commonly known) was published in black and white, so the vast majority of the colour photographs he took were never published. It is believed that the originals and the negatives were later destroyed in a house fire.

Stewart Wells remained as editor until issue 6 with Bernie (Bernadette) Jaye assuming the position from issue 9. Ian Kennedy was involved in a road traffic accident and the last comic strip he drew appeared in issue 6. Despite the new editor indicating in issue 9 that Kennedy would return with issue 10, he never did. Subsequent comic strips were drawn by a roster of artists with no strips appearing in issues 21 and 22, possibly in a move to save money.

Other contributors included Jacki Thorn (art assistance; issues 3, 4 and 6), Neil Diamond (art; issues 9-14) and Floron Florenzo (art; issues 9-23).

Kennedy drew an initial comic strip to be used by Marvel in promotional material, but not run in the magazine. It depicted Avon, Vila, Dayna and Tarrant aboard a ship realising they were being followed by Servalan, who was standing in the ruined hulk of the *Liberator* (see page 66).

The changing roster of staff was perhaps the clearest indicator at the time of behind the scenes turmoil at the magazine as it coped with a calamitous drop in sales following the poor reception of the initial issues and the unexpected end of the series with the transmission of 'Blake'. The question is not so much why the magazine only lasted 23 issues (and 2 specials) but more how did it survive so long?

The original line up of the magazine was extremely similar to that of the early unsuccessful issues of *Doctor Who Weekly* and *Blake's 7 Monthly* was aimed at a young audience, despite the fact that *Blake's 7* was more adult in tone than *Doctor Who*. 'Vila's Gags!' was a notable example of the childish tone and lasted just three issues.

With the exception of the covers and

the colour posters (where included) the magazine was printed on low grade paper, approximating newsprint. This had several drawbacks not least of which was that the black and white photos that were published were often extremely dark, murky and out-of-focus.

With the exception of issue one (where the strip ran to 10 pages) and issues 19 and 20 (where a two-part comic strip was published), the comic strips were hampered by the short page count allotted to each (8 pages) and the fact that each issue contained a self contained story.

BBC Enterprises expressed concern at the content of the first issue prior to publication, and requested changes, which Stewart Wells confirmed had taken place by letter dated 2 September 1981. It was also agreed that Wells and artist Ian Kennedy would attend a meeting to discuss the strip at Television Centre. Meanwhile Vere Lorrimer congratulated Ken Armstrong for 'so speedily absorbing the mood and characters of the piece' when reviewing the script of the first comic strip 'Mission of Mercy'.

Issue one was dated October 1981 and published as season 4 debuted on BBC1 with the episode 'Rescue' (transmitted on 28 September 1981). The debut issue sold in excess of 37,000 copies, considerably more than *Doctor Who Monthly* was averaging at the time. Issue two saw the print run increased to 42,213 copies but 9,737 were returned by newsagents.

Issue three had a larger print run still at 44,209 but a disastrously high 19,884 copies were returned leading to net sales of 24,325 just below *DWM*'s average. Readers had sampled the magazine and many had not liked what they saw. Vere Lorrimer however

in a note to BBC Enterprises dated 22 October 1981 regarding issue 3 wrote 'It's better than ever. Terrific action feature to start with, with really good articles on Tarrant. An amusing feature on Vila and very informative film reviews. Your artist has succeeded admirably in conveying the style and character of our stars and the drawings of *Scorpio* are superb. The matching dialogue is most amusing and Terry Nation will love it!'

Issue four dated January 1982 was published almost concurrently with the final ever episode of the series, 'Blake' (21 December 1981). This issue saw the largest print run of all issues at 44,489 but net sales of 25,954.

The magazine now faced an uphill battle to entice back those readers it had so quickly lost and maintain interest in a magazine where the main characters had been gunned down in the final episode. Their position was not aided by the BBC who made repeated public statements that 'Blake' was the final episode of the series and would not be returning.

The BBC had retained very few photographs from the first three seasons, making it difficult to visually represent these earlier episodes in the magazine. The quality of the magazine improved with incoming editor Bernie Jaye but the lack of new material and the initial alienation of some readers sounded the death knell for the magazine whose sales continued to decline sharply.

The BBC made an official announcement that the repeats of season 4 to be shown through June, July and August 1983 would be the final broadcast of the programme and that there would be neither a new series nor a spin-off involving characters from the show. Vere Lorrimer thought it best that the magazine tie its last issue in with the repeat run and the declining sales would not have led Marvel to any other conclusion. Consequently, in issue 20, an editorial comment from Bernie Jaye and Ken Armstrong announced to readers that the magazine would draw to a close with issue 23, a bumper double length issue published in August 1983.

A full listing of sales information for the magazine, and the associated Summer and Winter Specials is provided in Appendix B.

MAG-001   **MAG-002**

MAG-001 Issue 1

Cover Date: October 1981

Cover Price: 45p

Pages: 36 (including the cover)

Gift: Free transfer of the season 4 logo.

  With Transfer:

The first few pages of the launch issue set out the background to the series ('Blakes 7 – The Facts Behind The Smash-Hit TV Series') and a who's who to season 4 ('The Aftermath') including descriptions of the Scorpio, the clip guns, teleport bracelets and Xenon Base.

Regular features were 'Vila's Gags!' (generic illustrated sci-fi gags), a book review, film review, 'Ask Orac' (generic questions and answers on a space related theme), a 'Star Profile' (Paul Darrow is interviewed), a comic strip ('Mission of Mercy'), a short story ('Credit Transfer') and a colour poster across on the centre pages on glossy paper ('Paul Darrow as Avon').

Additionally in this issue was a game ('Prisoners of Carpaxia'), a space shuttle competition and 'Heads and Tails' (an interview with stuntman Nick Joseph).

There were no credits on either interview or on the short story. The comic strip was written by Armstrong and drawn by Kennedy. While Kennedy struggled to accurately capture the likenesses of the actors who portrayed the crew, his layouts and depiction of the series hardware were meticulous.

MAG-002 Issue 2

Cover Date: November 1981

Cover Price: 45p

Pages: 36

The comic strip, 'Autona… Planet of Lies!' was drawn by Kennedy and the there were two text stories; 'A Fracture in Time' and 'Queen of the Bankalls' both written by Armstrong. Michael Keating was interviewed (again by Armstrong), as was stuntmen Mike Potter. The colour poster was of Michael Keating as Vila.

The regular features of 'Ask Orac' (which now included questions related to the series itself), 'Vila's Gags!', the book review and the film review remained. A new regular feature was 'Blake's 7 Scrapbook'. This was a photo article of behind the scenes photographs taken during the making of season 4.

Other features included a quiz 'Time Warp Sequence' and a Blake's 7 word search. A photograph of Avon adorned the back cover together with some questions and answers with Paul Darrow.

MAG-003

MAG-004

MAG-005

MAG-006

MAG-007

MAG-003 Issue 3

Cover Date: December 1981

Cover Price: 45p

Pages: 36

The comic strip, 'Renegade', was drawn by Kennedy and the text story was 'Vila's Big Score'. Steven Pacey was interviewed in 'Star Profile' and the actor featured on the colour poster as Tarrant. 'Zap! Kam! Pow! A Sci-Fi Punch Up!' was a pictorial article on the work of the series stuntmen.

'Ask Orac' reverted to answering questions unrelated to the series, 'Vila's Gags!', the book and film review were generic in nature and 'Blake's 7 Scrapbook' completed the regular line up. A new regular feature was the letters page called 'Blake's 7 Points of View' (named after the long running BBC television show Points of View).

A quiz was entitled 'Can You Fly the Scorpio?' and there was a competition to win a video game computer and a one page article on the space shuttle. Again there were no credits as to the feature articles, story and comic strip.

MAG-004 Issue 4

Cover Date: January 1982

Cover Price: 45p

Pages: 36

The comic strip was entitled 'Battle Cruiser' and was again drawn by Kennedy in his distinctive style. The short story was 'Loop of Death' and Jacqueline Pearce was the latest cast member to be interviewed in 'Star Profile' and to appear on the colour poster. 'The Impossible Department' was an article on the series' special effects.

There was no 'Vila's Gags!' in this or any other issue (save for the Summer Special 1982) 'purely as a result of what you [the readers] told us'. 'Ask Orac' was rested for this and the following issue. The other regular features remained and for the first time, a book was reviewed that contained *Blake's 7* content (*Heroes of the Spaceways*).

A charity walk by the cast in aid of Doctor Barnardo's Homes was showcased over two pages. The back cover was a full page colour photograph of Stratford Johns as Belkov.

MAG-005 Issue 5

Cover Date: February 1982

Cover Price: 45p

Pages: 36

The issue was listed as Vol. 1 No. 5 and that style of numbering continued up to and including issue 8.

This month's comic strip was 'Interception' with the story again drawn by Kennedy. A six page story was entitled 'Blood on his Hands' and the 'Star Profile' and colour poster showcased Josette Simon. Script editor Chris Boucher was interviewed by Armstrong.

'Points of View' printed contact information for *Blake's 7* fan clubs and publications, 'Scrapbook' printed more behind the scenes photographs (still very poorly reproduced and dark) and while there was a film review there was no book review or 'Ask Orac'.

'A Star Studded Day' was an article on the magazine's readers attending the studio to watch filming of the series, 'If It's Worn… It's Costume' was a two page interview with costume designer Nicky Rocker and there was a competition in which the prizes were two home computers. The back cover featured a glossy photograph of Betty Marsden as Verlis.

MAG-006 Issue 6

Cover Date: March 1982

Cover Price: 45p

Pages: 36

This issue contained the last comic strip drawn by Kennedy, 'Sacrifice', and 'Wanderlust' was the short story. Glynis Barber was interviewed by Armstrong and the colour poster was a publicity shot of the actress as Soolin from the episode 'Blake'.

There were no reviews this issue but 'Scrapbook', 'Ask Orac' and 'Points of View' were joined by new regular feature 'Paul Darrow Writes…' where Paul Darrow reminisced on the making of the series. In this first instalment he discussed the initial filming of season 1.

'The Unsung Heroines' was an article on the BBC Make-Up department and included photographs from the episodes 'Stardrive', 'Warlord' and 'Blake'. 'Death in the Evening' was a picture article showcasing the final moments of the episode 'Blake' in which Blake and the *Scorpio* crew are shot, with the exception of Avon. The back cover was a colour photograph of Avon and 'Guest artist Roy Kinnear'.

MAG-007 Issue 7

Cover Date: April 1982

Cover Price: 45p

Pages: 36

No artist was attributed to the comic strip 'The Flying Bomb' with the short story being 'The Trap'. Armstrong interviewed Gareth Thomas and this month's colour poster was of Blake from the final episode.

The book review returned as did 'Ask Orac'. Paul Darrow continued to review the first season and 'Points of View' was again a full page.

'Yes… But Will It Fly?' looked at the work of visual effects designer Jim Francis and 'The Image Makers' investigated the role of the camera crew during filming. The back cover poster was of Zeeona.

MAG-008 Issue 8

Cover Date: May 1982

Cover Price: 45p

Pages: 36

This month 'Crossed Wires' was just four pages in length and no artist or author was credited. The story 'The Red Moon' was written by Armstrong who also interviewed Peter Tuddenham. The central colour poster was of Slave.

'Ask Orac' and 'Paul Darrow Writes' were the only regular features this month, with the latter covering the start of season 2 up to Gan's death in 'Pressure Point'.

'Death of a Spaceship' was another picture spread, this time detailing the filming of the crash landing of *Scorpio* on Gauda Prime. 'Setting the Scene' was a very short photo article on the work of the set designers. Four pages were devoted to black and white season 4 publicity shots of Josette Simon, Jacqueline Pearce, Steven Pacey and Glynis Barber (in what was to become standard page filler). The rear cover was a colour photograph of 'Soolin and Dayna' meeting some fans on the *Scorpio* flight deck set.

MAG-009 Issue 9

Cover Date: June

Cover Price: 45p

Pages: 36

New editor Bernie Jaye introduced a fresh take on the season 4 logo on the front cover, renamed 'Points of View' as simply 'B7 Letters' (although it would continue to be called 'Points of View' in the contents page) and abandoned both the film and book reviews. Credits now appeared in the magazine regularly.

'Treachery' was this month's comic strip (written by Armstrong and drawn by Steve Dillon), and the short story, 'Diamond Death' ran to seven pages. The 'Star Profile' was on Terry Nation (but was generic in nature) and the colour poster was of the season 4 crew.

'B7 Letters', 'Ask Orac' and 'Scrapbook' (behind the scenes photographs from 'Blake') were supplemented by Paul Darrow revisiting the end of season 2, the loss of Blake, and Jenna and Dayna joining the crew.

'Blasts from the Past' was a photo feature on weaponry seen in the series, 'Shuttle Payload' revisited the space shuttle, and two pages were devoted to black and white photographs of Avon and Tarrant. The back cover featured a colour photograph of Richard Hurndall as Nebrox in 'Assassin'.

MAG-010 Issue 10

Cover Date: July

Cover Price: 45p

Pages: 40

The page count was nominally increased to forty pages but there were more full page adverts and the back page colour photograph was eliminated (except for issue 12) for the remainder of the run.

'Prey' was both written and drawn by Jerry Paris and ran to five pages. 'The Golden Book (part 1)' was this month's story. Mary Ridge was interviewed by Armstrong in the first of two parts and the colour poster was of the *Liberator*.

The regular features comprised 'Scrapbook', 'B7 Letters', black and white full page photos of Servalan, Dayna and Tarrant and Avon (all from season 3) and Paul Darrow reached the third season in his column.

MAG-011 Issue 11

Cover Date: Aug.

Cover Price: 45p

Pages: 40

The comic strip was entitled 'Cranpax Core' (and was once again eight pages in length) and the short story featured the conclusion to 'The Golden Book'. It was drawn by Steve Dillon (not credited). The second part of the Mary Ridge interview was published as was a colour poster of the *Scorpio*.

'Scrapbook' for the first time included some photos from the earlier seasons, 'B7 Letters' and 'Ask Orac' ran as usual. Paul Darrow concluded his overview of the third season.

MAG-008　　　　**MAG-009**

MAG-012 Issue 12

Cover Date: Sep.

Cover Price: 45p

Pages: 40

'Rendezvous' was written by Armstrong and the artist was Steve Dillon. The two part short story 'Quantum Jump' commenced this issue and Armstrong himself was interviewed. The colour poster was of Avon and Tarrant from 'Stardrive'.

The regular features appeared as normal including 'Ask Orac' for the final time. Paul Darrow covered most of the fourth season in 'Paul Darrow Writes'. The final back cover colour photograph of the run depicted Larry Noble and John Savident as Pinder and Egrorian in 'Orbit'.

MAG-010　　　　**MAG-011**

MAG-013 Issue 13

Cover Date: Oct.

Cover Price: 45p

Pages: 40

Dave Lloyd drew Armstrong's script in 'Alliance' and 'Quantum Jump' concluded. The colour poster was a season 4 photograph of Avon.

Of the regular features, Paul Darrow concluded his articles on the series with his thoughts on 'Blake', and black and white photographs of Soolin and a Federation Guard were published.

The space shuttle was revisited and 'So You Think You Know *Blake's 7*?' was a twenty one question quiz. An illustrated montage of season four imagery, drawn by Geoff Senior, adorned the inside back cover.

MAG-012　　　　**MAG-013**

MAG-014   **MAG-015**

MAG-016   **MAG-017**

MAG-018   **MAG-019**

MAG-014 Issue 14

Cover Date: Nov.

Cover Price: 45p

Pages: 40

The comic strip, scripted by Armstrong and drawn by Mick Austin, was entitled 'Stranded' and the short story was first instalment of 'Plague'. Author Tony Attwood was interviewed by Armstrong and the colour poster was of Servalan from season 4. Armstrong also interviewed Paul Darrow at the actor's home.

'Scrapbook', 'B7 Letters', black and white pin-ups of Slave, and Avon, Blake and Vila comprised the regular features.

'At the Edge of the World' was a six page report on the *Blake's 7* convention of the same name held on 7–8 August 1982.

MAG-015 Issue 15

Cover Date: Dec.

Cover Price: 45p

Pages: 40

'Overboard' written by Armstrong and drawn by Mick Austin was the latest comic strip which ran to just five pages. 'Plague' concluded with its second instalment. Armstrong caught up with Michael Keating and the colour poster was of Tarrant.

'Scrapbook', 'B7 Letters' (which printed a letter from Vere Lorrimer and included a request for fans to send in short stories for possible publication), black and white pin-ups of Cally, Vila and Dayna were joined by irregular column 'Fan Scene'. This set out detailed information on *Blake's 7* fan clubs.

The magazine offered a number of *Blake's 7* publicity photographs for sale (none were behind the scenes shots) and the advert ran across three pages. This advert was included in every issue up to and including issue 19.

MAG-016 Issue 16

Cover Date: Jan. [1983]

Cover Price: 45p

Pages: 40

'Debris' was scripted by Paul Neary and drawn by Phil Gascoine and was once again five pages in length. The text story was the single instalment 'The Comet' by Armstrong. The colour poster was of Vila, Tarrant and Dayna.

The regular 'Scrapbook', 'B7 Letters' and black and white pin-ups of Paul Darrow and Dayna were joined by 'Paul Darrow Loves', a three part article by Darrow on the loves of Avon's life (Meegat and Cally in this first part).

MAG-017 Issue 17

Cover Date: Feb.

Cover Price: 50p

Pages: 40

Gift: Free sticker 'Bring Terry Nation's *Blakes 7* Back'

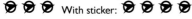

This month's five page comic strip, 'Hunted', was again drawn and scripted by Phil Gascoine and Paul Neary respectively. The text story was submitted by Harry Walter in response to the request for submissions in issue 15. Called 'A New Beginning' it picked up where the episode 'Blake' ended. Josette Simon was interviewed. The colour poster was of Servalan from 'Orbit' and the angle of the photograph showed some behind the scenes panels and cabling.

The remainder of the issue comprised 'Scrapbook', 'B7 letters', black and white pin-ups of Avon and Orac and the second part of (the renamed) 'For the Love of Avon' (this time discussing Anna Grant).

MAG-018 Issue 18

Cover Date: March

Cover Price: 50p

Pages: 40

'Hunger' saw Phil Gascoine and Paul Neary again at the helm of the comic strip, while this month's short story winner was Pamela Wright with 'Takeover'. The colour poster was of Servalan (from 'Rumours of Death').

The regular features were 'Scrapbook', black and white pin-ups of the *Liberator*, Blake (from 'Redemption'), Tarrant and *Scorpio*, 'B7 letters' and the final part of 'For the Love of Avon' (Servalan). 'Fanscene' began an episode guide, which this month covered the first season episodes of 'The Way Back', 'Space Fall' and 'Cygnus Alpha'.

MAG-019 Issue 19

Cover Date: April

Cover Price: 50p

Pages: 39

'Target Practice' was the initial instalment of a two-part comic strip, authored by Armstrong and drawn by Phil Gascoine which would run for ten pages over the two issues. Mary Moulden wrote the short story 'Stress Fracture'. David Jackson was interviewed by Armstrong and the colour poster was of Tarrant and Dayna.

'Scrapbook' featured an array of baddies from season 4, there were black and white posters of Dayna and Vila. 'Fanscene' expanded to two pages and published more fan club information and the announcement that season 4 was to be repeated over the summer (1983). The review of episodes was continued in the 'Episode Guide' and featured 'Time Squad', 'The Web' and 'Seek-Locate-Destroy'. 'Paul Darrow Writes' returned with an overview of the series' guest stars.

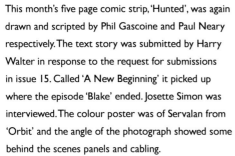

MAG-020 Issue 20

Cover Date: May

Cover Price: 50p

Pages: 36

This issue saw the page count reduce to 36 pages. 'Target Practice' concluded and there was no text story this issue or colour poster. Armstrong interviewed Jan Chappell.

'Scrapbook' continued its look at baddies from season 4, Paul Darrow concluded his review of guest stars in the series. 'Fanscene' contained the official announcement from the BBC that the series was not to return and the editorial comment that the magazine would cease publication with issue 23. The episode guide reviewed 'Mission to Destiny', 'Duel' and 'Project Avalon'. Finally there were black and white pin-ups of Steven Pacey, Avon and a scene from 'Headhunter'.

MAG-021 Issue 21

Cover Date: June

Cover Price: 60p

Pages: 36

There was no comic strip and the short story 'The Hand of Death' was written by Armstrong and concluded next issue. There was no colour poster.

'Scrapbook' continued, as did the episode guide which covered 'Bounty', 'Deliverance' and 'Orac' (called 'Oac' here) and the first five episodes of the second series. 'Paul Darrow Writes' was about his favourite eight episodes ('Time Squad', 'Horizon', 'Star One', 'Aftermath' and 'Sarcophagus' being the first five). In 'All Set …?' the studio sets of the fourth season were showcased. 'Costume Cuts' reviewed some of the costumes created by Nicky Rocker. Black and white pin-ups of Paul Darrow and Jenna (from season 1) rounded out the issue.

MAG-022 Issue 22

Cover Date: July

Cover Price: 60p

Pages: 36

With no comic strip, the only fiction was the conclusion to 'Hand of Death'. Again there were no interviews and no colour poster.

With no 'Scrapbook' either, the page count was made up with a six page *Blake's 7* quiz, with a further page set aside for the answers. 'B7 letters' dealt with the aftermath of the announcement in issue 20 that the magazine was to cease publication. 'Paul Darrow Writes' was about two more of his favourite episodes ('Terminal' and 'Power'). The episode guide covered the second half of the second season, with black and white pin-ups of Servalan and Federation troopers, Dayna and Blake rounding out this issue.

Blake's 7 Monthly was notorious for printing dark, blurry, out-of-focus and badly cropped photographs during its run but this issue saw the nadir. Dayna's head was almost completely shrouded in black ink on page 11 and on page 14, only the most ardent of fans would be able to tell that the almost completely black picture was in fact Bek and Largo from 'Shadow' (which was reviewed in the previous issue).

MAG-023 Issue 23

Cover Date: August

Cover Price: 45p

Pages: 68

This 'Collector's Edition' did not contain the issue number on the front cover. The final comic strip was the five page 'The Omen' by Armstrong and drawn by Phil Gascoine, in which Avon foresees his encounter with Blake in the final episode. There were two text stories 'Altered Image' and 'Probe' both of which were not credited. There was no final colour poster or interview.

'Scrapbook' emerged one final time as did

'Fanscene' (which expanded to three pages with one complete page set aside for the Horizon fan club) and 'Paul Darrow Writes' was about his final favourite episode ('Blake'). There were episode guides to seasons 3 and 4. Black and white pin-ups of Gan, a scene from 'Cygnus Alpha' and the final shot from 'Blake' increased the page count.

One-off features were 'The Rebel's Refrain' in which Vere Lorrimer's words and music to the marching song that appeared in the season 3 episode 'Moloch' were published for the first time; an open letter from Paul Darrow, and 'Star Round Up' updating readers on what the cast had been up to professionally since the end of the programme.

MAG-020

MAG-021

MAGAZINES, BLAKE'S 7 POSTER MAGAZINE

Following the success of the 1994 Winter Special, Gary Russell was keen to continue to publish *Blake's 7* related material, particularly photographs, but realised there was insufficient material, and probably interest, to sustain a regular magazine. A *Doctor Who Poster Magazine* was in development at the time and he obtained the agreement of all parties to produce a *Blake's 7* version. The experiment was not a success and publication ceased after seven issues.

MAG-022

MAG-023

The editor throughout the run was Gary Russell. There was no associate editor for the first two issues with Marcus Hearn being appointed for issue 3 with Gary Gillatt being co-credited for issues 4 through 7. The assistant editors were Marcus Hearn (1 and 2), Gary Gillatt (3), Warwick Gray (3, 4 and 5), and Scott Gray (6 and 7). The designers were Peri Godbold (1), Gary Gilbert (2 – 5), Paul Vyse and Gary Gilbert (6), and Paul Vyse (7).

The publisher was Marvel Comics UK Ltd and each issue had an ISSN of 1355-3879. The magazine had a front cover tagline of 'The Continuing Adventures of the *Liberator* Crew!' with reference to the *Scorpio* crew instead on issues 4 and 6. There was no exclamation mark on issue 1. Each issue comprised 16 pages. Character profiles of original crew members commenced in issue 4 and would have continued to include all crew members, recurring characters, the mutoids, the spaceships, the Federation and gadgetry on the series had the magazine not been cancelled. The character profiles were written by Andrew Pixley. The initial short stories had been commissioned for an abandoned *Blake's 7 Yearbook*.

MBP-001

MBP-002

MBP-003

MBP-004

MBP-001 Issue 1

Cover Date: Dec 1994

Cover Price: £1.50

Centre Poster: Season 2 Crew (8 pages)

Article: 'Cause and FX' by Mat Irvine (Part 1)

Fiction: 'The Harvest' by Ness Bishop

MBP-002 Issue 2

Cover Date: None

Cover Price: £1.50

Centre Poster: Season 3 Crew and Servalan (8 pages)

Article: 'Cause and FX' by Mat Irvine (Part 2)

Fiction: 'Faceless on Ghazar' by Andy Lane

MBP-003 Issue 3

Cover Date: Jan 1995

Cover Price: £1.50

Centre Posters: Servalan (4 pages), Avon (4 pages)

Article: 'Guiding the Seven'. Originally a five page BBC press release issued by the BBC to announce the series and to incentivise merchandisers to purchase licences.

Fiction: 'Widmanstatten's World' by Paul Cornell

MBP-004 Issue 4

Cover Date: Feb 1995

Cover Price: £1.50

Centre Posters: Soolin (4 pages), Vila (4 pages)

Character Profile: Roj Blake

Fiction: 'You Can't Take It With You' by Kate Orman

MBP-005 Issue 5

Cover Date: Mar. 1995

Cover Price: £1.50

Centre Posters: Blake (4 pages), Jenna (4 pages)

Character Profile: Jenna Stannis, Vila Restal

Fiction: 'The Pirates of Pelagos' by Gareth Roberts

MBP-006 Issue 6

Cover Date: Apr. 1995

Cover Price: £1.50

Centre Posters: Tarrant (4 pages), Cally (4 pages)

Character Profile: Kerr Avon

Fiction: 'Done Deal' by Justin Richards

MBP-007 Issue 7

Cover Date: May 1995

Cover Price: £1.75

Centre Posters: Gan (4 pages), Dayna (4 pages)

Character Profile: Servalan

Fiction: 'Suffer the Little Children' by Glenn Langford

MBP-005

MAGAZINES, *BLAKE'S 7* SPECIALS

MBS-001 *Blake's 7 Summer Special 1982*

Cover Date: Summer

Cover Price: 55p

Editor: Stewart Wales

Pages: 48

MBP-006

MBP-007

Published in June 1982, the *Summer Special* repeated material from the first three issues of *Blake's 7 Monthly* with the remainder of the magazine largely showcasing behind the scenes material.

'Blake's 7 – The Facts Behind the Smash-Hit TV Series' was a direct reprint of the article of the same name from issue 1 of the parent magazine, as was 'The Aftermath'. 'Vila's Gags!' appeared twice, the first page being an exact reprint of the gags page from issue 2 and the second reprinting the jokes found in issue 3, down to the exact page layout in each case.

There was no comic strip and the text story was 'Mind Over Matter'. A photo-novel type approach was taken to the final article in the magazine 'And So … To Death!', a retelling of 'Blake' with numerous photographs. The colour poster was of the season 4 crew and the back cover featured a colour photograph of Tarrant and Servalan from 'Sand'.

MBS-001

The behind-the-scenes picture features were 'The Preparations Begin …', 'And So to Location …', 'Studio Works Begins …', 'Guest Artists', 'Studio Recording Commences …', 'Back on Location …' and 'Bangs and Things …' There were black and white pinups of Avon and Vila.

MBS-002 *Blake's 7 Winter Special 1982*

Cover Date: Winter '82

Cover Price: 60p

Editor: Bernie Jaye

Pages: 40

While some of the material in the winter special, published in November 1982, may have been new to readers of the parent magazine, readers of *Starburst* would have found the majority of the contents were direct lifts from previous issues of that magazine.

There was no comic strip and the text story was 'Cipher' which was referred to in issue 15 as appearing 'next month'! The colour poster was of Vila and Avon (holding Orac) from 'Orbit'.

The interview with producer David Maloney was an exact reprint of the interview that appeared in *Starburst* 18, down to the page layout and photographs used. In the *Starburst* version many of the photographs were printed on glossy paper and in full colour unlike here. Its origins are betrayed by making reference to this interview being 'part 2' in the title (part 1 was an interview with the season 3 cast also printed in *Starburst* 18). Also the footnote included the phrase 'We at *Starburst* …' Similarly the interview with Paul Darrow was previously printed in *Starburst* 28. Again the page layout and photographs used in the winter special were identical except for a full page glossy photograph of Avon from season 2 was reprinted in black and white on standard stock paper. Both interviews were by John Fleming.

The article 'Interview Highlights' reprinted excerpts from interviews previously found in the monthly magazine and there was a two page quiz entitled 'Place That Phrase'. The magazine also contained one black and white pin-up of Blake at the *Liberator* flight controls (with Jenna in the background).

MBS-003 *Blake's 7 Winter Special 1994*

Cover Date: Winter 1994

Cover Price: £2.99

Pages: 51

ISSN: 1353 761X

By the summer of 1994, *Blake's 7* was enjoying a resurgence in popularity. All four seasons of the series had been released on VHS and sales had been healthy. Reviews of the individual releases were not confined to 'cult' magazines or fanzines but the mainstream media was reviewing them too. Gareth Thomas, Michael Keating, Jacqueline Pearce and Peter Tuddenham appeared on the Jonathan Ross' Channel 4 chat show on 19 April 1991. Gary Russell was the editor of *DWM* at the time and was aware of the existence of many colour photographs from the series that had never been published and thought a publication showcasing them could do well. Gareth Roberts, who provided comic strips for *DWM* was keen to write a comic script based on *Blake's 7*. Aware that Andrew Pixley had written a substantial amount for an aborted *Blake's 7* book, Russell approached him to ascertain Pixley's interest in editing this work to comprise an episode guide. Pixley readily agreed. Russell had regular contact with both the BBC and the Terry Nation Estate (for the use of the Daleks in *DWM*) and found a licence quickly and easily obtained.

The editor was Gary Russell, the assistant editor was Warwick Gray and it was designed by Gary Gilbert and published by Marvel Comics UK Ltd. The cover illustration was by Colin Howard. The magazine contained an episode guide to all four season, each written by Pixley and a comic strip entitled 'Blockade!' This was set during season 2 and after the episode 'Pressure Point'. It was the first time a comic strip of *Blake's 7* outside of season 4 had been published. It was written by Gareth Roberts with black and white artwork by Martin Geraghty. A late addition were the aborted lyrics written for the end credits of season 4. The magazine included over 50 photographs in full colour and sold well.

MBS-004 *Blake's 7 Summer Special 1995*

Cover Date: None

Cover Price: £2.99

Pages: 51

ISSN: 1353 761X

By 1995, Marvel Comics had acquired the rights to produce a yearbook for *Doctor Who*, a licence that had formerly been held by World Distributors. This was to be edited by Gary Russell who suggested a *Blake's 7* yearbook which was approved. Following the failure of the poster magazine, there was concern that the yearbook would sell in insufficient quantities to recoup costs. By this time the yearbook had been fully written and designed. Rather than have the work go to waste, it was released as a summer special which had lower costs of production and so less copies needed to be sold to make a profit. One unfortunate consequence of the format change was that the magazine had been designed by Paul Vyse for a yearbook format whose pages would have been 7¾" x 11¼". The summer special format had page sizes of 8¼" x 11" which resulted in the layout appearing to be slightly squashed.

Gary Russell was the editor; the associate editor was Gary Gillatt and the designer, Paul Vyse. The magazine contained a detailed review of the production of each season of the series, again written by Andrew Pixley. It contained numerous previously unpublished colour photos. The magazine's origins as a yearbook can be clearly seen when its cover is compared to that of the *Doctor Who Yearbook 1996* which has an identical layout.

MBS-002

MBS-003

**MBS-004
(w/DW Yearbook)**

MCT-001

MAGAZINES, MISCELLANEOUS

MCT-001 Magazines, *Cult Times*

A sister publication to *TV Zone*, *Cult Times* was a monthly genre magazine that differentiated itself from other periodicals by including a detailed television listing guide for the coming month for cult television in the United Kingdom. Each issue would also include a selection of articles. Owned by Visual Imagination it ceased publication with issue 158 in November 2008.

Blake's 7 was regularly mentioned on the listing pages (for showings on UK Gold) but are not included here. Issues that contained significant mention of the series were: 6 (a one page instant guide to *Blake's 7*), 12 (Michael Keating), 23 (Michael Keating again), 44 ('Dead Weight' the episode 'Orbit' is revisited), and 53 (Paul Darrow on *The Strangerers* and *Blake's 7*). *Cult Times* also published seasonal specials. *Blake's 7* was only mentioned significantly in two: S1 – Winter Special (Peter Tuddenham) and S4 – Winter Special (Paul Darrow and an episode guide to the series).

MDR-001 #13

MDW-001 #91

MDW-001 #108

MFE-001

MRT-001 #2824

MRT-001 #2878

MRT-001 #3020

MDR-001 Magazines, *Dreamwatch*

Previously published as amateur magazine *DWB*, the magazine was renamed *Dreamwatch* and launched as a professional title in 1994. Issue one was published with a cover date of October 1994 by DreamWatch Publishing. The magazine was sold to Titan Magazines in 1991. The final issue was issue 150 (of the renumbered series) published in January 2007.

Blake's 7 content could be found in: 2 (Jan Chappell Cover with insert of Brian Croucher for *Shakedown*, James Follett), 7 (Paul Darrow), 13 (cast reunion; pull out poster of Blake on Gauda Prime complete with full episode listing), 14 (Sally Knyvette), 21 (Gareth Thomas), 25 (Jan Chappell), 41 (seven page article on the series), 58 (*The Syndeton Experiment*), 109 (*Blake's 7* 25th anniversary; Gareth Thomas), and 128 (Paul Darrow).

MDW-001 Magazines, *DWB*

Originally called *Doctor Who Bulletin* (or *DWB* for short), this popular amateur fanzine was first published in July 1983 and exclusively reported on *Doctor Who*. In 1989 its remit expanded to include other genre film and television series and it was renamed *DreamWatch Bulletin* allowing its abbreviated title of *DWB* to remain. In 1994 it was re-launched as a professional newsstand magazine, *Dreamwatch* (see separate entry).

Substantive Blake's 7 articles appeared in; 64 (a one page 'News Special'), 66 (reviews of *Avon: A Terrible Aspect*, the US reprints of the *Blake's 7* novels and the compilation videos, in the form of a 'pull out' supplement), 69 (complete ratings guide), 71 (news report on, and full colour back cover advert for, the Comet Miniatures *Liberator* kit), 73 (Gareth Thomas), 76 (front cover, season 1 crew; merchandise guide), 77 (a review of the reissued compilation video tapes, together with 'Aftermath' which was released in the UK for the first time), 81 (Jacqueline Pearce, part 1), 82 (Jacqueline Pearce, part 2), 85 (Paul Darrow), 86 (a two page review of the first eight episodes to coincide with the release of the first four VHS tapes in 1991),

88 (front cover artwork of Blake, Servalan and Travis by Paul Richardson), 91 (Jacqueline Pearce as Servalan from the episode 'Pressure Point' on the front cover), 92 (Ian Scoones, part 1, no *Blake's 7*), 93 (Ian Scoones, part 2, no *Blake's 7*), 94 (front cover; lower half Ian Scoones with the *Liberator* model; Ian Scoones, part 3 on *Blake's 7*), 95 (Ian Scoones, final part), 97 (*Blake's 7* survey results; Michael Keating), 101 (Brian Croucher), 104 (Viktors Ritelis – the director of 'Warlord'), 107 ('*Blake's 7*'s Finest Hour' – a one page review of 'Gold' and 'Orbit'), 108 (front and back cover, season 4 crew; *Blake's 7* special – numerous articles, illustrated two page pull-out poster by Pete Wallbank, David Maloney, Chris Boucher), 109 (article on the Federation), 110 (*Blake's 7* article), 112 (a behind the scenes article on *The Making of Hitchhiker's Guide to the Galaxy* including information and a photograph of the model shoot of the *Liberator*), 116 (DWB 10th anniversary issue – cover artwork by Pete Wallbank of Avon, Lister, Picard, the Seventh Doctor and Spock), 125 (front cover, Blake; back cover, Jenna; five articles on the series including survey results), 126 (series survey continued) and 128 (Terry Nation article).

MFE-001 Magazines, *Fantasy Empire*

Published by Hal Schuster's company New Media Publishing, Inc the magazine ran for several years from the early 1980's. While published in the United States it concentrated on British genre television. The first few issues were published under the title *Fantasy Empire Limited* before it was shortened to simply *Fantasy Empire*. It was unusual in that it made frequent use of illustrations as opposed to photographs.

Blake's 7 articles of note were: 1 (article on American fans, front cover photograph of season 4 crew), 2 (Michael Keating), 3, (episode guide to the first eight episodes of season 1), 7 (a lengthy introduction to the series and characters and a season 1 episode guide), 8 (season 2 episode guide), and 15 (a continuation of the first season episode guide found in issue 3). *Fantasy Empire* Collector's Edition, Issue 2 (yet another season 1 episode guide).

MRT-001 Magazines, *Radio Times*

Each episode of the series broadcast (including the season 3 and 4 repeats) had the usual daily listing, together with the broadcasts of *The Sevenfold Crown* and *The Syndeton Experiment* radio plays. Occasionally the magazine printed reader's letters on the series and was inundated with correspondence following the broadcast of the final episode.

Substantive articles were found in the issues that coincided with the début of seasons 1, 2 and 4 on BBC1 and the premiere of *The Sevenfold Crown* on Radio 4.

Issue	Cover Date	Feature
2824	24 December 1977 – 6 January 1978	'Roaming a Naughty Universe' – a three page feature (including colour photographs) on the series development and début.
2878	6 – 12 January 1979	'Seven up' – a two page interview with Terry Nation coinciding with the start of season 2.
3020	26 September – 2 October 1981	'Watch this space' – a two page article on the basic plot of the series together with an interview with members of the fan club, the *Liberator* Popular Front. Colour photographs of both the fans and crew publicity shots.

3738	9 – 15 September 1995	'Where Are They Now?' looks at what the actors who played the season 1 crew (Peter Tuddenham was not included) were then doing. A 'Bonanza for *Blake's 7* Fans', offered the opportunity for two first prized winners to receive a BBC Video poster signed by all of the original *Liberator* crew (including Peter Tuddenham), a complete set of videos and the Harvard Associates Video Cabinet. Six second prize winners were to receive a signed poster, plus the video of the first two episodes. Fifteen runners up won just the video. Entrants had to answer the question 'What special powers does Cally have?'
3858	17 – 23 January 1998	A one page colour photograph of the actors from *The Sevenfold Crown* together with quotes from each.

MSC-001 Magazines, *Sci-Fi and Fantasy Modeller*

A follow-up title to the defunct *Sci-Fi & Fantasy Models*, this quarterly glossy magazine, from Happy Medium Press, has high production values and covers all aspects of sci-fi and fantasy modelling. *Blake's 7* featured regularly with reviews of the Titan Find kits as well as a scratch built Federation Pursuit Ship amongst other articles.

Volume	Date Issued	Feature
2	2006	'Building Titan Find's *Blake's 7* – DSV-1 *Liberator*'. Andy Pearson builds and reviews this model kit in an eight page colour feature. ISBN: 0 9549964 2 9; RRP: £12.95
6	2007	There are two articles in this issue. 'Here Come the Feds! Scratch-building a *Blake's 7* Pursuit Ship' by Gary R Welsh is a ten page colour article with numerous photographs. In 'The Thrill of the Chase Craft' Andy Pearson assembles the Titan Find release in a three page article. ISBN: 0 9549964 6 1; RRP: £12.95
11	2008	Barry Ford builds a '*Blake's 7* Pursuit Ship' yet another of Titan Find's kits in this five page article. ISBN: 978 0 9558781 2 1; RRP: £12.95
15	October 2009	Barry Ford tackles Titan Find's *Scorpio* resin kit in '*Scorpio* Rising' a seven page article that also covers Titan's *Blake's 7* logo stand. ISBN: 978 0 9558781 8 3; RRP: £13.95
16	January 2010	'Bling for People Going Places'. Andrew Viner scratch-builds a *Liberator* teleport bracelet. ISBN: 978 0 955 8781 9 0; RRP: £13.95
18	July 2010	'2001: Filming the Future'. An interview with Simon Atkinson including details of his work on *Blake's 7*. The article includes photos of the *London* and the *Liberator*. ISBN: 978 0 9564306 3 2; RRP: £13.95
19	October 2010	'Brain Box'. Kevin Davies recreates Orac in a six page article with numerous photographs. ISBN: 978 0 9564306 4 9; RRP: £13.95

22	July 2011	'Conceptually Alien'. James Costello scratch-builds The *Liberator* in this twelve page full colour article, including one full page of magnificent photos of the completed model. ISBN: 978 0 9564306 9 4; RRP: £14.95

MSF-001 Magazines, *Sci-Fi & Fantasy Models*

Edited by M G Reccia this magazine, like its successor *Sci-Fi and Fantasy Modeller*, covers all aspects of science fiction and fantasy modelling. Issues of particular interest are: 1 (Kevin Davies scratch builds a *Liberator* handgun and *Scorpio* bracelet), 7 (Martin Bowers covers the *Liberator*, Federation Pursuit Ships, the *Ortega*, the *FT7*, one of Servalan's ships, and *Liberator* teleport bracelets), 8 ('Scratchbuilding a *Blake's 7 Scorpio* Clip Gun' by Kevin Davies) and 10 ('Life with the Beeb – 1'. Bill Pearson recalls his time working on the final season of *Blake's 7*).

MRT-001 #3738

MRT-001 #3858

MSI-001 Magazines, *SciFi Now*

Launched in April 2007 by Imagine Publishing, *SciFi Now* is a monthly UK publication covering all aspects of science fiction, fantasy and horror. The magazine has contained a few *Blake's 7* related articles, notably in issues 4 ('The Bluffer's Guide to *Blake's 7*') and 29 ('Modern Classic: *Blake's 7*'). Additionally, a two page article appeared in *SciFi Now, The Timewarp Collection: Volume 1*.

MSC-001

MSF-001

MSM-001 Magazines, *SFX*

Launched in 1995 by Future Publishing, *SFX* has become the best selling science fiction and fantasy magazine in Europe. A regular feature was 'Couch Potato' where a group of writers watched and dissected various episodes of genre television. Introduced over a decade after the final season of *Blake's 7* the magazine has featured only limited coverage of the series. Substantive material can be found in the following issues: 4 (cast reunion, Couch Potato: How Good (or Bad) was *Blake's 7?*, 'Blueprint: The *Liberator*' and a one page review of ships from season 4), 9 (Paul Darrow), 32 (news article confirming the recording of *The Sevenfold Crown*), 34 (*The Sevenfold Crown* article and review),

MSI-001

MSM-001

MSP-001

MSR-001

MST-001

MSU-001

MSU-001 alternate

36 (Paul Darrow, Couch Potato: 'Pressure Point'), 39 (the *Liberator*), 44 (*The Sevenfold Crown*, Chris Boucher reviews volume 8 of the VHS tapes), 49 (an article on a Blake-less series, Couch Potato: 'Rumours of Death'), 50 (top 50 genre shows includes *Blake's 7* at number 16, Couch Potato: 'Orbit' and a 'What If?' *Blake's 7* movie poster), 53 (proposed TV movie), 69 ('Probe: Paul Darrow', the actor answers reader's questions), 72 (Couch Potato; Brian Blessed — including a 'review' of 'Cygnus Alpha'), 75 (Couch Potato: 'Stardrive'), 88 (ten best *Blake's 7* episodes) and 197 (a four page article on the series with numerous photographs). *SFX* also releases special issues and *Blake's 7* is included in; *SFX Collector's Edition* (numerous mentions in a themed issue on the best sci-fi and fantasy shows), *SFX Collection 22* (the Top 50 British Telefantasy shows, with *Blake's 7* at number 4), and *SFX Collection 49* (substantively included in an essay on 'Brits in Space' and a full page on the *Liberator* — including a lovely photo — in an article on SF craft entitled 'Britannia Rules the Stars').

MSP-001 Magazines, *Space Voyager*

The first issue was printed by Map Publication in 1982, with Mat Irvine acting as technical editor. The magazine failed to find a sustained readership and ceased publication after a few years. It is most notable for printing, for the first time, the original Roger Murray-Leach blueprints of the *Liberator* in its premiere issue. This clearly shows that the green engine compartment at the rear of the ship was not to be spherical but was built as a sphere to reduce costs of construction of the three *Liberator* models used for filming.

Those issues containing *Blake's 7* related material were: 1 (*Blake's 7* feature, including *Liberator* blueprints, photographs and a quick guide to the series), 5 (Michael Keating), 7 (a modelling article on a scene from 'Time Squad'), 12 (Tony Attwood on *Afterlife*) and 13 (Brian Croucher, Tanith Lee including her work on *Blake's 7* and BBC costume designer Dee Robson whose interview was accompanied by sketches of various costumes including two for Avon from season 3).

MSR-001 Magazines, *Starburst*

Starburst's first issue was published by Starburst Publishing Ltd in January 1978 but the magazine was sold to Marvel Comics UK Ltd from issue 4. From issue 88 (1985) the magazine was bought and published thereafter by Visual Imagination Limited until issue 365 in October 2008 when the magazine and company folded.

Issues of note are: 6 (front cover, the *Liberator*; Terry Nation interview), 17 (Mat Irvine), 18 (front cover, *Liberator* approaching a planet; interviews with members of the season 3 cast; David Maloney), 20 (Jim Francis and Steve Drewett), 28 (Paul Darrow), 30 (Mitch Mitchell), 32 (Jacqueline Pearce), 34 (Martin Bower), 36 (Vere Lorrimer on season 4), 38 (front cover, Soolin; Glynis Barber), 39 (Jim Francis), 89 (Vere Lorrimer), 110 (a two thirds page interview with Ann Bown of the Avon Club), 115 (mistakenly labelled as 114 – March 1988, ten years of *Blake's 7* – numerous errors), 196 (part 1 of a *Blake's 7* retrospective), 197 (part 2 of the retrospective article), 205 (cast reunion), 224 (Terry Nation tribute), 231 (*The Sevenfold Crown* on the radio), 233 (article on *The Sevenfold Crown*), 317 (Blake's Junction 7 article), 350 (article on the recording of the re-imagined audio series), 352 (*Blake's 7* reappraised), and 360 ('Avon Calling' – Paul Darrow). *Starburst Special 21* (six page *Blake's 7* article).

MST-001 Magazines, *Starlog*

The first issue was published in the United States in August 1976 by The Starlog Group Inc. It was announced in April 2009 that the publication had folded. *Starlog* focused on both films and television shows, with an emphasis on American productions. Most *Blake's 7* references are relatively short interviews with cast and crew.

Issues to note are: 106 (Terry Nation), 114 (Gareth Thomas), 116 (Paul Darrow), 117 (Terry Nation), 118 (Michael Keating), 121 (Jacqueline Pearce), 126 (Jan Chappell), 128 (Paul Darrow), 130 (Sally Knyvette), 135 (Stephen Pacey), 138 (Brian Croucher), 139 (Gareth Thomas), 140 (David Jackson), 147 (episode guide of seasons 1 and 2), 148 (episode guide of seasons 3 and 4), 150 (Terry Nation), 163 (Vere Lorrimer), 172 (Stephen Grief), 200 (article on Terry Nation) and 259 (article on Terry Nation). *Starlog Poster Magazine*, Volume 8 contained a large fold out poster of the season 3 crew.

MSU-001 Magazines, Sundry

Blake's 7 has appeared in numerous other magazines over the years from episode, video and DVD reviews to potential news of its return in one form or another and these fall outside of the scope of this guide. More substantive articles can be found in: *Acorn User* (issue 199, Judith Proctor writes about *Blake's 7* fandom and how computers are making life easier for the fanzine editor), *Action TV* (issue 3, programme and episode guides on seasons 1 and 2 and issue 9, episode guide to seasons 3 and 4, front cover included the original *Blake's 7* logo and a season 3 cast photo), *Bowerhouse* (issue 3, a 12 page full colour article by Martin Bower on the construction of a 25" long *Liberator* model with numerous photographs), *Classic Television* (issue 13, article on Roj Blake), *Collect It!* (issue 50 includes *Blake's 7* in a feature on Sci-Fi collectibles entitled 'Brave New Worlds'), *Cult TV* (issue 1:2, *Blake's 7* reviewed as it is shown again on satellite channel UK Gold and issue 2:1: *The Sevenfold Crown*), *Epi-Log* (issue 12, summary of episodes but 'Gambit' and 'The Keeper' omitted and issue 29, *Liberator* on front cover and complete episode summary), *Fantastic Films* (issue 29, series overview and episode guide to seasons 1 and 2), *Fantasy Image* (issue 1, report on the Scorpio II *Blake's 7* convention and issue 2, Vere Lorrimer), *Idols* (issue 26, a guide to the first two seasons of the series and the start of the third), *Infinity* (issue 3, Jan Chappell), *New Voyager* (issue 1, first season episode guide), *SFM:UK Yearbook 2007* ('1011 Models Later' – a 10 page interview with Martin Bower that encompassed *Blake's 7* and had numerous colour photographs), *TV Comic* (issues 1650 and 1651, an overview of the series in 'Star Line', which coincided with the repeat showing on BBC 1 of season 4), and *What Video*, August 1991 (a 3½ page interview with Terry Nation and Paul Darrow).

MTI-001 Magazines, *Time Screen*

Originally published in the late 1980's to the mid 1990's, 21 issues were produced together with a special issue 21, making 22 issues in total. Since that date, the earlier issues have been reprinted to a higher quality. Noted television historian Andrew Pixley contributed numerous articles, while Alice Hendry wrote the majority of the *Blake's 7* features.

Blake's 7 content can be found in the following issues: 2 (a two page article on 'The Way Back'), 5 (Paul Darrow), 8 ('From Script to Screen: Shadow') and 21 ('Seven Up' – a short article on *Blake's 7 – A Marvel Monthly*, in an edition devoted to British telefantasy in comics).

MTM-001 Magazines, *TV Zone*

The first issue of *TV Zone* was published in September 1989, by Visual Imagination Limited. It ran for 323 issues with the final issue being published in December 2008, just prior to the collapse of the publishers in early 2009. A regular feature was 'Fantasy Flashback' an in-depth review of an episode of a chosen television show.

Blake's 7 appeared in numerous issues and most substantively in: 4 (four page review of the series), 5 ('Fantasy Flashback – The Way Back'), 13 ('Fantasy Flashback – Redemption'), 14 (Brian Croucher and June Hudson), 18 (Chris Boucher), 19 (Peter Tuddenham), 21 (Jacqueline Pearce, with artwork by Pete Wallbank), 23 ('Fantasy Flashback – Power'), 24 (Peter Miles), 27 (front cover, Vila from season 4; Michael Keating), 28 (Stephen Pacey), 30 (Stephen Grief), 31 (Sheelagh Wells), 32 (David Jackson), 33 (Terry Nation, part 1), 34 (Terry Nation, part 2), 43 (David Maloney), 44 (Mary Ridge, part 1), 45 (Mary Ridge, Part 2), 53 (Pennant Roberts), 58 (front cover, Vila, Cally and Avon from season 3; Jan Chappell interview), 63 (a two page episode guide to season 1), 64 (a two page episode guide to season 2), 69 (Allan Prior), 70 (a one page picture dominated news article on the BBC Video cast gathering on 1st August 1995), 99 (a two page article

on *The Sevenfold Crown* including quotes from the returning cast; 'Fantasy Flashback – Sarcophagus'), 109 (Vere Lorrimer), 125 ('Fantasy Flashback – Gambit'), 146 ('Fantasy Flashback – Killer'), 156 (a nine page review of the series), 163 (Andrew Pixley explores the original season 1 episode 'The Invaders' that was subsequently replaced by 'Breakdown'), 179 ('Fantasy Flashback – Shadow'), 187 ('Fantasy Flashback – Star One'), 215 (a six page article on the recording of the re-imagined audio adventures) and 218 (a two page obituary for, and article on, Peter Tuddenham).

MTS-001 Magazines, *TV Zone Specials*

In addition to its regular issues *TV Zone* also published numerous specials with each being a themed issue.

S2 (Jim Francis), S4 (Gareth Thomas), S5 (Sally Knyvette), S8 (Vere Lorrimer), S9 (Reprint of Brian Croucher interview from *TV Zone* 14), S14 ('Fantasy Flashback – Orac'), S18 (Fiona Cumming), S27 (Terry Nation remembered), S30 (episode guide to seasons 3 and 4), S44 (a villains special with a four page article on Servalan and a two page interview with Jacqueline Pearce), S53 (Paul Darrow on a proposed TV movie), S76 (an interview, in studio, with the writers and cast of the re-imagined audio adventures).

MZN-001 Magazines, *Zenith*

This was a one-off magazine that was billed as a *Blake's 7* special which was published in 1998 with a cover illustration of Travis II by Pete Wallbank. It contained interviews with Brian Croucher, Paul Darrow, Vere Lorrimer and Peter Miles. There was a 'spotlight' article on the season 2 episode 'Trial'. Other material included fiction by Nickey Barnard and Alan Stevens.

MODELS, GARAGE KITS

Garage kits are so called because they are usually fan produced kits or models made in someone's garage. While many are of professional quality, because they are unlicensed products, it is difficult to

MTI-001

MTM-001

MTS-001

MZN-001

ascertain the completeness and accuracy of the production details.

MGA-001 Federation Trooper

Manufacturer: Kevin Davies (1991)

RRP: £20

A six inch tall model of a Federation trooper which was painted black. The trooper was in a standing pose, gun in arm waiting to fire. The model was mounted on an oak base. Only very limited quantities were made.

MGA-002 Federation Storm Trouper Blaster

Manufacturer: Unknown (1994)

RRP: £85

The manufacturer of this item is unknown but could possibly have been Reshape/GBH. The item came fully assembled and painted and was available by mail order. The kit was available for only a limited period of time and had a short production run. The rifle was approximately to scale. It was primarily made of plastic, while the extending stock was constructed from a car or radio aerial. The box was illustrated with a drawing taken from *The Horizon Blake's 7 Technical Manual* and was labelled as a 'Trouper' blaster as opposed to 'Trooper'.

MGA-001

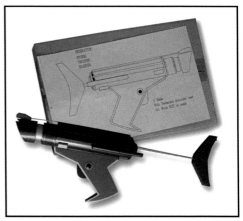
MGA-002

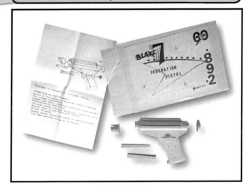

MGA-003

MGA-003 Federation Officer's Pistol

Manufacturer: Reshape/GBH (1999)

RRP: £40

This garage kit was available only for a very limited time and had a small production run. The resin kit comprised seven parts and came complete with photocopied handwritten instructions and assembly diagram. The constructed kit was a full size replica. The box referred to a 'Blake 7 Federation Pistol'.

MGA-004 Federation Trooper Head Bust

Manufacturer: Head-Up Display (1999)

RRP: £18.50

Head-Up Display made predominately handcrafted, painted plaster busts of characters and monsters from Doctor Who but also occasionally made a Blake's 7 or Star Wars item. The Federation Trooper Head Bust is made of plaster, weighs less than half a pound and is 3" high.

MGA-004

MGA-005 Miniature White Metal *Liberator* Starships

Manufacturer: S Couldings (2010)

RRP: £10

Scratch-built and hand-cast *Liberator* models. They were cast in soft white metal and required cleaning, filling, assembly and painting. Each model was 2" in length.

MGA-006 Miniature White Metal Federation Pursuit Ships – Starburst Class

Manufacturer: S Couldings (2010)

RRP: £10

Scratch-built and hand-cast Federation Pursuit Ships that were sold as being 'Starburst Class'. The models were cast in soft white metal and required cleaning, filling, assembly and painting. Each model was 2" in length.

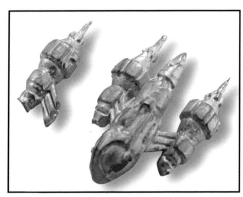

MGA-005

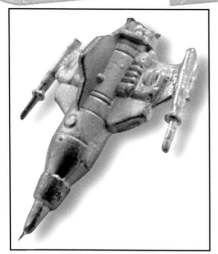

MGA-006

MGA-007 *Liberator* Miniature for Role Playing Game

Manufacturer: Adam Schwaninger (April 2011)

RRP: None

Amazingly detailed in hard-wearing white plastic, this gaming miniature of the *Liberator* was produced in a plastics workshop that was able to cut parts from digital 3D design models. Only three were produced as it was not cost effective to produce a larger batch.

The model is unpainted and around two inches long from the engine ball to the forward neutron blaster tips. There is a small hole in the bottom for mounting on a gaming miniature vehicle/spacecraft stand.

MGA-008 Federation Pursuit Ship for Role Playing Game

Manufacturer: Adam Schwaninger (2011)

RRP: None

This plastic gaming miniature of a Federation Pursuit Ship was produced in the same workshop as the *Liberator* RPG model.

The model is unpainted and just over one inch long. There is a small hole in the bottom for mounting on a gaming miniature vehicle/spacecraft stand.

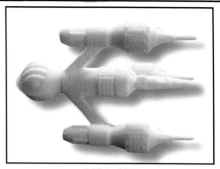

MGA-007

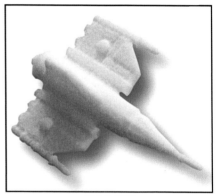

MGA-008

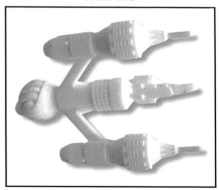

MGA-009

MGA-009 *Liberator* Miniature for Role Playing Game

Manufacturer: Adam Schwaninger (June 2011)

RRP: None

Detailed in hard-wearing white plastic, this 4" miniature of the *Liberator* is twice the length of the previous version. Only a very small number were produced.

MGA-010

MGA-011

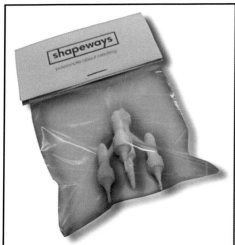

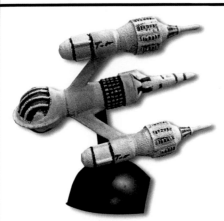

MGA-012

MGA-010 System Ship for Role Playing Game

Manufacturer: Adam Schwaninger (June 2011)

RRP: None

This white plastic gaming miniature of a System Ship is unpainted and is 2" long. There is a small hole in the bottom for mounting on a gaming miniature vehicle/spacecraft stand.

MGA-011 *Scorpio* for Role Playing Game

Manufacturer: Adam Schwaninger (June 2011)

RRP: None

This white plastic gaming miniature of the *Scorpio* is unpainted and is 2.4" long. There is a small hole in the bottom for mounting on a gaming miniature vehicle/vspacecraft stand.

MGA-012 LRV-7 Insurgent Ship

Manufacturer: Shapeways (2011)

RRP: US $8.71 for the 2 inch version;
US $35.71 for the 4 inch version.

Described as an alien fugitive starship for space miniatures gaming, this model is very clearly the *Liberator*. It is available in two sizes, approximately two inches, and four inches long respectively.

MGA-013 Alliance Pursuit Frigate

Manufacturer: Shapeways (2011)

RRP: US $4.43 for the 1 inch version;
US $8.23 for the 2 inch version.

This craft is described by Shapeways as 'always chasing after the Insurgent's crew,' and is an exact copy of a Federation Pursuit Ship. This model for role playing games is available at just over one inch long, or just over two inches long.

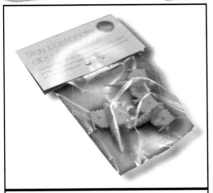

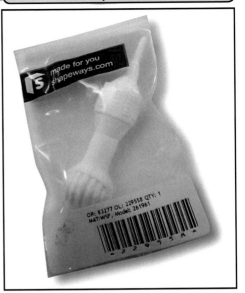

MGA-014

MGA-013

MGA-014 Alien Pursuit Ship

Manufacturer: Shapeways (2011)

RRP: US $5.70 for the 2 inch version;

US $18.77 for the 4 inch version.

Like the LRV-7 Insurgent Ship this model, based on the System Chase Craft, is available in two inch and four inch versions.

MGA-015 Wandering Scorpion

Manufacturer: Shapeways (2011)

RRP: US $3.70 for the 1.3 inch version;

US $9.20 for the 2.3 inch version.

It doesn't take a genius to realise the Wandering Scorpion is in fact the *Scorpio*, which is described by Tarrant as being "Wanderer Class" in the episode 'Rescue.' Shapeways describe both versions (1.3 inches long, and 2.3 inches long) as being in scale with their Insurgent craft.

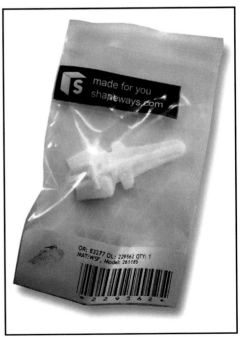

MGA-015

MKT-001

MODELS, KITS

MKT-001 DSV 1 – The *Liberator* (9" Plastic Kit)

Manufacturer: Comet Miniatures (December 1989; Clear version 1995)

ISBN: 0 935 706233

Ref: CM006; Clear Version CM006A

RRP: £18.95; Clear Version: £29.50

 Clear version: 🛸 🛸 🛸 🛸

Comet Miniatures sought the licence from the BBC to produce the first *Liberator* model kit, after attempts to interest Airfix in 1978 had proved unsuccessful. An unusual stumbling block was the insistence of Comet Miniature's owner Tony James that the box needed to include the original series logo. The BBC wanted the season 4 logo to be used (as they had with the then recent US reprints of the *Blake's 7* novels). James was eventually able to persuade the BBC that the original logo was synonymous with the *Liberator* and a deal was finalised. The proportions of the three models that were used during filming all varied, so the kit design was based on the largest which was some three feet in length. Fine detail was added with the assistance of Mat Irvine and *The Horizon Blake's 7 Technical Manual*. Highly detailed (with over 200 parts) and accurate this item remains highly collectible, particularly in the original box untouched. Two versions were produced; a standard version in white and several years later a limited edition of 50 kits moulded in clear plastic.

MKT-002

MKT-003

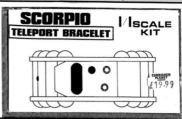

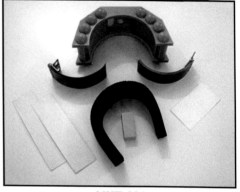

MKT-004

MKT-002 Clip Gun Kit

Manufacturer: Comet Miniatures (November 1990)

RRP: £35.00

This was a limited edition resin kit in four pieces that when assembled was a full size replica of the season 4 handgun. Only 100 were produced.

MKT-003 *Liberator* Teleport Bracelet

Manufacturer: Comet Miniatures (1992)

Ref: GBH

RRP: £19.99

This was a full size resin model with a particularly high level of detail. It was hinged so it could be opened and closed and came fully painted and assembled.

MKT-004 *Scorpio* Teleport Bracelet

Manufacturer: Comet Miniatures (1992)

Ref: GBH

ISBN: 60984 81800

RRP: £19.99

A resin model in twelve pieces that when assembled was highly detailed. It was full size. There was a hinge so it could be opened and closed.

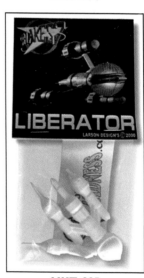

MKT-005

MKT-005 The *Liberator*

Manufacturer: Larson Designs (2000)

RRP: £3.00

This was a resin recast of the 3" Comet Miniatures metal kit that was released in 1988.

MKT-006

MKT-006 The *Liberator*

Manufacturer: Masterpiece Models (2006)

Ref: MSCF70112

RRP: US $69.95

This kit was easy to assemble and comprised just five main parts. It came complete with decals and a display stand. The finished model was 12" in length.

MKT-007 The *Liberator*

Manufacturer: Titan Find (24th June 2005)

RRP: US $130

Other Editions: The original edition could subsequently be purchased from Scale Model Technologies. A reissue of a slightly modified kit with a more accurate engine housing is scheduled for 2012.

The *Liberator* model includes 46 resin parts and is almost 14" in length when built (excluding antennae). Two transparent half domes are included to allow for lighting of the engine section. Also included are comprehensive decals and brass rods for the antennae.

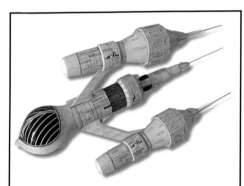

MKT-007

MKT-008 Chase Craft

Manufacturer: Titan Find (2nd October 2006)

RRP: US $65

The Chase Craft model, which is approximately 10" long, includes 21 resin parts and is in scale with the Titan Find *Liberator*. The kit includes two transparent red half domes to allow for lighting of the engine section. Also included are decals and brass rods for the antennae.

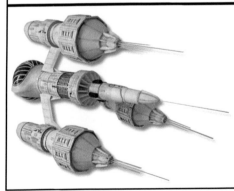

MKT-009 Federation Pursuit Ship

Manufacturer: Titan Find (25 September 2007)

RRP: US $110

The model includes 32 resin parts and decals and when completed is approximately 11" in length.

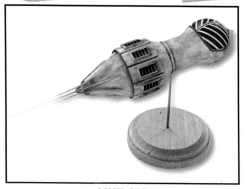

MKT-008

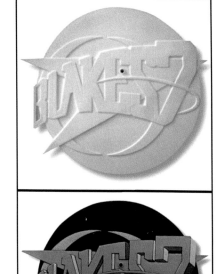

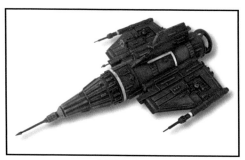

MKT-009

MKT-010

MKT-010 *Blake's 7* Logo Model Stand

Manufacturer: Titan Find (8 February 2009)

RRP: US $40

This is a stand to display all of the Titan Find *Blake's 7* models. It is approximately 8.5" in diameter and when painted is the original series logo.

MKT-011 *Scorpio*

Manufacturer: Titan Find (14 March 2009)

RRP: US $190

The *Scorpio* model comprises 37 resin parts and decals and when completed was 13" in length and just over 5" wide. The run was limited to forty-five kits; thirty-five in 2009 and a further ten in December 2011.

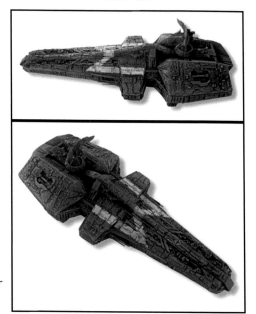

MKT-011

MODELS, METAL MINIATURES

These were produced as 3" models by Comet Miniatures which were licensed and 2" models by Imar Models (Ian Marchant) which were not. Consequently the Imar Model kits were not

labelled as *Blake's 7* merchandise instead they were called 'Personality Figures' and were 1:32 scale. Each came supplied with a painting and assembly guide. Other 'Personality Figures' produced by Imar Models included characters from such television programmes as *Dad's Army*, *Xena, Warrior Princess* and *Space: 1999*. Model makers and fan clubs offered fully built and painted versions. The prices quoted are for the original unpainted kits.

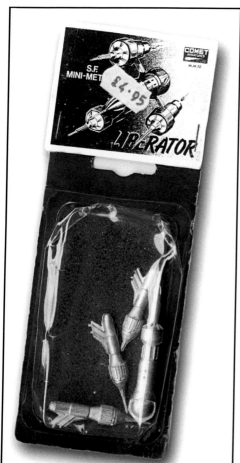

MMM-001

MMM-001 The *Liberator*

Manufacturer: Comet Miniatures (June 1988)

Ref: RB701

RRP: £4.95

This was a 3" model in four parts and made of silver metal. It had a poor finish that detracted from an otherwise accurate design. It was produced in at least three different types of packaging.

MMM-002 Federation Trooper

Manufacturer: Comet Miniatures (November 1992)

Ref: RB701

RRP: £7.00

This 1:24, 3" white metal model kit depicted a Federation trooper in a standing pose, gun in arm, waiting to fire. The kit comprised four parts and only 100 were produced, although a later 'reshaped' batch were also made.

MMM-003 Avon

Manufacturer: Imar Models (1998)

RRP: £8.30

A 1:32 white metal kit that is approximately 2" high when constructed. This model was unlicensed and was figure number 8 in Imar's 'Personality Figure' range.

MMM-004 Blake

Manufacturer: Imar Models (1998)

RRP: £8.30

A 1:32 white metal kit that is approximately 2" high when constructed. This model was unlicensed.

MMM-005 Jarriere

Manufacturer: Imar Models (1998)

RRP: £8.30

A 1:32 white metal kit that is approximately 2" high when constructed. This model was unlicensed. The character of Jarriere appeared in the season 2 episode 'Gambit'.

MMM-006 Servalan

Manufacturer: Imar Models (1998)

RRP: £8.30

A 1:32 white metal kit that is approximately 2" high when constructed. This model was unlicensed and very few went on sale.

MMM-007 Travis

Manufacturer: Imar Models (1998)

RRP: £8.30

A 1:32 white metal kit that is approximately 2" high when constructed. This model was unlicensed and is detailed after the season 2 character so the likeness is that of Brian Croucher.

MMM-002

MMM-003

MMM-004

MMM-005

MMM-006

MMM-007

MMM-008

MWD-001

MWD-002

MMM-008 Vila

Manufacturer: Imar Models (1998)

RRP: £8.30

A 1:32 white metal kit that is approximately 2" high when constructed. This model was unlicensed.

MODELS, WOODEN

MWD-001 *Liberator* Model

Manufacturer: Various companies based in the Philippines (2009)

RRP: US $135 – US $170 (dependent upon size and the prevailing exchange rate)

There are several companies, such as Scale Model Company and Custom Made Models that are making science fiction models out of mahogany, including the *Liberator*. Each is hand-sculpted and painted and made to order. They vary in size from 9" to 12". These models are unlicensed.

MWD-002 *Scorpio* Model

Manufacturer: My Asian Art (May 2011)

RRP: US $175

An 11" model made from mahogany. Each is individually hand-sculpted and painted and made to order. This model is unlicensed.

SUNDRIES, BOOKMARKS

SBK-001 Set of Original Crew Bookmarks

Manufacturer: Minor Miracles/Goode Intentions (1997)

RRP: £6.50 (including postage)

The set comprised seven black and white postcards of the *Liberator* crew, 6" in length and 1.5" in diameter. Each depicted a lithographic portrait of a member of the original crew, together with the name of the character and the appropriate actor, but with Peter Tuddenham being shown with Zen in the background.

SBK-002 Servalan Bookmark

Manufacturer: Minor Miracles/Goode Intentions (1997)

RRP: £1.50 (including postage)

An individual bookmark in the same size and style of the original crew bookmarks.

SUNDRIES, GREETING CARDS

SGC-001 *Blake's 7* Greetings Cards

Manufacturer: Marcus Young Images (2009)

RRP: US $2.59 and US $3.90

Marcus Young Images sold greetings cards in two sizes; 4" x 6" and 5" x 7½". The cards were blank inside with a montage cover featuring the *Liberator* in the style of Russian constructionist art

SUNDRIES, PHOTOGRAPHS

Almost all photographs offered for sale are official BBC publicity photographs taken while the series was in production. In the 1970's and 1980's these could be purchased direct from the BBC photographic library. This practice ended in the 1990's when the library was reorganised and access restricted to BBC staff and licensees.

Other photographs taken 'behind-the-scenes' during production of other series or audios featuring members of the *Blake's 7* actors and crew have also been offered for sale periodically as have BBC photographs through dealers such as Star Framers and Movie Market. These private sales fall outside of the scope of this guide.

SBK-001

SBK-002

SGC-001

SPH-001

SPH-001 *Blake's 7* Magazine Photo Packs

From December 1982 until 7 April 1993 *Blake's 7 Monthly* offered a selection of official BBC photographs to their readers. Two packs were available:

Pack 1 comprised six 10" x 8" black and white photographs of individual shots of Avon, Tarrant, Vila, Soolin, Dayna and Servalan. Also included was one 10" x 8" colour print from a selection of a potential eighteen season 4 photographs: a group shot in front of Slave, a group shot with Orac, a group shot at flight controls, teleport trio (Vila, Dayna and Soolin), Avon with gun, Avon at controls, Tarrant in close-up, Tarrant standing, Vila with gun creeping, Vila smiling, Soolin standing and smiling, Soolin with gun, Dayna with gun, Dayna smiling, Blake and Avon, Slave, *Scorpio* and the *Liberator* (the only photograph not from season 4).

Pack 2 comprised six 10" x 8" black and white photographs of the *Scorpio*, the *Liberator*, Slave, Orac, Blake and the *Scorpio* Crew. An additional 10" x 8" colour photograph was also included which was selected as for pack one.

Each pack cost £7.00 which included postage and packing. Additional colour photographs (from the pack selection) could be bought at a cost of £1.60.

Readers could also order any photograph that had appeared in the magazine at a cost of £1.00 per print. These were also 10" x 8" and black and white.

SPH-002 Lionheart Television Photographs

Lionheart Television, a subsidiary of BBC Enterprises, distributed 8" x 10" glossy black and white photographs from season 4.

SPH-003 Together Again Photographs

Photographs were made available by the producers of the 'Together Again' series of audios. The first two were taken during production of the television series, with the remainder being taken during the recording of interviews. The first seven were made available in late 1997, with the remainder following over the next few months.

Boys in the Hood (Gareth Thomas and Paul

SPH-002

Darrow on location); 6" x 4" at £1.50

Avon in Silver (Paul Darrow on location for 'Hostage'); 6" x 4" at £1.50

Action (Stephen Grief with patch and parrot); 6" x 4" at £1.50

Bound and Gagged (Gareth Thomas, Paul Darrow and Michael Keating); 6" x 4" at £1.50

Blake's Back Cover shot (Gareth Thomas and Paul Darrow); 7" x 5" at £2.00

SPH-003

Wanted (Michael Keating with wanted poster); 7" x 5" at £2.00

Blake's '97 (Gareth Thomas reprises his role as season 4 Blake); 7" x 5" at £2.00

Portrait of Paul Darrow (in garden); 7" x 5" at £2.00

David and the Three Monkeys (David Maloney with Gareth Thomas, Paul Darrow and Peter Tuddenham); 7" x 5" at £2.00

Behind You! (Gareth Thomas behind Jacqueline Pearce); 7" x 5" at £2.00

SPH-004 Autographed BBC Library Photographs

10th Planet Events organise signing sessions and conventions where cast and crew, mainly from *Doctor Who*, but also from *Blake's 7* and other genre shows will appear and sign copies of official merchandise. Since 2001 they have had official access to the BBC photo library and their guests often sign official photographs as well as merchandise. These licensed autographed photos were originally offered for sale at an RRP of £8.00, but the cost has since risen to £10.00. Unsigned photographs are not offered for sale

GARETH THOMAS
"Blakes 7"
© BBC WorldWide 2002   10th Planet

SPH-004

SPI-001

SPI-001 *Blake's 7* Launch Cover No. 1

Manufacturer: The Stamp Centre (6 March 2004)

RRP: £14.95

This is a first day cover, of composite design, depicting Servalan and signed by Jacqueline Pearce. The run was limited edition to 1,000 copies. The back of the cover depicted a photograph of Servalan from 'Aftermath' and generally described the series and the character of Servalan in particular. A brief biography of Jacqueline Pearce was also included. The artwork was by Ian F Burgess.

SPI-002

SPO-001

SPO-002

SPI-002 *Blake's 7* **First Day Cover No. 2**

Manufacturer: The Stamp Centre (15 July 2007)

RRP: £24.95

A first day cover for the story 'The City at the Edge of the World', signed by Colin Baker and Paul Darrow. The cover was limited to 1,000 copies. The artwork was by Ian F Burgess.

SUNDRIES, POSTCARDS

SPO-001 BBC Postcards

Manufacturer: BBC (1978 – 1981)

These publicity cards were printed to promote the series and were often given away to fans that contacted the BBC. Each season a new set of postcards were issued. The cards for the first three seasons were in black and white (5.5" x 3.5") and colour for the final season (6" x 4"). Each set comprised a group shot of the principle cast and individual shots of the regulars (which included Servalan from season 2 onwards, and Travis for just season 2), and bore the actors names, the characters names and the appropriate series logo. The first set also included a postcard of the *Liberator*, and the fourth set included an individual postcard of Peter Tuddenham with Orac. A further postcard was given away free to purchasers of the compilation video tape *Orac*.

SPO-002 Fabulous Films Postcards

Manufacturer: Fabulous Films (1997)

Two colour postcards were produced and given away with the first two VHS episodic releases. The first was of the series logo, the second a season 2 publicity photograph. On the back of each was a list of the episodes on the first seven tapes.

SUNDRIES, POSTERS, PRINTS & CANVAS ARTWORK

SPP-001 Blake Lithographic Portrait

Manufacturer: Minor Miracles/Good Intentions (1997)

RRP: £6.50

🌀 🌀 🌀 🌀

A4 sized black and white print officially approved by Gareth Thomas.

SPP-002 Avon Lithographic Portrait

Manufacturer: Minor Miracles/Good Intentions (1998)

RRP: £6.50

🌀 🌀 🌀 🌀

A4 sized black and white print officially approved by Paul Darrow.

SPP-001   **SPP-002**

SPP-003 Servalan Print

Manufacturer: The Stamp Centre (2002)

RRP: £14.95

🌀 🌀 🌀

A limited edition 8¼" x 11¾" composite design print featuring Servalan which was signed by Jacqueline Pearce.

SPP-004

SPP-003

SPP-004 Avon Canvas Artwork – Variant 1

Manufacturer: 10th Planet Events (2009)

RRP: £114

🌀 🌀 🌀

A limited edition 24" x 32" x 2" canvas artwork featuring a close up portrait of Avon from season 3 on stretched canvas with a wooden frame. It was signed by Paul Darrow.

SPP-005 Avon Canvas Artwork – Variant 2

Manufacturer: 10th Planet Events (2009)

RRP: £114

🌀 🌀 🌀

SPP-005

A limited edition 24" x 32" x 2" canvas artwork featuring Avon from season 3 holding a *Liberator* gun on stretched canvas with a wooden frame. It was signed by Paul Darrow.

SPP-006

SPP-007

SPP-008

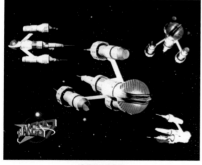

SPP-009

SPP-006 Avon Print

Manufacturer: 10th Planet Events (2009)

RRP: £28

A limited edition (of 40) 10" x 15" print of Avon and the *Scorpio*.

SPP-007 Season 3 Cast Canvas Artwork

Manufacturer: 10th Planet Events (2009)

RRP: £213

Limited edition 24" x 32" x 2" canvas artwork of the season 3 cast on stretched canvas with a wooden frame. The canvas was signed by Paul Darrow, Jacqueline Pearce, Jan Chappell, Michael Keating and Steven Pacey.

SPP-008 *Blake's 7* Cast Montage Canvas Artwork

Manufacturer: 10th Planet Events (2009)

RRP: £213

This montage was a limited edition 24" x 32" x 2" composite canvas artwork of main cast members and the *Liberator* on stretched canvas with a wooden frame. It was signed by Paul Darrow, Jacqueline Pearce, Glynis Barber, Brian Croucher, Gareth Thomas, Jan Chappell, Michael Keating, Mat Irvine and Steven Pacey.

SPP-009 *Liberator* Montage Canvas Artwork

Manufacturer: 10th Planet Events (2009)

RRP: £213

This composite artwork was a limited edition 24" x 32" x 2" montage of four images of the *Liberator*, together with the original series logo. It was produced on stretched canvas and mounted on a wooden frame. It was signed by Paul Darrow, Jacqueline Pearce, Glynis Barber, Brian Croucher, Gareth Thomas, Jan Chappell, Michael Keating, Mat Irvine and Steven Pacey.

SPP-010 *Blake's* **7 Artwork**

Manufacturer: Gauda Prime Designs (April 2011)

Designer: Damien May

RRP: £5 for all prints, except size A3 at £7.

P&P was £3 within the UK

A 12" x 10" print of Avon launched this line of original artwork, produced under licence from B7 Media. A total of three 12" x 10" prints, two 10" x 8" prints (of Cally and Vila respectively) and ten A3 prints (mainly of the *Liberator, Scorpio* and *Federation Pursuit Ships*) were made available. The prints were available by mail order.

    The first 150 purchases also received a free 10" x 8" or 12" x 10" print of an unseen design.

SPP-010

SUNDRIES, TRADING CARDS

STR-001 Strictly Ink Promotional Card

Manufacturer: Strictly Ink (2005)

RRP: Free

This was a promotional card for a proposed series of *Blake's* 7 trading cards. The trading cards were never issued.

STR-002 Argentinean Trading Cards

Manufacturer: Unknown Argentinean Company (circa 1985-90 or 2010)

RRP: ???

Three sets of cards were produced and sold in boxes, labelled 'Serie A, Serie B' and 'Serie C'. The cards were of poor quality and measured 1½" by 2¼". They contained photos from the series, often with incorrect aspect ratios to 'fit' the designated space on the card. The boxes did not correspond to the first three seasons of the show as might be expected. These may very well be bootleg items, and should be viewed with suspicion.

STR-001

STR-002

TOYS

Despite a large marketing push by the BBC and Roger Hancock on behalf of Terry Nation and initial interest from numerous companies, an extensive catalogue of toys based on the series failed to materialise. The success of the Corgi *Liberator* toy provides a glimpse of what might have been.

TYA-001

TYA-002

TOYS, ARGENTINIAN

Small toys were apparently manufactured in Argentina. While they were produced to professional quality it has proven impossible to confirm their provenance, so great care should be taken when purchasing any of these products. Many of the items state 'Industria Argentina' indicating that they were manufactured in the country.

It is claimed that some of the smaller items were distributed as free gifts inside breakfast cereal boxes, but this is also unverified.

TYA-001 Dominos
Manufacturer: Unknown Argentinean Company
(circa 1985-90 or 2010)
RRP: ???

A set of 28 plastic dominos with photos of Blake, Cally, Avon, Vila, Servalan, the *Liberator* and the original logo.

TYA-002 Ludo Board Game
Manufacturer: Unknown Argentinean Company
(circa 1985-90 or 2010)
RRP: ???

The game comprised a plastic ludo board with sixteen pieces, and centre section to 'throw' the dice. The board had four distinct images from the series – Blake, the *Liberator*, the original logo and the Season 3 cast.

TYA-003 Mini Pinball Machine

Manufacturer: Unknown Argentinean Company

(circa 1985-90 or 2010)

RRP: ???

A plastic, handheld, pinball machine. The background image was of the Season 2 crew from 'Redemption'.

TYA-004 Pinball Machine

Manufacturer: Unknown Argentinean Company

(circa 1985-90 or 2010)

RRP: ???

A handheld pinball machine that was 11" by 4¾". The background image was a Season 1 publicity photo of the crew.

TYA-005 Plastic Ring

Manufacturer: Unknown Argentinean Company

(circa 1985-90 or 2010)

RRP: ???

The ring was a white hexagon with a circular face. The outer plastic was white and the front of the ring was adorned with the original logo on a light blue background.

TYA-006 Spinning Tops (Small)

Manufacturer: Unknown Argentinean Company

(circa 1985-90 or 2010)

RRP: ???

Six of these miniature spinning tops were produced. Each had a white base and a circular photograph of a main cast member, together with the appropriate character and actor's name and the original series logo. The characters were Roj Blake (Gareth Thomas), Jenna Stannis (Sally Knyvette), Kerr Avon (Paul Darrow), Vila Restal (Michael Keating), Cally (Jan Chappell) and Servalan (Jacqueline Pearce).

TYA-003

TYA-005

TYA-004

TYA-006

TYA-007

TYA-007 Spinning Tops (Large)

Manufacturer: Unknown Argentinean Company (circa 1985-90 or 2010)

RRP: ???

Two sets of three spinning tops were produced. Each set came in a clear plastic bag with a cardboard fastener, which depicted Jenna, Blake and Cally from Season 1, the *Liberator* and the original logo. Each spinning top had a photographic image of a member of the crew together with the logo.

Set one comprised Blake, Servalan and Vila and set two Tarrant, Avon and Jenna.

TOYS, GENERAL

TYG-001 Corgi *Liberator* (2" Toy)

Manufacturer: The Mettoy Co Ltd sold under the Corgi Junior Line (January 1979)

RRP: £0.75; Corgi Double-pack; £1.25

Corgi's parent company, The Mettoy Co Ltd, showed immediate interest in the series and originally intended to develop a large die cast *Liberator* which would incorporate the voice of Zen. In November 1977, it was agreed that Mettoy would also develop a smaller version with 'working features' for their Corgi Junior Line. When Mettoy decided not to proceed with the larger version, they suggested packaging the Corgi version three different ways to maximise sales and royalty payments. By this time, the toy was a static model only. All three versions were included in the 1980 catalogue that Corgi distributed to retailers to give them advance notice of new product lines, presumably having missed the print deadline for the 1979 catalogue.

TYG-001a E2 *Blake's 7 Liberator*

This was the original design of the Corgi model and the *Liberator* was faithfully reproduced with a white hull, gold panelling and a green tinted engine compartment to the rear. An early prototype contains the same hull design but a bulbous non-spherical engine, which may have

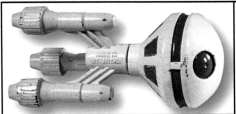

TYG-001a (prototype)

TYG-001a

been a result of the initial lack of visual material.

The diecast metal spaceship is sealed within a plastic blister and cardboard pack, with the original logo prominently displayed at the top of the packaging. All editions are stamped ©1977 on the underside of the main hull. Width: 101 mm, Depth: 33 mm. It went on sale in January 1979 and before it was discontinued when Mettoy went into administration, over 445,000 were sold worldwide.

In total over 910,000 Corgi *Liberator* toys were sold between January 1979 and June 1982.

The original version (E2) was re-released in 2005 as part of a limited DVD box set of the third season. Originally intended to be released with the season two DVD, the ships were delivered unpainted and already sealed in their dome shaped blister packs. As the hull and weapon pods were in silver and the central section black, these were scrapped by BBC Worldwide, and the decision taken to release correctly painted versions with the season 3 set. Some of the unpainted versions made their way onto the market.

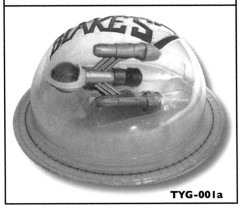

TYG-001a

TYG-001b E44 Starship *Liberator*

Released in the second quarter of 1979, this edition was simply entitled 'Starship *Liberator*' and had no reference to the series on the packaging other than through the use of the name *Liberator* and the copyright line. There were three versions of this edition:

(1) the toy comprised a metallic silver hull, gold collar, yellow probes and engine housing and the front section of the central hull was white plastic;

(2) this variant was identical except for a silver (not gold) collar; and

TYG-001b

(3) this version was the same as the first variant except the hull was metallic blue as opposed to metallic silver.

Like the original version 'Starship *Liberator*' was extremely successful with nearly 320,000 being sold.

TYG-001c

TYG-002

TYG-003

TYG-001c E2512 Starship *Liberator* and NASA Space Shuttle Twin Pack

Released in the first quarter of 1980, this twin pack comprised the metallic silver version of E44 (with the gold collar) and the NASA Space Shuttle Enterprise. Again the only reference to the series on the packaging was the use of the name *Liberator* and the copyright line.

The twin pack sold in excess of 145,000 units.

On 17 May 1982, Mettoy sought approval to market the Corgi *Liberator* internationally in a five model gift set that would comprise the USS Enterprise (*Star Trek*), a Klingon Warship (*Star Trek*), a Starfighter (*Buck Rogers*), the *Liberator* and a NASA Space Shuttle. Production was due to commence in July 1982 for sales later that year. Draft packaging was passed to the BBC for approval and the set was to be known as 'Space Flight'.

Approval was readily given by the BBC and the 'Copyright Owner' on 25 May 1982 but the gift set never went into production as Mettoy's financial difficulties mounted.

TYG-002 Federation Interceptor

Manufacturer: Blue Box Toys (c. 1978)

Whilst described as a 'Federation Interceptor' the toy bears no resemblance to the Federation Pursuit Ships seen on screen. As little visual material was available for review by merchandisers, it is likely that the toy was produced without reference to the actual models. Stickers of the *Blake's 7* logo are the only element that links the interceptor to the series.

It is not known whether a pre-existing toy line was adorned with these stickers to sell as *Blake's 7* merchandise, or following the end of the licence, the toys continued to be sold but without reference to the series or the incorporation of the logo.

This item is extremely hard to find, but is less marketable than it otherwise would be as the model was never seen in the series.

TYG-003 Neutron Space Rifle

Manufacturer: Jotastar (c. 1979)

ISBN: None

Jotastar originally intended to produce three toys; a Federation guard helmet (which quickly ran into development problems), a *Liberator* handgun that was to be sold as 'Blake's Blaster' and a Federation toy rifle. Only the latter was produced. It fired white ping pong balls (six were included with the toy) and had a detachable clip. It was available in both blue and gold and was approximately to scale.

TYG-004 Plastic Spaceships

Manufacturer: Blue Box Toys (c. 1978)

Three ships were released by Blue Box Toys in addition to the 'Federation Interceptor'. While the circular spaceship had not appeared on screen at the time of its manufacture, it does bear a striking resemblance to the Gauda Prime ships that shot down the *Scorpio* in the season 4 episode 'Blake'. Each was driven by a friction motor and were available in multiple colours. Many were sold without the *Blake's 7* logo.

TYG-004

VIDEO, BBC VIDEO COMPILATION RELEASES

VBB-001a *Blake's 7: The Beginning*

Format: VHS, and Betamax: 121 minutes approx

Publisher: BBC Video (1985, re-release 5 March 1990)

RRP: £24.95; Re-release: £9.99

Rating: PG

Cover: Tony Geddes

Ref: BBCV 2000 (VHS) / BBCB 2000 (Betamax); Re-release: BBCV 4326

Other Editions: Japanese laserdisc, BBC Episodic Release, Fabulous Films Episodic Release, Fabulous Films 25th Anniversary VHS Release, DVD releases

An edited 'movie' format release of the first four episodes. With a total running time of a little over two hours substantial cuts were made. 'The Way Back'

is reduced to just 15 minutes; 'Space Fall' remained nearly intact at 45 minutes; 'Cygnus Alpha' fares less well at 35 minutes, with 'Time Squad' being reduced to 25 minutes in duration. With both 'Cygnus Alpha' and 'Time Squad' there was some reordering of scenes which would seem to be an attempt to maintain a balance between the various plot strands following the edits.

While substantial cuts were clearly made, one scene was left intact that would not be seen again until the DVD release in 2004. In 'Space Fall', after the scene in which Gan forces the guard to open the door, the action cuts back to Avon's fight with the technician. Avon is shown being strangled and the technician is banging Avon's head against the wall. To

VBB-001a

VBB-001b

make the technician release his grasp, Avon uses both hands to smack the technician around the ears. On subsequent releases, after the previous scene in the cell, the fight with the technician resumes with Avon slamming him into the wall.

All of the original compilation releases came in a thick black video case, while subsequent releases were in thinner, clear cases. This video was re-released in 1990 in VHS format only. It was also released in Japan in 1985 with Japanese subtitles, Australia and New Zealand in March 1987, and in Greece with Greek subtitles.

VBB-001b *Blake's 7: The Beginning*
Format: Laserdisc (Japan only): 121 minutes approx
Publisher: Pony Vision (1985)
RRP: Unknown
Other Editions: BBC Compilation Tape Release, BBC Episodic Release, Fabulous Films Episodic Release, Fabulous Films 25th Anniversary VHS Release, DVD releases

The laserdisc was only distributed in Japan and was in NTSC format with Japanese subtitles. It was released complete with inner sleeve notes by Pony Vision in association with BBC Video.

VBB-002a *Blake's 7: Duel*
Format: VHS, and Betamax: 120 minutes approximately
Publisher: BBC Video (15th July 1985;
re-release 5 March 1990)
RRP: £24.95; Re-release: £9.99
Rating: PG
Cover: Tony Geddes
Ref: BBCV 2031 (VHS) / BBCB 2031 (Betamax);
Re-release: BBCV 4327
Other Editions: Japanese laserdisc, BBC Episodic Release, Fabulous Films Episodic Release, Fabulous Films 25th Anniversary VHS Release, DVD releases

An edited 'movie' format release of the season 1

episodes 'Seek-Locate-Destroy', 'Duel' and 'Project Avalon'. With the same running time as *The Beginning* but only comprising three episodes the cuts were minor in comparison. This was re-released in VHS format only in March 1990 and was released in Japan in 1986 with Japanese subtitles and Australia and New Zealand in September 1987.

VBB-002b *Blake's 7: Duel*

Format: Laserdisc (Japan only):

120 minutes approximately

Publisher: Pony Vision (1986)

RRP: Unknown

Other Editions: BBC Compilation Tape Release, BBC Episodic Release, Fabulous Films Episodic Release, Fabulous Films 25th Anniversary VHS Release, DVD releases

The laserdisc was only distributed in Japan in NTSC format with Japanese subtitles. It was released complete with inner sleeve notes in 1986 by Pony Vision in association with BBC Video.

VBB-002a

VBB-002b

VBB-003 *Blake's 7: Orac*

Format: VHS and Betamax: 120 minutes approximately

Publisher: BBC Video (21st July 1986;

re-release 5 March 1990)

RRP: £24.95; Re-release: £9.99

Rating: PG

Cover: Tony Geddes

Ref: BBCV 2037 (VHS) / BBCB 2037 (Betamax);

Re-release: BBCV 4328

Other Editions: BBC Episodic Release, Fabulous Films Episodic Release, Fabulous Films 25th Anniversary VHS Release, DVD releases

An edited 'movie' format release of the season 1 and 2 episodes 'Deliverance', 'Orac' and 'Redemption'. This was re-released in VHS format only in March 1990 and was released in and was released in Japan in 1986 with Japanese subtitles and Australia and New Zealand in

VBB-003

VBB-004a

VBB-004b

Other Editions: BBC Episodic Release, Fabulous Films Episodic Release, Fabulous Films 25th Anniversary VHS Release, DVD releases

An edited 'movie' format release of the season 3 episodes 'Aftermath', 'Powerplay' and 'Sarcophagus'. 'Sarcophagus' was written by Tanith Lee and was the first episode the BBC released not written by Terry Nation.

This video was originally only released in Australia. The cover was a front photograph of the *Liberator* beneath the original logo. To the bottom left of the cover is an inset photograph of Dayna fighting Section Leader Clegg in the teleport room. It was released in New Zealand in February 1989.

VBB-004b *Blake's 7: Aftermath*
Format: VHS: 120 minutes approximately
Publisher: BBC Video (5 March 1990)
RRP: £9.99
Rating: PG
Cover: Unknown
Ref: BBCV 4329
Other Editions: BBC Episodic Release, Fabulous Films Episodic Release, Fabulous Films 25th Anniversary VHS Release, DVD releases

This video was originally released in Australia under the title *The Aftermath* in 1987, appearing in the UK three years later as simply *Aftermath*.

Unlike *The Aftermath*, this tape was only available in VHS, not Betamax, and had a different cover to the Australian release. The new cover was a side shot of the *Liberator* being struck by two green laser beams. The cover reduces the title to simply *Aftermath* although the cassette itself and the on screen credits still refer to *The Aftermath*.

October 1987. A postcard of the cover art was also included for a limited time with the latter release, with a sticker on the cover highlighting its inclusion in many cases.

VBB-004a *Blake's 7: The Aftermath*
Format: VHS and Betamax: 120 minutes approximately
Publisher: BBC Video (1987 in Australia, 1989 in New Zealand)
RRP: AUS $29.95
Rating: PG
Cover: Unknown but stated to be a 'BBC Video Presentation by Susan Thorne'
Ref: BBC2040 2

VIDEO, BBC VIDEO EPISODIC RELEASES

BBC Video released the entire series of fifty two episodes between January 1991 and January 1993. Each video cassette contained two episodes; twenty-six tapes were released in total. The first four cassettes were released on 7 January 1991, with two tapes being released every other month thereafter.

Each episode of the series was announced as being released uncut, except for the episode 'Space Fall'. To avoid the BBFC certifying the tape the relatively new rating of '12' (which was introduced on 1 August 1989) an edit was made to the scene that followed Gan forcing the guard to open the door. On the VHS tape, Avon is seen throwing the technician against the wall and knocking him unconscious. The few preceding seconds in which Avon is being strangled by the technician who is also banging Avon's head against the wall was cut, together with Avon smacking the technician around the head forcing him to release his grip.

Although the cover to tape 20 which comprised the episodes 'Terminal' and 'Rescue' stated it contained 'Two Complete Unedited Episodes' there were some cuts made towards the end of 'Rescue'. When Vila emerges from hiding and finds the Federation rifle, the scene is cut short where he appears to way up the bottle and the gun. After Dorian's death, Dayna goes over to the body of Dorian's late partner. On the VHS tape the scene is edited and she is no longer seen looking back at her comrades and Soolin leaving the cavern is also cut. This appears to have been a genuine oversight as this was the episode as broadcast for the 1983 repeat. An unedited version of 'Rescue' would not be released until the DVD release in 2006.

If tape 17 was purchased from Woolworths it included an interview with Paul Darrow. Unlike other BBC Video releases, the *Blake's 7* videos had a consistent design throughout the run.

The entire range was deleted on 1 February 1996, with BBC Video intending to release the range again at a reduced price of £7.99 per tape in July of that year. This never occurred.

The exact same tapes with identical cover illustrations were released in Australia and New Zealand virtually concurrently between May 1991 and June 1993.

In the United States, BFS Video distributed the tapes in NTSC format between 12 June 1991 and the autumn of 1993, originally under licence of BBC Enterprises, and from tape 17 onwards under licence from Lionheart Television International (which was a division of BBC Enterprises). These too had identical cover illustrations, but the covers were cardboard slip covers as opposed to the plastic cases of the BBC releases.

VBC-001

VBC-002

VBC-003

VBC-004

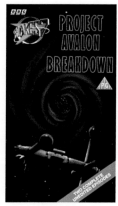

VBC-005

VBC-006

VBC-007

VBC-001 *Blake's 7: Cassette 1: The Way Back /*
Space Fall
Format: VHS: 102 minutes approximately
Publisher: BBC Video (7 January 1991);
BFS Video (NTSC)
RRP: £9.99
Rating: PG
Cover: Barry Jones
Ref: BBCV 4447; 99877 (BFS)
Other Editions: BBC Compilation Release, Fabulous
Films Episodic Release, Fabulous Films 25th
Anniversary VHS Release, DVD releases

'Space Fall' was the only episode that was cut
for video release (the edits to 'Rescue' being an
oversight not intentional cuts to obtain a lower
BBFC certificate) when a small edit was made to
remove part of the scene where Avon attacks the
technician.

VBC-002 *Blake's 7: Cassette 2: Cygnus Alpha /*
Time Squad
Format: VHS: 104 minutes approximately
Publisher: BBC Video (7 January 1991);
BFS Video (NTSC)
RRP: £9.99
Rating: PG
Cover: Barry Jones

Ref: BBCV 4448; 99878 (BFS)

Other Editions: BBC Compilation Release, Fabulous Films Episodic Release, Fabulous Films 25th Anniversary VHS Release, DVD releases

VBC-003 Blake's 7: Cassette 3: The Web / Seek-Locate-Destroy

Format: VHS: 102 minutes approximately

Publisher: BBC Video (7 January 1991); BFS Video (NTSC)

RRP: £9.99

Rating: PG

Cover: Barry Jones

Ref: BBCV 4449; 99879 (BFS)

Other Editions: BBC Compilation Release, Fabulous Films Episodic Release, Fabulous Films 25th Anniversary VHS Release, DVD releases

VBC-004 Blake's 7: Cassette 4: Mission to Destiny / Duel

Format: VHS: 103 minutes approximately

Publisher: BBC Video (7 January 1991); BFS Video (NTSC)

RRP: £9.99

Rating: PG

Cover: Barry Jones

Ref: BBCV 4450; 99880 (BFS)

Other Editions: BBC Compilation Release, Fabulous Films Episodic Release, Fabulous Films 25th Anniversary VHS Release, DVD releases

VBC-005 Blake's 7: Cassette 5: Project Avalon/ Breakdown

Format: VHS: 105 minutes approximately

Publisher: BBC Video (5 March 1991); BFS Video (NTSC)

RRP: £9.99

Rating: PG

Cover: Barry Jones

Ref: BBCV 4468; 99881 (BFS)

Other Editions: BBC Compilation Release, Fabulous Films Episodic Release, Fabulous Films 25th Anniversary VHS Release, DVD releases

VBC-006 Blake's 7: Cassette 6: Bounty / Deliverance

Format: VHS: 102 minutes approximately

Publisher: BBC Video (5 March 1991); BFS Video (NTSC)

RRP: £9.99

Rating: PG

Cover: Barry Jones

Ref: BBCV 4469; 99882 (BFS)

Other Editions: BBC Compilation Release, Fabulous Films Episodic Release, Fabulous Films 25th Anniversary VHS Release, DVD releases

VBC-007 Blake's 7: Cassette 7: Orac / Redemption

Format: VHS: 102 minutes approximately

Publisher: BBC Video (7 May 1991); BFS Video (NTSC)

RRP: £10.19

Rating: PG

Cover: Barry Jones

Ref: BBCV 4497; 99890 (BFS)

Other Editions: BBC Compilation Release, Fabulous Films Episodic Release, Fabulous Films 25th Anniversary VHS Release, DVD releases

The price rise was caused by the UK VAT rate increasing from 15% to 17½% on 1 April 1991.

VBC-008

VBC-009

VBC-010

VBC-008 *Blake's 7: Cassette 8: Shadow /*
Weapon
Format: VHS: 103 minutes approximately
Publisher: BBC Video (7 May 1991); BFS Video (NTSC)
RRP: £10.19
Rating: PG
Cover: Barry Jones
Ref: BBCV 4498; 99891 (BFS)
Other Editions: Fabulous Films Episodic Release,
Fabulous Films 25th Anniversary VHS Release, DVD
releases

VBC-009 *Blake's 7: Cassette 9: Horizon /*
Pressure Point
Format: VHS: 100 minutes approximately
Publisher: BBC Video (2 July 1991); BFS Video (NTSC)
RRP: £10.19
Rating: PG
Cover: Barry Jones
Ref: BBCV 4628; 99892 (BFS)
Other Editions: Fabulous Films Episodic Release,
Fabulous Films 25th Anniversary VHS Release, DVD
releases

VBC-010 *Blake's 7: Cassette 10: Trial / Killer*
Format: VHS: 103 minutes approximately
Publisher: BBC Video (2 July 1991); BFS Video (NTSC)
RRP: £10.19
Rating: PG
Cover: Barry Jones
Ref: BBCV 4629; 99893 (BFS)
Other Editions: Fabulous Films Episodic Release,
Fabulous Films 25th Anniversary VHS Release, DVD
releases

VBC-011 *Blake's 7: Cassette 11: Hostage /*
Countdown

Format: VHS: 103 minutes approximately

Publisher: BBC Video (3 September 1991);

BFS Video (NTSC)

RRP: £10.19

Rating: PG

Cover: Barry Jones

Ref: BBCV 4662; 99894 (BFS)

Other Editions: Fabulous Films Episodic Release, Fabulous
Films 25th Anniversary VHS Release, DVD releases

VBC-011

VBC-012 *Blake's 7: Cassette 12: Voice from*
the Past / Gambit

Format: VHS: 101 minutes approximately

Publisher: BBC Video (3 September 1991);

BFS Video (NTSC)

RRP: £10.19

Rating: PG

Cover: Barry Jones

Ref: BBCV 4663; 99895 (BFS)

Other Editions: Fabulous Films Episodic Release, Fabulous
Films 25th Anniversary VHS Release, DVD releases

VBC-012

VBC-013 *Blake's 7: Cassette 13: The Keeper /*
Star One

Format: VHS: 101 minutes approximately

Publisher: BBC Video (5 November 1991);

BFS Video (NTSC)

RRP: £10.19

Rating: PG

Cover: Barry Jones

Ref: BBCV 4641; 99910 (BFS)

Other Editions: Fabulous Films Episodic Release, Fabulous
Films 25th Anniversary VHS Release, DVD releases

VBC-013

VBC-014 *Blake's 7: Cassette 14: Aftermath / Powerplay*
Format: VHS: 103 minutes approximately
Publisher: BBC Video (5 November 1991);
BFS Video (NTSC)
RRP: £10.19
Rating: PG
Cover: Barry Jones
Ref: BBCV 4644; 99911 (BFS)
Other Editions: BBC Compilation Release, Fabulous Films Episodic Release, Fabulous Films 25th Anniversary VHS Release, DVD releases

VBC-015 *Blake's 7: Cassette 15: Volcano / Dawn of the Gods*
Format: VHS: 103 minutes approximately
Publisher: BBC Video (7 January 1992);
BFS Video (NTSC)
RRP: £10.99
Rating: U
Cover: Barry Jones
Ref: BBCV 4716; 99912 (BFS)
Other Editions: Fabulous Films Episodic Release, Fabulous Films 25th Anniversary VHS Release, DVD releases
 Poster:
While the front cover correctly displayed the episodes in transmission order, on the spine 'Dawn of the Gods' preceded 'Volcano'. This error was replicated on the BFS Videos and the releases in other territories.

   If this video was purchased from Woolworths a full colour poster, produced by BBC Enterprises, was available for free. Measuring 24" x 17" it was a photo montage of the main cast (minus Travis) set against a star background with both the *Liberator* and *Blake's 7* logo. This offer was an incentive by BBC Enterprises to have Woolworths stock the tapes.

VBC-016 *Blake's 7: Cassette 16: The Harvest of Kairos / City at the Edge of the World*
Format: VHS: 104 minutes approximately
Publisher: BBC Video (7 January 1992);
BFS Video (NTSC)
RRP: £10.99
Rating: U
Cover: Barry Jones
Ref: BBCV 4717; 99913 (BFS)
Other Editions: Fabulous Films Episodic Release, Fabulous Films 25th Anniversary VHS Release, DVD releases
 Poster:
If this tape was bought from Woolworths then the same colour poster given to customers with cassette 15 was given to purchasers.

VBC-017 *Blake's 7: Cassette 17: Children of Auron / Rumours of Death*
Format: VHS: 101 minutes approximately
Publisher: BBC Video (7 April 1992); BFS Video (NTSC)
RRP: £10.99
Rating: PG
Cover: Barry Jones
Ref: BBCV 4738 or BBCV 4804 (Woolworths exclusive); 99914 (BFS)
Other Editions: Fabulous Films Episodic Release, Fabulous Films 25th Anniversary VHS Release, DVD releases
With Paul Darrow interview:
If cassette 17 was purchased from Woolworths, the tape contained an interview with Paul Darrow at the end of the tape.

VBC-014

VBC-015

VBC-016

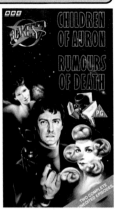

VBC-017

VBC-018 *Blake's 7: Cassette 18: Sarcophagus /*
Ultraworld

Format: VHS: 102 minutes approximately

Publisher: BBC Video (7 April 1992); BFS Video (NTSC)

RRP: £10.99

Rating: PG

Cover: Barry Jones

Ref: BBCV 4739; 99915 (BFS)

Other Editions: BBC Compilation Release, Fabulous
Films Episodic Release, Fabulous Films 25th
Anniversary VHS Release, DVD releases

VBC-017
(w/interview)

VBC-018

VBC-019 *Blake's 7: Cassette 19: Moloch /*
Death-Watch

Format: VHS: 103 minutes approximately

Publisher: BBC Video (2 June 1992); BFS Video (NTSC)

RRP: £10.99

Rating: PG

Cover: Barry Jones

Ref: BBCV 4744; 99916 (BFS)

Other Editions: Fabulous Films Episodic Release,
Fabulous Films 25th Anniversary VHS Release, DVD
releases

VBC-019

VBC-020

VBC-021

VBC-022

VBC-023

VBC-024

VBC-025

VBC-026

VBC-020 *Blake's 7: Cassette 20: Terminal /*
Rescue

Format: VHS: 104 minutes approximately

Publisher: BBC Video (2 June 1992); BFS Video (NTSC)

RRP: £10.99

Rating: PG

Cover: Barry Jones

Ref: BBCV 4745; 99917 (BFS)

Other Editions: Fabulous Films Episodic Release,
Fabulous Films 25th Anniversary VHS Release, DVD
releases

The source print used for 'Rescue' was that used for
the 1983 repeat and contained some edits. When Vila
emerges from hiding and finds the Federation rifle, the
scene is cut short where he appears to way up the
bottle and the gun. After Dorian's death, Dayna goes
over to the body of Dorian's late partner. The scene is
edited to remove the shot of her looking over at the
others and Soolin leaving the cavern is also cut.

VBC-021 *Blake's 7: Cassette 21: Power / Traitor*

Format: VHS: 100 minutes approximately

Publisher: BBC Video (7 July 1992); BFS Video (NTSC)

RRP: £10.99

Rating: PG

Cover: Barry Jones

Ref: BBCV 4824; 99918 (BFS)

Other Editions: Fabulous Films Episodic Release, Fabulous Films 25th Anniversary VHS Release, DVD releases

VBC-022 *Blake's 7: Cassette 22: Stardrive / Animals*

Format: VHS: 100 minutes approximately

Publisher: BBC Video (7 July 1992); BFS Video (NTSC)

RRP: £10.99

Rating: PG

Cover: Barry Jones

Ref: BBCV 4825; 99919 (BFS)

Other Editions: Fabulous Films Episodic Release, Fabulous Films 25th Anniversary VHS Release, DVD releases

VBC-023 *Blake's 7: Cassette 23: Headhunter / Assassin*

Format: VHS: 100 minutes approximately

Publisher: BBC Video (1 September 1992); BFS Video (NTSC)

RRP: £10.99

Rating: PG

Cover: Barry Jones

Ref: BBCV 4858; 99920 (BFS)

Other Editions: Fabulous Films Episodic Release, Fabulous Films 25th Anniversary VHS Release, DVD releases

VBC-024 *Blake's 7: Cassette 24: Games / Sand*

Format: VHS: 99 minutes approximately

Publisher: BBC Video (1 September 1992); BFS Video (NTSC)

RRP: £10.99

Rating: PG

Cover: Barry Jones

Ref: BBCV 4859; 99921 (BFS)

Other Editions: Fabulous Films Episodic Release, Fabulous Films 25th Anniversary VHS Release, DVD releases

VBC-025 *Blake's 7: Cassette 25: Gold / Orbit*

Format: VHS: 97 minutes approximately

Publisher: BBC Video (5 January 1993); BFS Video (NTSC)

RRP: £10.99

Rating: PG

Cover: Barry Jones

Ref: BBCV 4886; 99922 (BFS)

Other Editions: Fabulous Films Episodic Release, Fabulous Films 25th Anniversary VHS Release, DVD releases

VBC-026 *Blake's 7: Cassette 26: Warlord / Blake*

Format: VHS: 99 minutes approximately

Publisher: BBC Video (5 January 1993); BFS Video (NTSC)

RRP: £10.99

Rating: PG

Cover: Barry Jones

Ref: BBCV 4887; 99923 (BFS)

Other Editions: Fabulous Films Episodic Release, Fabulous Films 25th Anniversary VHS Release, DVD releases

VBF-001

VBF-002

VBF-001 & 002 box

VIDEO, FABULOUS FILMS EPISODIC RELEASES

Starting in March 1998, Fabulous Films Ltd released all episodes of *Blake's 7* on VHS and like their BBC predecessors the releases consisted of two episodes per tape. For season 1 only there was a limited edition of 7,000 shiny foil wrapped sleeves of each tape. These were phased out as they interfered with the scanning of barcodes. The spines of the 26 tapes showed a montage of the *Blake's 7* logo (seasons 1 to 3), the *Liberator*, the season 3 crew and the *Scorpio*. The only edited episode was 'Space Fall' for the same reason as the BBC release in 1991 (to obtain a PG certificate).

VBF-001 *Blake's 7: The Way Back / Space Fall*
Format: VHS: 102 minutes approximately
Publisher: Fabulous Films Ltd. (2 March 1998)
RRP: £10.99
Rating: PG
Cover: Form
Ref: FAB 4121
Other Editions: BBC Compilation Release, BBC Episodic Release, Fabulous Films 25th Anniversary VHS Release, DVD releases
🎞️ 🎞️   Boxed Set: 🎞️ 🎞️ 🎞️ 🎞️ 🎞️
'Space Fall' was the only episode that was cut for video release when a small edit was made to remove part of the scene where Avon attacks the London technician. This tape was also available in a boxed set with tape 2: *Blake's 7: Cygnus Alpha / Time Squad.*

VBF-002 *Blake's 7: Cygnus Alpha / Time Squad*

Format: VHS: 104 minutes approximately

Publisher: Fabulous Films Ltd. (2 March 1998)

RRP: £10.99

Rating: PG

Cover: Form

Ref: FAB 4122

Other Editions: BBC Compilation Release, BBC Episodic Release, Fabulous Films 25th Anniversary VHS Release, DVD releases

  Boxed set:

This tape was additionally released with *Blake's 7: The Way Back / Space Fall* in a boxed set.

VBF-003   **VBF-004**

VBF-003 *Blake's 7: The Web / Seek-Locate-Destroy*

Format: VHS: 102 minutes approximately

Publisher: Fabulous Films Ltd. (6 April 1998)

RRP: £10.99

Rating: PG

Cover: Form

Ref: FAB 4123

Other Editions: BBC Compilation Release, BBC Episodic Release, Fabulous Films 25th Anniversary VHS Release, DVD releases

VBF-005

VBF-004 *Blake's 7: Mission to Destiny / Duel*

Format: VHS: 103 minutes approximately

Publisher: Fabulous Films Ltd. (6 April 1998)

RRP: £10.99

Rating: PG

Cover: Form

Ref: FAB 4124

Other Editions: BBC Compilation Release, BBC Episodic Release, Fabulous Films 25th Anniversary VHS Release, DVD releases

VBF-005 *Blake's 7: Project Avalon/ Breakdown*

Format: VHS: 105 minutes approximately

Publisher: Fabulous Films Ltd. (25 May 1998)

RRP: £10.99

Rating: PG

Cover: Form

Ref: FAB 4125

Other Editions: BBC Compilation Release, BBC Episodic Release, Fabulous Films 25th Anniversary VHS Release, DVD releases

VBF-006

VBF-007

VBF-008

VBF-006 *Blake's 7: Bounty / Deliverance*

Format: VHS: 102 minutes approximately

Publisher: Fabulous Films Ltd. (29 June 1998)

RRP: £10.99

Rating: PG

Cover: Form

Ref: FAB 4126

Other Editions: BBC Compilation Release, BBC Episodic Release, Fabulous Films 25th Anniversary VHS Release, DVD releases

VBF-007 *Blake's 7: Orac / Redemption*

Format: VHS: 102 minutes approximately

Publisher: Fabulous Films Ltd. (27 July 1998)

RRP: £10.99

Rating: PG

Cover: Form

Ref: FAB 4127

Other Editions: BBC Compilation Release, BBC Episodic Release, Fabulous Films 25th Anniversary VHS Release, DVD releases

VBF-008 *Blake's 7: Shadow / Weapon*

Format: VHS: 103 minutes approximately

Publisher: Fabulous Films Ltd. (14 September 1998)

RRP: £10.99

Rating: PG

Cover: Form

Ref: FAB 4128

Other Editions: BBC Episodic Release, Fabulous Films 25th Anniversary VHS Release, DVD releases

VBF-009 *Blake's 7: Horizon / Pressure Point*

Format: VHS: 100 minutes approximately

Publisher: Fabulous Films Ltd. (14 September 1998)

RRP: £10.99

Rating: PG

Cover: Form

Ref: FAB 4129

Other Editions: BBC Episodic Release, Fabulous Films 25th Anniversary VHS Release, DVD releases

VBF-009

VBF-010 *Blake's 7: Trial / Killer*

Format: VHS: 103 minutes approximately

Publisher: Fabulous Films Ltd. (5 October 1998)

RRP: £10.99

Rating: PG

Cover: Form

Ref: FAB 4130

Other Editions: BBC Episodic Release, Fabulous Films 25th Anniversary VHS Release, DVD releases

VBF-010

VBF-011 *Blake's 7: Hostage / Countdown*

Format: VHS: 103 minutes approximately

Publisher: Fabulous Films Ltd. (9 November 1998)

RRP: £10.99

Rating: PG

Cover: Form

Ref: FAB 4131

Other Editions: BBC Episodic Release, Fabulous Films 25th Anniversary VHS Release, DVD releases

VBF-011

VBF-012

VBF-012 *Blake's 7: Voice from the Past /*
Gambit
Format: VHS: 101 minutes approximately
Publisher: Fabulous Films Ltd. (18 January 1999)
RRP: £10.99
Rating: PG
Cover: Form
Ref: FAB 4132
Other Editions: BBC Episodic Release, Fabulous Films
25th Anniversary VHS Release, DVD releases

VBF-013 *Blake's 7: The Keeper / Star One*
Format: VHS: 101 minutes approximately
Publisher: Fabulous Films Ltd. (18 January 1998)
RRP: £10.99
Rating: PG
Cover: Form
Ref: FAB 4133
Other Editions: BBC Compilation Release, BBC
Episodic Release, Fabulous Films 25th Anniversary VHS
Release, DVD releases

VBF-013

VBF-014

VBF-014 *Blake's 7: Aftermath / Powerplay*
Format: VHS: 103 minutes approximately
Publisher: Fabulous Films Ltd. (22 February 1998)
RRP: £10.99
Rating: PG
Cover: Form
Ref: FAB 4134
Other Editions: BBC Compilation Release, BBC
Episodic Release, Fabulous Films 25th Anniversary VHS
Release, DVD releases

VBF-015 *Blake's 7: Volcano / Dawn of the Gods*

Format: VHS: 103 minutes approximately

Publisher: Fabulous Films Ltd. (22 February 1998)

RRP: £10.99

Rating: U

Cover: Form

Ref: FAB 4135

Other Editions: BBC Episodic Release, Fabulous Films 25th Anniversary VHS Release, DVD releases

VBF-015

VBF-016 *Blake's 7: The Harvest of Kairos / City at the Edge of the World*

Format: VHS: 104 minutes approximately

Publisher: Fabulous Films Ltd. (29 March 1999)

RRP: £10.99

Rating: U

Cover: Form

Ref: FAB 4136

Other Editions: BBC Episodic Release, Fabulous Films 25th Anniversary VHS Release, DVD releases

VBF-016

VBF-017 *Blake's 7: Children of Auron / Rumours of Death*

Format: VHS: 101 minutes approximately

Publisher: Fabulous Films Ltd. (3 May 1999)

RRP: £10.99

Rating: PG

Cover: Form

Ref: FAB 4137

Other Editions: BBC Episodic Release, Fabulous Films 25th Anniversary VHS Release, DVD releases

VBF-017

VBF-018

VBF-019

VBF-020

VBF-018 *Blake's 7: Sarcophagus / Ultraworld*

Format: VHS: 102 minutes approximately

Publisher: Fabulous Films Ltd. (3 May 1999)

RRP: £10.99

Rating: PG

Cover: Form

Ref: FAB 4138

Other Editions: BBC Compilation Release, BBC Episodic Release, Fabulous Films 25th Anniversary VHS Release, DVD releases

VBF-019 *Blake's 7: Moloch / Death-Watch*

Format: VHS: 103 minutes approximately

Publisher: Fabulous Films Ltd. (7 June 1999)

RRP: £10.99

Rating: PG

Cover: Form

Ref: FAB 4139

Other Editions: BBC Episodic Release, Fabulous Films 25th Anniversary VHS Release, DVD releases

VBF-020 *Blake's 7: Terminal / Rescue*

Format: VHS: 104 minutes approximately

Publisher: Fabulous Films Ltd. (7 June 1999)

RRP: £10.99

Rating: PG

Cover: Form

Ref: FAB 4140

Other Editions: BBC Episodic Release, Fabulous Films 25th Anniversary VHS Release, DVD releases

'Rescue' had the same edits as the 1992 BBC Video release.

VBF-021 *Blake's 7: Power / Traitor*

Format: VHS: 100 minutes approximately

Publisher: Fabulous Films Ltd. (5 July 1999)

RRP: £10.99

Rating: PG

Cover: Form

Ref: FAB 4141

Other Editions: BBC Episodic Release, Fabulous Films
25th Anniversary VHS Release, DVD releases

VBF-021

VBF-022 *Blake's 7: Stardrive / Animals*

Format: VHS: 100 minutes approximately

Publisher: Fabulous Films Ltd. (6 September 1999)

RRP: £10.99

Rating: PG

Cover: Form

Ref: FAB 4142

Other Editions: BBC Episodic Release, Fabulous Films
25th Anniversary VHS Release, DVD releases

VBF-022

VBF-023 *Blake's 7: Headhunter / Assassin*

Format: VHS: 100 minutes approximately

Publisher: Fabulous Films Ltd. (6 September 1999)

RRP: £10.99

Rating: PG

Cover: Form

Ref: FAB 4143

Other Editions: BBC Episodic Release, Fabulous Films
25th Anniversary VHS Release, DVD releases

VBF-023

VBF-024

VBF-025

VBF-026

VBF-024 *Blake's 7: Games / Sand*

Format: VHS: 99 minutes approximately

Publisher: Fabulous Films Ltd. (4 October 1999)

RRP: £10.99

Rating: PG

Cover: Form

Ref: FAB 4144

Other Editions: BBC Episodic Release, Fabulous Films 25th Anniversary VHS Release, DVD releases

VBF-025 *Blake's 7: Gold / Orbit*

Format: VHS: 97 minutes approximately

Publisher: Fabulous Films Ltd. (4 October 1999)

RRP: £10.99

Rating: PG

Cover: Form

Ref: FAB 4145

Other Editions: BBC Episodic Release, Fabulous Films 25th Anniversary VHS Release, DVD releases

VBF-026 *Blake's 7: Warlord / Blake*

Format: VHS: 99 minutes approximately

Publisher: Fabulous Films Ltd. (17 January 2000)

RRP: £10.99

Rating: PG

Cover: Form

Ref: FAB 4146

Other Editions: BBC Episodic Release, Fabulous Films 25th Anniversary VHS Release, DVD releases

VBF (spines)

VIDEO, FABULOUS FILMS 25th ANN. RELEASES

Each episode of the series was digitally remastered and released over 13 volumes, with four episodes per volume between 18 October 2003 and 7 February 2004. Each was priced at £12.99. These sold in very limited quantities, with the exception of tapes 1, 2, 9 and 10.

Four season box sets were also released by Fabulous Films Ltd, each comprising the appropriate individual releases. They were released on 18 October 2003 (FHEBLAKE 1/VFB 03495), 15 November 2003 (FHEBLAKE 2/VFB 05934), 24 January 2004 (FHEBLAKE 3/VFB 08567) and 30 January 2004 (FHEBLAKE 4/VFB 09268), each with an RRP of £39.99.

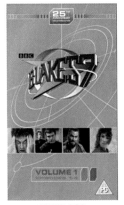

VBT-001

VBT-001 *Blake's 7: Volume 1: The Way Back / Space Fall / The Web/ Seek-Locate-Destroy*

Format: VHS

Publisher: Fabulous Films Ltd. (18 October 2003)

RRP: £12.99

Rating: PG

Other Editions: BBC Compilation Release, BBC Episodic Release, Fabulous Films 20th Anniversary VHS Release, DVD releases

VBT-002 *Blake's 7: Volume 2: The Web / Seek-Locate-Destroy / Mission to Destiny / Duel*

Format: VHS

Publisher: Fabulous Films Ltd. (18 October 2003)

VBT-002

RRP: £12.99   Ref: FHEV1723/VFB 03897

Rating: PG

Other Editions: BBC Compilation Release, BBC Episodic Release, Fabulous Films 20th Anniversary VHS Release, DVD releases

VBT-003   **VBT-004**

VBT-003 *Blake's 7: Volume 3: Project Avalon /*
Breakdown / Bounty / Deliverance
Format: VHS
Publisher: Fabulous Films Ltd. (15 November 2003)
RRP: £12.99
Rating: PG
Other Editions: BBC Compilation Release, BBC
Episodic Release, Fabulous Films 20th Anniversary VHS
Release, DVD releases

VBT-004 *Blake's 7: Volume 4: Orac /*
Redemption / Shadow / Weapon
Format: VHS
Publisher: Fabulous Films Ltd. (15 November 2003)
RRP: £12.99
Rating: PG
Other Editions: BBC Compilation Release, BBC
Episodic Release, Fabulous Films 20th Anniversary VHS
Release, DVD releases

VBT-005   **VBT-006**

VBT-005 *Blake's 7: Volume 5: Horizon /*
Pressure Point / Trial / Killer
Format: VHS
Publisher: Fabulous Films Ltd. (3 January 2004)
RRP: £12.99   Ref: FHEV1726
Rating: PG
Other Editions: BBC Compilation Release, BBC
Episodic Release, Fabulous Films 20th Anniversary VHS
Release, DVD releases

VBT-010   **VBT-011**

VBT-006 *Blake's 7: Volume 6: Hostage /*
Countdown / Voice from the Past / Gambit
Format: VHS
Publisher: Fabulous Films Ltd. (3 January 2004)
RRP: £12.99
Rating: PG
Other Editions: BBC Compilation Release, BBC
Episodic Release, Fabulous Films 20th Anniversary VHS

Release, DVD releases

VBT-007 *Blake's 7: Volume 7: The Keeper /*
Star One / Aftermath / Powerplay
Format: VHS
Publisher: Fabulous Films Ltd. (24 January 2004)
RRP: £12.99
Rating: PG
Other Editions: BBC Compilation Release, BBC
Episodic Release, Fabulous Films 20th Anniversary VHS
Release, DVD releases

VBT-008 *Blake's 7: Volume 8: Volcano / Dawn*
of the Gods / The Harvest of Kairos / City at
the Edge of the World
Format: VHS
Publisher: Fabulous Films Ltd. (24 January 2004)
RRP: £12.99
Rating: PG
Other Editions: BBC Compilation Release, BBC
Episodic Release, Fabulous Films 20th Anniversary VHS
Release, DVD releases

VBT-009 *Blake's 7: Volume 9: Children of*
Auron / Rumours of Death / Sarcophagus /
Ultraworld
Format: VHS
Publisher: Fabulous Films Ltd. (7 February 2004)
RRP: £12.99
Rating: PG
Other Editions: BBC Compilation Release, BBC
Episodic Release, Fabulous Films 20th Anniversary VHS
Release, DVD releases

VBT-010 *Blake's 7: Volume 10: Moloch /*
Death-Watch / Terminal / Rescue
Format: VHS

Publisher: Fabulous Films Ltd. (7 February 2004)
RRP: £12.99
Rating: PG
Other Editions: BBC Compilation Release, BBC
Episodic Release, Fabulous Films 20th Anniversary VHS
Release, DVD releases

VBT-011 *Blake's 7: Volume 11: Power /*
Traitor / Stardrive / Animals
Format: VHS
Publisher: Fabulous Films Ltd. (7 February 2004)
RRP: £12.99
Rating: PG
Other Editions: BBC Compilation Release, BBC
Episodic Release, Fabulous Films 20th Anniversary VHS
Release, DVD releases

VBT-012 *Blake's 7: Volume 12: Headhunter /*
Assassin / Games / Sand
Format: VHS
Publisher: Fabulous Films Ltd. (7 February 2004)
RRP: £12.99
Rating: PG
Other Editions: BBC Compilation Release, BBC
Episodic Release, Fabulous Films 20th Anniversary VHS
Release, DVD releases

VBT-013 *Blake's 7: Volume 13: Gold / Orbit /*
Warlord / Blake
Format: VHS
Publisher: Fabulous Films Ltd. (7 February 2004)
RRP: £12.99
Rating: PG
Other Editions: BBC Compilation Release, BBC
Episodic Release, Fabulous Films 20th Anniversary VHS
Release, DVD releases

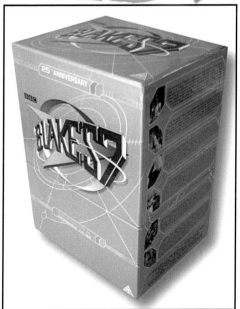

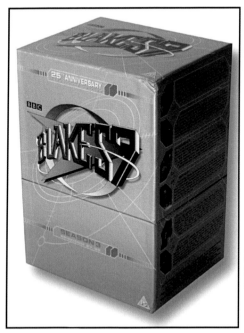

VBT (season box sets)

VIDEO, FABULOUS FILMS AND 2ENTERTAIN DVD

Each episode was digitally remastered for DVD release and released in season boxed sets. Each boxed set comprised a cardboard sleeve and a digi-pack within containing the disks. These sets have also been released in Australia, New Zealand and The Netherlands.

The Netherlands releases had alternate covers upon which the photographs used often did not match the season contained within. For example, the front cover of 'Serie 2' had three publicity shots from 'Cygnus Alpha'. The four rear cover photographs were season 1 publicity shots of Avon and Gan, a scene from 'The Web' and a photograph from the season 3 episode 'Dawn of the Gods'.

VDV-001

VDV-001 *Blake's 7: Series One*

Format: DVD (5): 663 minutes approximately

Publisher: Fabulous Films Ltd. (1 March 2004)

RRP: £49.99

Rating: PG

Other Editions: BBC Compilation Tapes, BBC Episodic Releases, Fabulous Films Episodic Releases, Fabulous Films 25th Anniversary VHS Releases

Ref: BBCDVD 1176

Extras included outtakes, a missing scene, a blooper, a *Blue Peter* feature (Lesley Judd makes a *Liberator* teleport bracelet) and a trailer for season 2. There were commentary tracks on three episodes: 'Space Fall' (Michael Keating, Sally Knyvette, and David Maloney); 'Seek-Locate-Destroy' (Stephen Grief, Michael Keating, and Jacqueline Pearce) and 'Project Avalon' (Stephen Grief, Sally Knyvette, and Jacqueline Pearce). The CGI sequences were created by Qurios Entertainment.

The DVD was released in Australia in 2004, the Netherlands on 9 August 2007 and New Zealand on 5 August 2004. There has been no release in the United States.

VDV-002

VDV-002
(Dutch release)

VDV-002 *Blake's 7: Series Two*

Format: DVD (5): 650 minutes approximately

Publisher: Fabulous Films Ltd. (17 January 2005)

RRP: £49.99

Rating: PG

Other Editions: BBC Compilation Tapes, BBC Episodic Releases, Fabulous Films Episodic Releases, Fabulous Films 25th Anniversary VHS Releases

Ref: BBCDVD 1184

Extras included an extract from *Multi-Coloured Swap Shop* (10 March 1979), *Saturday Superstore* (8 January 1983) and *Scene Today* (24 January 1991). There were features on June Hudson's Costume Collection feature, Mat Irvine's Models, Orac and the Mutoids and a trailer for season 3. There are commentary tracks on three episodes: 'Shadow' (Jan Chappell, Brian Croucher, David Maloney); 'Trial' (Chris Boucher, Jan Chappell, David Maloney); and 'Gambit' (Brian Croucher, Michael Keating, Jacqueline Pearce). The CGI sequences were created by Qurios Entertainment.

A limited edition variant including a replica of the Corgi Liberator toy from 1978 was to be released, but was scrapped when the toys were delivered unpainted and sealed in blister packs. The toys were discarded but a few have made their way onto the market.

The DVD was released in Australia in 2005, the Netherlands on 12 March 2009 and New Zealand on 14 April 2005. There has been no release in the United States.

VDV-003 *Blake's 7: Series Three*

Format: DVD (5): 662 minutes approximately

Publisher: Fabulous Films Ltd. (20 June 2005)

RRP: £49.99

Rating: PG

Other Editions: BBC Compilation Tapes, BBC Episodic Releases, Fabulous Films Episodic Releases, Fabulous Films 25th Anniversary VHS Releases

Ref: BBCDVD 1185;

BBCDVD 1789 (Limited release with Corgi *Liberator*)

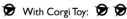 With Corgi Toy:

A limited edition variant of 5,000 copies included a replica of the Corgi *Liberator* toy. These were correctly painted and 'housed' in a dome shaped plastic casing in the middle of the DVD sleeve. Extras included an extract from *Nationwide: Look North* (31 July 1979), features on Stuart Fell's stunt work, Sheelagh Wells' make-up, introductions to the characters of Dayna and Tarrant, a blooper reel, season 3 clean titles and a trailer for season 4. Commentary tracks were provided for: 'Death-Watch' (Chris Boucher, Jacqueline Pearce); 'Rumours of Death' (Chris Boucher, Jan Chappell, Paul Darrow) and 'Terminal' (Paul Darrow, David Maloney, Jacqueline Pearce, Gareth Thomas). The CGI sequences were created by Qurios Entertainment.

The DVD was released in Australia in 2005, the Netherlands on 11 August 2007 and New Zealand on 1 September 2005. There has been no release in the United States.

VDV-004 *Blake's 7: Series Four*

Format: DVD (5): 640 minutes approximately

Publisher: Fabulous Films Ltd. (24 April 2006)

RRP: £49.99

Rating: 12

Other Editions: BBC Episodic Releases, Fabulous Films Episodic Releases, Fabulous Films 25th Anniversary VHS Releases

Ref: BBCDVD 1186

Extras included extracts from *Pebble Mill* (11 April 1979), *Blue Peter* (6 June 1983; how to make a *Scorpio* teleport bracelet), features on Terry Nation on season 4, Ken Ledsham's *Blake's 7* designs, the Radiophonic Workshop, Avon, introductions to the characters of Soolin and Slave, season 4 clean titles, season 4 studio recordings, a blooper reel. Commentary tracks were provided for the episodes 'Assassin' (Paul Darrow, Jacqueline Pearce) and 'Blake' (Chris Boucher, Paul Darrow, Gareth Thomas). The CGI sequences were created by Qurios Entertainment.

The DVD was released in Australia in 2006, the Netherlands in February 2010 and New Zealand on 20 July 2006. To date this season has not been released in the United States.

VDV-005 *Blake's 7: The Complete Collection*

A DVD box set of all four seasons was issued on 6 November 2006, by 2 Entertain Video exclusively through Amazon's UK website. The set was rated 12 and comprised 20 disks. The extras were the same as the individual season sets.

VIDEO, MYTH MAKERS

Reeltime Pictures is an independent video production company that was established by Keith Barnfather a fan of *Doctor Who*. Since 1984 Reeltime have released a series of video interviews with the cast and crew of *Doctor Who*. In 2000, with *Doctor Who* having been off-air since 1989 (save for the 1996 TV movie) it became apparent there were a finite number of interviewees and so the range was expanded to include *Blake's 7*. The first interviewee was Jacqueline Pearce in the same year. While the releases were primarily aimed at the UK market, tapes were made available in the NTSC format with the videos being available from May 2000, at US retailers Mike's Comics, WhoNa and Ambrosia Books & Collectibles.

VDV-003
(limited edition)

VDV-003

VDV-004

VMM-001 *Myth Makers: Jacqueline Pearce:*
Servalan – Blake's 7

Format: VHS: 55 minutes approximately

Publisher: Reeltime Pictures Ltd. (May 2000)

RRP: £12.99 (PAL); US $14.95 (NTSC)

Rating: E

Cover: Benjamin Smith

Ref: RTP0229

Nicholas Briggs interviews Jacqueline Pearce in her central London flat. Indicating that this release fell outside of the main *Doctor Who* range of tapes, this video was not numbered unlike the *Doctor Who* releases. There were 200 limited edition signed copies.

VDV-005

JACQUELINE PEARCE
Servalan – Blake's 7

VMM-001

STEPHEN GREIF
The First Travis – Blake's 7

VMM-002

MAT IRVINE
Visual Effects Supervisor

VMM-003

GARETH THOMAS
Blake - Blake's 7

VMM-004

PETER TUDDENHAM
Zen, Orac & Slave - Blake's 7

VMM-005

VMV-001

GARETH THOMAS Blake - Blake's 7

VMV-002

VMM-002 *Myth Makers: Stephen Grief: 1st Travis – Blake's 7*

Format: VHS: 50 minutes approximately
Publisher: Reeltime Pictures Ltd. (June 2000)
RRP: £12.99 (PAL); US $14.95 (NTSC)
Rating: E
Cover: Benjamin Smith
Ref: RTP0231

Stephen Grief was the second *Blake's 7* cast member to be approached and he too was interviewed in 2000. Nicholas Briggs interviewed Grief in the New Forest, where the location filming for 'Duel' took place. The production incorporated a framing device of an alien (clearly the character of Sinofar from the same episode) setting up the meeting. The alien was played by Beverley Cressman. There were 200 limited edition signed copies.

VMM-003 *Myth Makers: Mat Irvine: Visual Effects Supervisor*

Format: VHS: 55 minutes approximately
Publisher: Reeltime Pictures Ltd. (November 2000)
RRP: £12.99 (PAL); US $14.95 (NTSC)
Rating: E
Cover: Benjamin Smith
Ref: RTP0230

Mat Irvine was interviewed at his home by Nicholas Briggs. In addition to discussing his working on *Doctor Who* Irvine discussed his time on *Blake's 7* and showcased the original *Liberator* model (complete with fungus from its final episode 'Terminal') and the original Orac prop. There were 200 limited edition signed copies.

VMM-004 Myth Makers: Gareth Thomas: Blake – Blake's 7

Format: VHS (PAL and NTSC): 50 minutes approximately

Publisher: Reeltime Pictures Ltd. (31 July 2003)

RRP: £12.99 (VHS); US $14.95 (NTSC)

Rating: E

Cover: Benjamin Smith. Cover photo by Mark Spencer.

Ref: RTP0286

Gareth is interviewed by Nicholas Briggs at Gatton Park, Surrey (where location filming for 'Trial' took place) and at Betchworth Quarry, Surrey (which has been used in numerous episodes). In addition to Thomas and Briggs, two extras dressed as Federation guards are interspersed throughout.

VMM-005 Myth Makers: Peter Tuddenham: Zen, Orac and Slave – Blake's 7

Format: VHS (PAL and NTSC): 50 minutes approximately

Publisher: Reeltime Pictures Ltd. (31 August 2003)

RRP: £12.99 (VHS); US $14.95 (NTSC)

Rating: E

Cover: Benjamin Smith

Ref: RTP0289

Nicholas Briggs is credited as interviewer but is only onscreen for a few minutes at the start and end of the interview. Instead, Peter Tuddenham reprises his role of Orac and Tuddenham answers questions put to him by a working Orac prop. There was a limited edition of 200 signed copies.

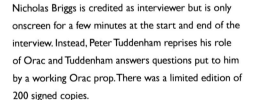

VIDEO, MYTH MAKERS DVD

Commencing in 2003, Reeltime began releasing their *Myth Makers* series of interviews on DVD. Initially these were rereleases of interviews only available on VHS with two interviews per disk. Eventually single issue releasers became the norm. The DVD releases were not numbered unlike the VHS releases.

VMV-001 Myth Makers: Jacqueline Pearce: Servalan – Blake's 7 and Stephen Greif: 1st Travis – Blake's 7

Format: DVD-R (Region 0): 120 minutes approximately

Publisher: Reeltime Pictures Ltd. (July 2003)

RRP: £15.99

Rating: E

Cover: DVD Design Anastasia Stylianou. Ben Smith's cover adapted by Stellenstar.

Ref: RTP0288

This DVD rereleased the separately available interviews released on VHS in 2000. Two short new introductions for each interview were included with Keith Barnfather and Nicholas Briggs.

VMV-002 Myth Makers: Gareth Thomas: Blake – Blake's 7

Format: DVD-R (Region 0): 50 minutes approximately

Publisher: Reeltime Pictures Ltd. (31 July 2003)

RRP: £15.99 (DVD);

Rating: E

Cover: DVD Design Anastasia Stylianou. Ben Smith's cover adapted by Stellenstar. Cover photo by Mark Spencer.

Ref: RTP0287

Gareth Thomas is interviewed by Nicholas Briggs at Gatton Park, Surrey (where location filming for 'Trial' took place) and at Betchworth Quarry, Surrey (which has been used in numerous episodes). In addition to Thomas and Briggs, two extras dressed as Federation guards are interspersed throughout. There was a limited edition of 200 signed copies.

VMV-003 *Myth Makers: Peter Tuddenham: Zen, Orac and Slave – Blake's 7*

Format: DVD-R (Region 0): 50 minutes approximately

Publisher: Reeltime Pictures Ltd. (31 August 2003)

RRP: £15.99 (DVD)

Rating: E

Cover: DVD Design Anastasia Stylianou. Ben Smith's cover adapted by Stellenstar.

Ref: RTP0298

Nicholas Briggs is credited as interviewer but is only onscreen for a few minutes at the start and end of the interview. Instead, Peter Tuddenham reprises his role of Orac and answers questions put to him by a working Orac prop. There was a limited edition of 200 signed copies.

VMV-004 *Myth Makers: Louise Jameson and Mat Irvine*

Format: DVD-R (Region 0): 120 minutes approximately

Publisher: Reeltime Pictures Ltd. (July 2004)

RRP: £15.99

Rating: E

Cover: DVD Design Anastasia Stylianou. Ben Smith's cover adapted by Stellenstar.

Ref: RTP0320

This DVD rereleased the separately available interviews released on VHS. Two short new introductions for each interview were included with Keith Barnfather and Nicholas Briggs.

VMV-005 *Myth Makers: Dudley Simpson: Composer*

Format: DVD-R (Region 0): 70 minutes approximately

Publisher: Reeltime Pictures Ltd. (February 2005)

RRP: £15.99

Rating: E

Cover: DVD Design Anastasia Stylianou. Ben Smith's cover adapted by Stellenstar.

Ref: RTP0338

Nicholas Briggs presents an interview with Dudley Simpson. Simpson's impressive wide-ranging career is discussed from his time serving in the army during World War II to finding himself working on *Doctor Who*. Simpson composed the *Blake's 7* theme as well as providing the incidental music for all episodes of the series, except 'Duel' and 'Gambit'. This is touched on in brief.

VMV-006 *Myth Makers: Jan Chappell: Cally – Blake's 7*

Format: DVD-R (Region 0): 50 minutes approximately

Publisher: Reeltime Pictures Ltd. (2005)

RRP: £15.99

Rating: E

Cover: DVD Design Anastasia Stylianou. Ben Smith's cover adapted by Stellenstar.

Ref: RTP0351

Jan Chappell is interviewed by Nicholas Briggs at Quex Park in Kent the filming location for the episode 'Bounty'. The interview was recorded on 7 July 2005 and the DVD includes a biography of the actor and behind-the-scenes material. There were 200 limited edition signed copies.

VMV-007 Myth Makers: Stuart Fell: Stunt Arranger

Format: DVD-R (Region 0): 50 minutes approximately
Publisher: Reeltime Pictures Ltd. (April 2006)
RRP: £15.99
Rating: E
Cover: DVD Design Anastasia Stylianou. Ben Smith's cover adapted by Stellenstar.
Ref: RTP0374

Nicholas Briggs presents an interview with Stuart Fell, stunt coordinator on *Doctor Who* and *Blake's 7*.

VMV-008 Myth Makers: June Hudson: Costume Designer

Format: DVD-R (Region 0): 50 minutes approximately
Publisher: Reeltime Pictures Ltd. (September 2006)
RRP: £15.99
Rating: E
Cover: DVD Design Anastasia Stylianou. Ben Smith's cover adapted by Stellenstar.
Ref: RTP0383

Nicholas Briggs presents an interview with costume designer June Hudson, who discusses her time at the BBC including her work on *Doctor Who* and the second season of *Blake's 7*.

VIDEO, OTHER

VOT-001 The Making of Hitchhiker's Guide to the Galaxy

Format: VHS: 60 minutes approximately
Publisher: BBC Video (1 March 1993)
RRP: £12.99
VHS DVD
This video contained the *Liberator* in the opening sequence. The opening voiceover by Peter Jones was as

VMV-003

VMV-004

VMV-005

VMV-006

VMV-007

VMV-008

VOT-001 UK VHS

VOT-001 US VHS

VOT-001 UK DVD

follows: 'The planet Earth was an unusual place to film an inter-galactic adventure, but that had never stopped the BBC before ...' The sequence continues with a motion-controlled shot of the *Liberator* flying towards Earth being chased by the TARDIS. They pass a signpost on a little asteroid which reads: 'Earth Welcomes Careful Film Crews'.

Arthur Dent's voice is then heard saying: 'That's it – third left, just after that sun. Oh anywhere will do. Yes, the Northern hemisphere would be marvellous. Thank you very much. Oh, just drop me on the corner ...' implying that he's been given a lift back to Earth by one of these craft.

The *Liberator* model was built by *Blake's 7* and general SF fan Paul Holroyd, who was also responsible for *The Horizon Blake's 7 Technical Manual*.

The VHS release got a special commendation in the annual VHE awards in 1993, but lost out to a documentary on *The Dambusters*.

It was released in the US and distributed by Fox Video with an alternate cover illustrated by Peter Cross.

The documentary was included in the 2002 DVD release of the BBC Television adaptation of *The Hitchhikers Guide to the Galaxy*.

VOT-002 *Blake's Junction 7*
Format: DVD: 35 minutes approximately
Publisher: 2 Entertain Video (21 January 2008)
RRP: £15.99
Rating: 12

This is a comedy short parodying *Blake's 7*. It was released alongside *Ant Muzak* and *World of Wrestling*, two further parodies by the same writer and director (Tim Plester and Ben Gregor respectively). Peter Tuddenham reprised his role as the voice of Orac.

Extras included a behind-the-scenes feature on all three films, commentary on *Blake's Junction 7* with Paul Darrow and Mark Heap, an interview with Paul

Darrow and Mark Heap, an interview with Mackenzie Crook and Peter Tuddenham's recording session. The front cover predominantly featured the *Blake's Junction 7* publicity poster which was designed by Niel Bushnell of Qurios Entertainment.

VOT-003 *An Evening with Jacqueline Pearce*

Format: DVD-R: 90 minutes approximately

Publisher: Whoovers (March 2011)

RRP: £6 plus £1.50 postage and packing in the UK

Rating: E

VOT-002

The Whoovers are a *Doctor Who* related fan group based in the Derby area. They play host to stars from that show and release them in their 'An Evening With …' series. On Friday 4 February 2011, their guest was Jacqueline Pearce (who played the role of Chessene in the *Doctor Who* story 'The Two Doctors' (1985)). She talked about her life and career including *Blake's 7*. The DVD was available at the reduced price of £4 for members of the group.

VOT-003

VIDEO, STORAGE

VST-001 Video Cabinet

Manufacturer: Harvard Associates

Version: Standard (July 1992) and Deluxe (May 1995)

RRP: Standard: £19.95; Deluxe: £59.99

🗇 🗇 🗇 🗇 🗇 Deluxe: 🗇 🗇 🗇 🗇 🗇

A fully assembled black laminate video cabinet designed by BBC Video could be ordered through mail order, or by telephone, to house the complete set of 26 *Blake's 7* videos on two shelves. The cabinet was 17" across by 18" down by 5" deep. There was a limited run of the cabinets and they were subject to availability. The offer expired 30 June 1993.

A second 'deluxe' video cabinet was produced a few years later. The size was amended to 18" high by 17" wide by 8" deep to accommodate a smoked glass door etched with the *Blake's 7* logo seen in the first three seasons. The RRP of both models included postage and packing.

VST-001

APPENDIX A: UNRELEASED/CANCELLED ITEMS

An item is included in this section when it has reached a certain stage of development, rather than just being a proposal. So by way of example, the Letraset rub down transfers are not included as although a licence was purchased for their manufacture, no products were developed by the company. The board game by Denys Fisher is included as a prototype was both produced and tested.

Blake's 7 – The Board Game (1978)

In 1977, Denys Fisher signed a licence to produce a board game based on the series. In the summer of 1978 a prototype was made available to the BBC; the reasons for the delay were primarily the lack of visual material and Denys Fisher needing a firm grasp of the series format. The prototype game involved a Federation craft chasing the *Liberator* around the board and pieces included the Zen computer. Both the BBC and Terry Nation were pleased with the prototype but on 8 December 1978, Denys Fisher wrote to BBC Enterprises to inform them that the game would not be put into production. Over the preceding weeks Denys Fisher had 'both play-tested the game with children and shown the finished product to some major buyers. The reaction on both counts was far from good'.

Die Cast *Liberator* Toy with the Voice of Zen (1978)

Mettoy was one of the very first merchandisers to show an interest in the series and two early prototypes of a talking large scale model were shown to the BBC in November 1977. The model would have sound effects in the form of the voice of the Zen computer. Unusually the licence was to be for worldwide rights not just the United Kingdom. During the development process Mettoy also expressed an interest in developing a smaller version for its Corgi Junior line which was readily agreed to by the copyright holders. On the 5 January 1979, Mettoy Playcraft Ltd informed BBC Merchandising 'that in view of the fact that the *Blakes 7* series has not been successful in terms of overseas distribution to date, we have decided not to continue with the introduction of a large scale version of the *Liberator*'. Hope was expressed by Mettoy that the series would find its way into enough important territories to persuade them to resurrect the large scale model. While a licence for 'Die cast model vehicles' based on the series was entered into on 1 August 1979, this was primarily for the Corgi *Liberator* and the talking *Liberator* toy was permanently shelved.

Blake's 7 Colouring and Activity Books (1979)

When World Distributors enquired about the rights to produce a *Blake's 7* annual, they sought approval to produce a range of colouring and activity books. The lack of visual material that hampered the development of the first annual similarly affected this product line. On 5 October 1978, World wrote to reassure BBC Enterprises that the books would be included in their 1979 range. On 13 March 1979 World sent the BBC the artwork for the *Blake's 7 Annual 1980* and the cover of their *Blake's 7* Activity Book. Like the annual, the artwork of the activity book included the characters of Servalan and Travis, for which agreement hadn't been reached with either Jacqueline Pearce or Brian Croucher. The reduced sales of the 1980 annual led to the range being abandoned.

Blake's 7: State of Mind (1985)
Tony Attwood's brief for his published book *Afterlife* was that it was not to be self-contained allowing a continuation on screen or in a second book. By the time *Afterlife* was published, as there had been no movement on the television front, it was felt that a second book wouldn't be justified by potential sales. The book *State of Mind* was therefore never written but Attwood intended it to involve Vila and Avon fighting Tor and all three of them then battling the Federation. It would also have further elaborated the concept of MIND introduced in *Afterlife* and would have been published by Target Books. Attwood's notes on the book can be found on pages 233-235 of the second edition of *Blake's 7: The Programme Guide*.

The Complete Blake's 7 (1991)
Andrew Pixley was commissioned by Virgin Publishing in 1991 to write *The Complete Blake's 7*, a book on the production and history of the show. Neil Alsop joined the project at the request of Pixley but later both authors withdrew over licensing issues. At this point Una McCormack became actively involved in the project, primarily in an editorial capacity. After most of the text had been completed it became clear that the project would need to be shelved due to rights issues. Much of the material eventually saw the light of day when it was published in Marvel's *Blake's 7 Winter Special 1994* and the *Summer Special 1995*.

The Making of Blake's 7 (1993)
BBC Enterprises sought to produce a *Blake's 7* documentary for exclusive release through BBC video. The project was to be directed by Kevin Jon Davies who had recently produced *The Making of The Hitchhikers Guide to the Galaxy*, and was to include previously unseen archive footage.

The *Blake's 7* documentary was to follow a similar structure to that proposed by Mark Wing-Davey (who had played Zaphod in both the radio and television adaptations of *The Hitchhikers Guide to the Galaxy*) to Douglas Adams, when Adams was considering a third radio series of *Hitchhikers*. Adams foresaw a difficulty in developing a third radio series as the plots between the radio and television versions had become 'so thoroughly self-contradictory'. Adams thought that Wing-Davey's idea, which would tackle this issue head on, was 'terrific' and was keen to use it. The third series as proposed would involve two hour long episodes that would be simultaneously broadcast on two different radio stations. Each episode would contradict the other but both would end at the same point. A third radio series of *Hitchhikers* was never produced.

Davies's documentary was to comprise two linked documentaries, one entitled 'Good', the other 'Evil'. Dependent upon availability, Avon (and perhaps Vila) would be interrogated in a detention cell, recalling past events, which would lead into and out of clips of the series and talking head interviews with cast and crew. This tape would be subtitled 'Good'.

On the second tape ('Evil') two Federation guards would be on duty in the corridor outside the cell, and characters would be seen coming and going through the cell door. The more experienced guard relates to his colleague the stories he has heard or witnessed about Blake and his followers, which again would allow the introduction of further documentary elements.

In the finale, the interrogator would communicate to Servalan that Avon was loyal to Blake and that he and Vila should be killed, together with those still frozen. Servalan orders the guards outside the cell to kill the occupants. The viewer would see the operation as it played out in both the cell and the corridor. The guards would be overpowered and, wearing their uniforms, Avon and Vila would follow Servalan onto her ship as she departs. The interrogator was to be revealed as Blake who would then teleport away in the final seconds having contacted Orac. The drama segment was deliberately designed to leave unanswered questions.

The time codes of the drama scenes were to be matched so that both tapes could be played simultaneously side-by-side and the characters would appear to go from one screen to the other, with only the documentary elements differing. The VHS tapes could have been viewed in either order.

The documentary's structure was likened by BBC Video Producer David M Jackson (who is no relation to the actor that played the character of Gan) to the Alan Ayckbourn play *Bedroom Farce*. The play has three bedroom sets on stage, side-by-side, with characters moving from one bedroom to the next.

Videotaping took place on the 2 and 3 of June 1993 and comprised interviews with Vere Lorrimer, David Maloney, Chris Boucher, Jacqueline Pearce, Brian Croucher, Stephen Grief, Matt Irvine, Jan Chappell and Peter Tuddenham. Davies intended to reuse his *Liberator* footage from the *Hitchhikers* documentary in this programme.

Initial overtures were made to John Whiston at *The Late Show* and Alan Yentob and Michael Jackson (the controllers of BBC1 and BBC2) who had agreed in principle to show a cut-down version on television as part of the *Doctor Who* thirtieth anniversary celebrations in November.

The project stalled as the BBC wanted the video released in October 1993 to capitalise on the Christmas market. An agreement with Roger Hancock wasn't reached in time so Jackson decided to postpone its release and all work ceased. When Jackson left BBC Video in early 1994, production never resumed.

Federation Officer's Pistol (1994)

Comet Miniatures planned to release a 1:1 scale Federation Officer's Pistol in June 1994 (Ref: PHO14). The kit was to be made of resin and when complete would have been 8 inches long. The proposed RRP was £23.

Blake's 7 Novelisations (1994)

Virgin Publishing sought to obtain the rights to novelise the television episodes, but agreement was never reached and the idea scrapped after authors had been sought. Virgin

Publishing were also hoping to publish a line of *Blake's 7* original fiction, in a similar vein to their successful range of *Doctor Who* 'Missing Adventure' novels.

Blake's 7 Yearbook (1996)

In 1995 Marvel Comics UK Ltd acquired the licence to produce a *Blake's 7* yearbook, which would be a sister title to its *Doctor Who Yearbook 1996*. The publication was abandoned when poor sales of the *Blake's 7* poster magazine indicated that it was unlikely to recoup the costs of production. Gary Russell was the editor, Paul Vyse the designer, with Andrew Pixley contributing the majority of the text. The material was released instead as a summer special in the summer of 1995.

Rerelease by BBC Video of entire series on VHS (1996)

Following the deletion of all BBC *Blake's 7* videos on 1 February 1996, BBC Video intended to release the range again at a reduced price of £7.99 per tape in July of that year. This release never occurred.

Blake, Avon and Servalan Model Kits (1997)

Comet Miniatures intended to retail three resin kits of the characters of Blake, Avon and Servalan. They were to be 1:6 scale, released in the Spring of 1997 and were advertised in their catalogue but were never produced.

Blake's 7 Documentaries for DVD releases (2002)

Following a letter from Kevin Jon Davies in 2002, Joe Mahoney, a producer at BBC Worldwide, revived *The Making of Blake's 7* documentary that had been abandoned in 1993. The intention was to produce four documentaries, one per season, with each appearing on the appropriate DVD release of the series.

Davies was instructed to incorporate the 1993 interviews alongside new interview footage. The interviewees included Gareth Thomas, Michael Keating, Steve Pacey, Jan Chappell, Sally Knyvette, and David Jackson alongside members of the crew including Roger Murray-Leach (who designed the *Liberator*) and *Blake's 7* fans. With the documentaries on the first three seasons complete, the project was again cancelled due to rights issues. Some remnants of material shot for those documentaries did find their way onto the released DVDs either as Easter Eggs or featurettes.

Myth Makers VHS Release (2003)

Three *Blake's 7* themed releases were scheduled for 2003 by Reeltime Pictures to coincide with the 20th anniversary of *Blake's 7*. While interviews with both Gareth Thomas (August 2003) and Peter Tuddenham (September 2003) were released on VHS and DVD as scheduled, the proposed October 2003 VHS release with Jan Chappell was not. A *Myth Makers* interview with Jan Chappell was eventually released in 2005 on DVD only.

Blake's 7 Trading Card Set (2005)

A test promotional card for a proposed series of *Blake's 7* trading cards was produced in 2005 by Strictly Ink but a full set was never produced as the manufacturer was unable to secure enough images for the set.

Maximum Power! An Auton Guide to Blake's 7 by Andy Davidson, Robert Hammond, Andrew Orton, Chris Orton, Phil Ware and Matt West

A satirical book to be written by the same team behind the *Doctor Who* related book *Auton: Shock and Awe*. This was announced by Hirst Books to be published in December 2011. It was cancelled in July of the same year. Almost immediately it was announced that it would be published in January 2012 by Miwk Publishing, with the revised title *Maximum Power! The Complete Unauthorised Guide To All 64 Episodes of Blake's 7*.

APPENDIX B: *BLAKE'S 7 – A MARVEL MONTHLY* – CIRCULATION FIGURES

Issue	Date	Gross Sales	Returns	Net Sales
1	Sept 1981	37,852	816	37,036
2	Oct 1981	42,213	9,737	32,476
3	Nov 1981	44,209	19,884	24,325
4	Dec 1981	44,489	18,535	25,954
5	Jan 1982	36,450	61	36,389
6	Feb 1982	29,873	688	29,185
7	Mar 1982	27,155	2,689	24,466
8	Apr 1982	24,508	NR	24,508
9	May 1982	23,860	NR	23,860
10	June 1982	21,237	NR	21,237
11	July 1982	22,845	2,876	19,969
12	Aug 1982	18,599	1,552	17,047
13	Sept 1982	17,332	2,158	15,174
14	Oct 1982	16,039	2,062	13,977
15	Nov 1982	15,730	1,466	14,264
16	Dec 1982	14,728	1,093	13,635
17	Jan 1983	17,569	1,568	16,001
18	Feb 1983	14,783	1,537	13,246
19	Mar 1983	13,382	1,456	11,926
20	Apr 1983	12,307	586	11,721
21	May 1983	11,423	1,115	10,309
22	June 1983	11,616	602	11,014
23	July 1983	11,332	2,346	8,986
Summer Special	1982	30,924	11,717	19,207
Winter Special	1982	21,157	12,023	9,134

NR – Not Reported. Until the quarter ending June 1982, Marvel reported the returns for each issue in the following quarter. Beginning with the quarter ending September 1982, Marvel reported all returns for each issue in the same statement. During this cross-over, no returns were reported for issues 8, 9 and 10.

APPENDIX C: INTERVIEWS

ARTISTS

Ian Kennedy Interview, 21 May 2010

Ian Kennedy has been a freelance artist since 1954. His work has graced the pages of such high profile comics and magazines as Hotspur, Buster, 2000AD, Star Lord, Eagle *(primarily for the 'Dan Dare' strip) and* Commando *for over fifty years. He drew the first six comic strips in* Blake's 7 – A Marvel Monthly.

Where were you born and raised?
I was born in Dundee on 22 September 1932 and have lived in the area my entire life. My wife and I now live in a lovely little cottage, just outside of the city. During the war there were five airfields close to where I lived and like most boys my age I wanted to become a pilot in the RAF. It was the start of a lifelong fascination with aviation. I did well at school, and clearly had an artistic bent, but flying was wanted I wanted to do.

Did you consider a military career?
Very much so but an ear infection put an end to my aspirations to be a pilot. An old school friend of my mother's then introduced me to the DC Thompson's art department and he got me a job as an apprentice there. Although I did take some evening classes they weren't much use really and I mostly learnt my trade working at my job.

What led to you becoming a freelance artist?
I worked at DC Thompson until 1954 when, needing to earn more money to support my young family, I decided to chance my luck working freelance. I was extremely lucky as the comic book boom was just taking off and I never had difficulty finding work.

How did you network and find steady work in those early days?
Much of it was by recommendation, a letter would arrive in the post asking whether you were available to work on a project; having heard about you from another individual or company in the industry.

Following the war, comics moved away from the western and the war took on increasing importance thematically. How did you find this transition?
I was delighted. I truly loved drawing aerial combat scenes and could imagine myself up there with the pilots. My hobby had become my job.

Upon returning to DC Thompson as a freelancer you initially drew 'Red Skull Branson'.
This was in 1955, and it was a great job for me in particular, drawing the adventures of a wartime ace pilot.

In the 1970s you moved away from aviation to a certain extent and became more involved with Science Fiction.
I was drawing for *2000AD* and the 'Dan Dare' strip in *Eagle* which kept me busy. My style was well suited to the cut and thrust of space battles, as I was able to draw on my experience of drawing dogfights over the preceding twenty years.

How did you become involved in Blake's 7 Monthly?
Ken Armstrong is a contemporary of mine, perhaps a few years younger and we went to the same school. It was Ken that contacted me to ascertain my interest and availability.
I was a great fan of *Blake's 7* and was very excited to be involved.

The launch of the Blake's 7 *title coincided with the transmission of the fourth season. With the introduction of the* Scorpio, *new characters and costumes, how did you manage?*
There was very little lead time but I was invited to BBC Television Centre to meet with the cast on set. I was able to take photographs of the actors which were extremely useful. It was an exciting day as I was an avid viewer. I also had the opportunity to meet Vere (Lorrimer) who was a delightful man and couldn't have been more helpful.

Your strips captured the action sequences with the Scorpio *and the other vessels to great effect. Did you have the opportunity when visiting the BBC to see any of the models?*
Sadly no, but I was provided with a few photographs but not many. Luckily, my experience in aerial combat translated well and I think these parts of the *Blake's 7* strips were particularly suited to my abilities.

In addition, to the six strips you drew, you also drew a strip that was used in promotional material for the magazine.
Did I? You are stretching my memory now at this point …

It involved Avon, Vila, Dayna and Tarrant in a new vessel being pursued by Servalan, who was standing in the ruined hulk of the Liberator!
Ah yes, this was the first thing I drew before we were aware of the storylines for the new season.

Your involvement with Blake's 7 Monthly *came to an abrupt end following a car crash.*
Yes, it was in the winter of 1981 and my car skidded in snow and hit a wall. While my injuries were not life threatening, it sadly put paid to my continued involvement with *Blake's 7*. At the time, I was on friendly terms with the Red Arrows, who sent me a cartoon while I was convalescing. It featured my car being towed by the squadron! Like I told them, I had no trouble with the flying; it was the landing ...

Ian Kennedy continued to work consistently until his semi-retirement in 1997. He still contributes artwork to DC Thompson's Commando *magazine.*

NOVELISTS
Tony Attwood Interview, May 2010

What led to you becoming a writer?
I started my career as a musician and I thought I was going to become this great gift to worldwide music [laughs]. Of course, as in 99.9% of cases that didn't happen. For the first ten years, to supplement my income, I worked as a teacher in state schools as well as teaching students privately. I then progressed into theatre work and eventually taught music in higher education. As an academic you are expected to publish academic papers but additionally, I also wrote books for secondary schools. One day my royalty cheque arrived and much to my surprise it was for a staggering sum. The publisher of one of these books, Oxford University Press, had failed to mention that it had become a best seller and was now on its fifth printing. With that I moved fairly quickly into writing full time.

Why has much of your non-fiction writing dealt with learning difficulties?
One of my three daughters is profoundly dyslexic and when she was about 8 or 9 she wasn't able to read, yet we were quite a

literary household. My wife at the time and I soon came to realise that there wasn't that much educational material for dyslexics that was good and we quickly became disillusioned with available publications and even the charities of the day. So we decided to do something about it. We produced materials under the name 'Multi Sensory Learning' and they became hugely popular. Following this success I later looked at dyscalculia (difficulty in learning or comprehending mathematics) and realised that the work and methodology that we had applied to dyslexia was just as applicable to dyscalculia. Dyscalculia's profile is where dyslexia's was 20 years ago. Suddenly this became a revolutionary concept and a new company that I worked with to run a GCSE math course was getting dyscalculia students through their exams with high grades. My company which published books was equally successful and I became involved in International Dyscalculia Day, whose profile increased dramatically. Suddenly I was in demand to appear on television, radio spots and on breakfast shows.

The Improving Department *also seems to have been a ground breaking book.*
The purpose of the book was to demonstrate a way in which schools could improve from within. Up until this point, the overriding view was that a team of professionals were needed to turn schools around, which was costly and not always successful. The methodology suggested in my book was that you take the best department in the school and improve that department. If you try to improve the worst department or many departments at once you are setting the school up for failure. Then you take the template that has worked on that department and apply it to the next and so on. It has proved to be a very effective methodology and I'm particularly proud that many schools improved as a result as did the results of their pupils.

How did Blake's 7: The Programme Guide *come to be published?*
I had done bits and pieces with the BBC including some radio adaptations and I was looking for other books that I could do. I needed them to have a relatively quick turnaround as I had only recently transitioned to full time writing from academia at that point and bluntly I needed a regular income to pay the bills. I watched *Blake's 7* and enjoyed it, much as I had enjoyed other genre shows such as *The Prisoner, Doctor Who* and (particularly) *Survivors.* There had been a *Doctor Who* programme guide and basically though the grapevine it was suggested that writing the guide might be possible. I then approached Roger Hancock who was very keen on the project and it was he who really made it happen.

Roger informed me that while Terry Nation owned the rights to the characters, concepts and his scripts, the BBC and the writers of the other episodes also had rights in the material. I had plenty of experience of rights issues having previously written three volumes of 'Pop Songbooks'. I had suggested a book to my publisher which brought popular songs of the day into the school music room. While keen on the idea, Oxford University Press thought the rights issues would block it. I personally negotiated all of the necessary agreements (including as an example the rights to include the Beatles' 'Yesterday' for just £35) and the book became enormously successful. I went on to agree contracts with all of the interested parties in *Blake's*

7 which allowed the programme guide to proceed.

The initial idea was that as the season 4 was in production, the guide would cover the first four seasons and could be revised and updated after season 5. I spent several weeks at Television Centre in Shepherds Bush. Vere Lorrimer was delightful and arranged for me to have an (invaluable) BBC car park pass, a viewing room and access to tapes of every episode. Back then the filing systems weren't what they are now and I looked at all available scripts but that by no means included all of them. I conducted the interviews while I was there except for Michael Keating who I spoke to later. The photos in the book proved to be a bit of a problem as it was difficult to obtain photographs from the earlier seasons which is why there is a bias towards the fourth season in the shots chosen.

The BBC file on The Programme Guide *indicated they requested to see every advert for approval which you considered would seriously hamper attempts to market the book. In the end, it was agreed that only one 'general' advert would be submitted to them. Any comments?*
Ah – on the issue of seeing every advert – that is something that I have come up against all my life in working with other people's rights, or with other organisations.

So that is very much in keeping with my standard view – I probably would not even have gone back to W H Allen on that one if the BBC were asking for it – because I knew W H Allen would explode.

Blake's 7 – Afterlife *was your continuation of the series following the events of 'Blake' and was somewhat controversial …*
Like the programme guide this sold very well and was generally well received but sadly not by fandom.

Roger Hancock didn't know what Chris [Boucher] was writing in episode 52 and a few days after transmission Roger was on the 'phone asking how dare the BBC kill off characters that Terry owned the rights to. As I remember it, and some of this may be wrong as my recollection may be incorrect after nearly thirty years, but the BBC and Terry Nation were in dispute over the Daleks. Terry Nation took the view that the Daleks were his creation and only he could commission or write a Dalek script or book, while the BBC believed as long as they paid the correct royalties they could commission a Dalek story from anyone else. Roger Hancock as Terry's agent took the view that all cooperation with the BBC would stop until the matter was resolved. I was told that this was the reason season 5 'stopped' and the show went on hiatus. Nine months later Roger told me that it was all over and it wouldn't be returning.

The idea behind the timing of the book was that as a fifth season wasn't in pre-production by the time of transmission of 'Blake', there would be a good year of sales prior to any season 5. The book could then either be withdrawn, or if I was lucky, the book would form the basis of the first two and final two episodes of the next season. I approached W H Allen and they were very keen as not only would they generate profits from the book itself but hopefully it would also boost sales of the *Programme Guide*.

When I came to write the book I spoke to Chris as to what he was thinking when he wrote that ending and he was quite clear that he had written it to produce a strong cliff-hanger to the season and he hadn't any idea as to where it would go next. So I sat down and, thinking of the general public as my target audience, thought 'why did Avon shoot Blake?' and hopefully I came up with a rational explanation. Your average reader of a tie-in novel knows but a fraction of the details surrounding the show that a fan would know, and this certainly influenced how I approached it. Although I was free to use whichever characters I chose except Blake (who all concerned said was most definitely dead) other limitations were placed on the book. One was that it still needed to be *Blake's 7* despite Blake's death

and the fact they were no longer a 'seven', and the other was that a powerful spaceship was felt to be integral to the show and so such a ship needed to be included. I thought the latter point strained credibility (how likely was it that they would discover such a ship for the third time?) but that was non-negotiable. So I introduced the super powerful ship *Blake's 7* which name had come to symbolise the rebellion.

I decided (and all other parties agreed) that Avon and Vila were absolutely essential having been the mainstays of the series and they were a terrific double act to write for; 'one man and his dog' as Paul Darrow once described them. I found Servalan very difficult to write for as the character believed that 'where there is life, there's a threat' that made her very predictable. Yet by necessity there always had to be a rationale why the crew was linked to her yet neither killed the other. That is why I introduced Avon's sister, Tor. Their sibling relationship provided a link, a bond, that couldn't easily be broken.

As it was unclear what was happening with regard to the television show I deliberately wasn't clear as to the fate of the other characters so they could be written back in if necessary. So I included a cameo for Tarrant as he had become a very popular character in his two seasons and thought he warranted inclusion.

My brief made it clear that *Afterlife* was not to be self contained, and had to allow a continuation on screen or in a second book. By the time *Afterlife* was published there hadn't been any movement on the television front and having been off air for a few years, and with the dispute over rights still unresolved the second book never went ahead. It was to have been called *State of Mind* and would have further elaborated the concept of MIND. I no longer have my notes (I've moved house three times and had a divorce since then, and that

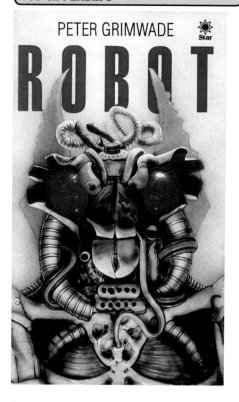

PETER GRIMWADE

Star

R O B O T

combination is guaranteed to destroy any filing system) but it would have involved Vila and Avon fighting Tor and all three of them fighting the Federation. That would have given the basis for alliances, possible alliances, alleged alliances and would leave the Federation ultimately saying to Avon, help us get Tor and we will drop all charges and let you out of prison; that sort of thing.

Of course if I wrote it now, it would be different, and maybe one day it will get written. A contemporary version of the story would have Entanglement Drives and every possibility of Entanglement would be happening.

For the uninitiated what exactly is Entanglement?
Entanglement is a term used in quantum theory to describe the way that particles of energy/matter can become correlated to interact with each other regardless of how far apart they are. So this either throws Einstein's relativity theory out of the window (as it provides that nothing can move faster than light, but entangled particles interact irrespective of distance) or there is some other explanation, such as the particles somehow involve time travel where effect can precede cause.

I am fascinated by physics and the latest discoveries and emerging technologies. Now the Large Hadron Collider has been switched on we are in one of the great periods of scientific discovery. What more could a writer want?

Another genre novel you wrote was Turlough and the Earthlink Dilemma.
This was for a short lived spin off range of original *Doctor Who* novels which also included the novelisation of 'K9 and Company' and Ian Marter's *Harry Sullivan's War*. Each book was to deal with former companions of the Doctor, who had now returned home.

Earthlink afforded me the opportunity to write a *Doctor Who* story that could be more complex than anything that the show could accommodate, and also I was able to write without the limitations of an effects budget or the need to film in a quarry in Surrey. I thought Turlough was an interesting character, very well played by Mark Strickson. After publication, there was an issue with Peter Grimwade who claimed that as the writer of 'Mawdryn Undead' he owned the rights to the Turlough character. I referred him to the BBC. The dispute went on for a long time and in fact Peter wrote a book [*Robot*, 1977] that included characters named after those people he had taken issue with over the character. So in this book there is a teacher called Tony Attwood. I never did discover the final outcome as Peter passed away.

What isn't widely known was that at the time of his untimely death, Ian Marter and I were working on a project to write more Harry Sullivan stories. Ian would come up with a storyline which I would then write and he would review to ensure the characterisation of Harry was spot on. I was shocked by his death; he had a young family and it was a terrible tragedy.

The range was stopped after these three books as someone at the BBC felt it was 'too confusing' to write about past companions. If you look at the new series and how it has addressed the post-Doctor life of some of his companions it seems to me that the idea was simply ahead of its time.

You have returned to writing fiction after over twenty years with Singles Night at the Museum *which you co-wrote with Fran Levitov.*

One thing I do regret is that after I started to write full time, I did not write more fiction. I have written around 100 books of which only a few are fictional. *Singles Night at the Museum* focuses on an advertising copywriter, and a lawyer, who between them uncover a series of conspiracies that threaten the whole of mankind.

I am slowly transitioning from working full time in my company Hamilton House Mailings Plc into retirement and that is affording me the opportunity to write more of what I want to write.

After a number of experiments with novels I published *Making the Arsenal* in 2009. It is a novel set in 1910 (obviously brought out in time for the centenary) and is written as the diary of a journalist. It deals with all the contemporary events (Halley's Comet being visible in the daytime, the fear of invasion from Germany and from space, spy fever), most importantly the issue of what to do with the unemployed (known in 1910 as the vortex). A proposal was put forward by some in government to sterilise them all – and the whole situation was akin to many a sci-fi novel – except that it actually all took place. The glue holding the book together is the decline and fall of a London football club, and the attempts by a right wing politician to buy it. All the situations are true, but the journalist and his friends who uncover the story are of course fictional.

I'm still working on a novel that has been on my computer for some time: *The Personality Shop* which is my attempt to merge the writing styles of two of my favourite authors: P G Wodehouse and Douglas Adams, although I could never hope to match their genius. In the Personality Shop of the title you can buy a new personality. Nearby shops sell viruses that alter who you are. This is not as far fetched as it might at first sound. A parasitic organism [Toxoplasma Gondii] has been discovered by scientists that affects the behaviour of rodents. It manipulates its host for its own benefit enhancing its transmission through the food chain by reducing a rat's innate fear of cats and their smells, and increasing reckless behaviour. So a rat is more likely to be eaten by the parasite's final host; the cat. This parasite is widespread in the human food chain but infection rates vary enormously from less than 15% in the

USA to 80-90% in France and Germany. The more complex human brain is more difficult to manipulate but research indicates a correlation between human infection and personality traits suggesting a potential explanation for cultural differences.

I love that story, but because of the success of *Making the Arsenal* I now have to do a follow up – which takes the great great grand daughter of the hero of that book, and has her working in a situation in which the whole economy of Britain is collapsing for a most extraordinary and unbelievable reason. It wasn't really the bankers after all...

Chris Boucher Interview, April 2010

Chris Boucher has written, and script edited, many television shows including Bergerac, Juliet Bravo *and* Shoestring. *He created the character of Leela in* Doctor Who *and has written four novels featuring her and the fourth Doctor. He acted as script editor on all four seasons of* Blake's 7.

Being a war baby, when you were growing up the war was very fresh in the minds of those around you. Do you think the closeness of the war and the impact of the Third Reich has had lasting influences on your writing?
I suppose it's possible but somehow I doubt it. Even at my most paranoid I can't believe they had it in for me personally. I would imagine that post-war austerity had more impact. I can actually remember rationing and a time when you learned the pleasures of deferred gratification. (I want it and I want it now? – well get over it there isn't any). I was horrified to realise recently that I was born before the NHS was started. We've got the war to thank for it and like everyone else I certainly benefitted. But I digress: if you're asking about militarism and nationalism and patriotism and all the other isms that flesh is heir to I am sure they affected me but how I have no idea. I hate them all of course but show me someone who hates something and I will show you someone who is afraid of whatever it is and quite probably attracted to it as well. Take a good look at the racists, the religious zealots, the gay-bashers – did you ever see such fear and confusion?

At what point growing up did your family obtain a television? What was it like, as a child or young adult at the time, to suddenly have access to this new medium?
I loved television from the first moment I saw it. It had a 12 inch black-and-white screen and mostly crappy dull programmes. Now my set has a 54 inch colour screen and mostly crappy dull programmes. And I still love it.

I think I was ten when the family clubbed together to buy my gran and granddad the first set so we could all sit round and watch the coronation. And what a really boring broadcast that was.

I also loved films (we didn't call them movies – back in the day it was called going to the pictures). I still love films though I have come to hate cinemas. Noisy, smelly and uncomfortable, and that's just the audience.

Has living through the birth of television affected how you view radio as opposed to its younger counterpart?
No. I don't remember there ever having not been radio (called the wireless by the way). I have listened to it all my life. On its day it is superior to all other forms. And if you don't believe me, consider *The Hitchhiker's Guide to the Galaxy*. It went from radio to television to film – and downhill all the way...

What was the first piece of writing you sold?
It was what I later discovered is called a three-line quickie: basically a three speech comedy sketch. I sold it to a Saturday night television magazine programme called *Braden's Week*. Bernard Braden was a major star back then. He phoned personally. I was out, so was my wife. My mum answered the phone – she was thrilled. The producer of the show was John Lloyd, a charming Welshman, died suddenly and sadly young. The quickie was performed by Chris Munds and Hilary Pritchard. We watched it that Saturday night. I was thrilled. That's more information than you wanted isn't it?

Each of your three Doctor Who *stories, 'The Face of Evil', 'Robots of Death' and 'Image of the Fendahl' has fairly overt references to God and other deities, with Xoanon, Taren Capel and the Fendahl respectively. Indeed the working title for 'The Face of Evil' was 'The Day God Went Mad'. This influence contrasts sharply with your, more secular, scripts for* Blake's 7. *Why the change and did this reflect any evolution of your own beliefs?*
I was an instinctive atheist before the full logic of evolution struck me, and that happened in my late twenties. Until then, though Godless, I was still wedded to the idea that our species was on some inevitable progression onwards and upwards to some higher destiny. And then I realised that our development was logical but it wasn't inevitable; that it was a progression but it wasn't upwards, and that there was no higher destiny as such.

Would you consider yourself a fan of science fiction in general and the work of the late Frank Herbert in particular?
Frank Herbert, Philip Dick, Harry Harrison, Walter Miller Jnr, Brian Aldiss, Robert Heinlein, Asimov, Clarke, Pohl – the list is long and full of wondrous cleverness. Back when I started reading

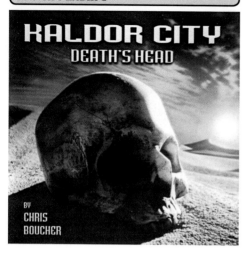

KALDOR CITY
DEATH'S HEAD

BY
CHRIS
BOUCHER

the stuff, which was back when I started reading, short stories were the dominant form. *Amazing, Astounding, New Worlds* were not just the names of magazines, they were accurate descriptions of what was inside them.

Destination: Void (Herbert, 1965) which introduced the concept of generational starships and the effect that extended periods of spaceflight has on a crew and their decedents would seem to be a direct influence on 'The Face of Evil'. Was this the case, and, if so what was it about this novel that inspired you to adapt some of the concepts for Doctor Who?

I've given up trying to remember where I got ideas from. You know what they say: one source is plagiarism, two and it's research. Having said that though I think Harry Harrison's *Captive Universe* was probably in there somewhere too. Most of us never have an original idea of any kind about anything (despite secretly believing we are unique). In fact there can be no such thing as a completely original idea – or rather it would be unrecognisable as an idea since, by definition, it would relate to nothing else that was known. So anyway providing you don't simply copy an idea, what matters is what you do with it, rather than where you got it from. Well that's my story and I'm sticking to it.

'Robots of Death' shares similar themes (such as desert planet, aristocratic/noble houses and a valuable spice/mineral) with Herbert's Dune *(1965) a novel widely regarded as perhaps the greatest science fiction novel of all time. Like its counterpart, 'Robots of Death' is considered one of the greatest* Doctor Who *stories of all time. Why do you think this is?*

I stole from a good source obviously. *Dune* is a great novel which has been very badly adapted for film and TV. I could have done it so much better. (Oh yes I could and since no-one's ever going to pay me to try, I'll say it again: I would have made a much better job of it!) As to 'Robots of Death': it had a good writer, a good script editor, a good director, a good producer, it had Tom Baker and Louise Jameson – what's not to like? It was the first onto DVD too – there's lucky. And just to show you how well I understand such things – I told the guys who were producing the disc that it was probably a bit pointless because DVDs would always be an expensive niche market.

How did you become the script editor of Blake's 7?

David Maloney offered the job to Bob Holmes originally but Bob didn't want to work with Terry Nation again, so he suggested me.

In June 1977 the BBC issued a five page press release to announce Blake's 7 and to act as an incentive to merchandisers to purchase licences. After fully describing the series, the release described the flexibility of the format and the 'specially designed equipment' that would be an essential part of the show. It concluded, 'in short, there is no limit to the product range that can be genuinely attributed to Blake's 7'. Were you aware of this drive towards merchandising? And did merchandise potential influence the scripts in any way?

No I wasn't; and no it didn't. My god did they really say that? And there was me thinking tasteless chancers had only recently got a toehold at the Beeb. Some people just don't pay attention do they?

Early drafts of some scripts are widely available such as the initial draft of 'The Way Back' then entitled 'Cygnus Alpha'. The changes from initial script to screen clearly seem intended to produce a more cost effective series such as the reduction in the principal cast. How agreeable was Terry to these changes and was there any difficulty within the BBC of having Blake convicted (wrongly) of kidnap and child molestation?

Terry was a very agreeable man, seriously charming and a talented self-promoter (with a very tough agent). Like all good freelancers he had to have an eye to the money. And the money comes from screen time. Extended screen time comes from being viable and watchable and, in my view, listenable (if the dialogue stinks so does the show).

David Maloney was a terrific producer and I was a good script editor. Terry was lucky to have us. As it goes I think we may well have hurt his feelings quite badly and I am genuinely sorry for that. However he made a lot more money than me and he took all the credit anyway. So not too sorry... The specific answers are: he had no real choice; and no there was no problem with the BBC.

You became the first person to write scripts for Blake's 7 after Terry Nation with your scripts for 'Shadow' and 'Weapon' and they seem to introduce a change in tone for the series. Travis is now more intense, with his previous discipline and servitude to the Federation weakened, and Blake displays a willingness to cooperate with criminal cartels and drug traffickers. What was the rationale for these changes?

I prefer my heroes and villains a little more nuanced. Heroes can be villainous at times and villains have heroic moments. It's all a bit predictable and dull otherwise, not to mention patronising. Was it Barnum who said nobody lost money underestimating the intelligence of the general public? Somebody said something along those lines anyway. Well I had the feeling that we'd all grown up a bit since then and you underestimated people at your peril. Mind you I thought religion was a thing of the past too...

The tonal shift was developed further in your next script, 'Trial'. Travis is now standing trial for the murder of 1,417 unarmed civilians on the planet Serkasta three years previously. His defence that he reacted instinctively and that his instincts were a product of his training echo some of the real life defences to the My Lai Massacre (16 March 1968) and Bloody Sunday (30 January

1972). How did the Vietnam conflict and the Northern Ireland 'troubles' influence the continued development of the series?
Only in so far as they were in the general background and affected mood and understanding. There's a poncy word for that isn't there? Zeitgeist? Can't remember how you spell it and my spell-checker doesn't seem to give a damn. I'm afraid I'm too old and weak to lift down a real dictionary. All right: I'm lazy.

'Trial' also sees a humanisation of the Federation as we are again introduced to Rontane and Bercol (from 'Seek-Locate-Destroy') and two troopers, Lye and Par who are seen, without helmets, going about their duties. Was this a deliberate attempt on your part to 'blur the lines' by showing another side of the Federation?
Not consciously. It was just story-telling.

In 'Star One', it is made clear that the destruction of the Federation's control complex will result in many, many deaths and Cally, the only other member of the resistance, raises grave reservations as to whether they can do such a thing. Blake attempts to justify his actions by telling her that it is the only way to prove that 'he was right'. This apparently fanatical behaviour had been seen in 1984 with both Winston and Julia agreeing to commit major acts of sabotage to destroy the Party. What were your thought processes here?
It was a passing thought. In my mind the emphasis should have been on the word 'right' not on the word 'I'. It was intended to be a dark moment of doubt for him rather than the rant of a fanatic. The winners are always right and they write the history. For what it's worth, which is very little, I feel that the end never justifies the means – because there are no ends, only means. Or to put it another way: the shit keeps on coming.

In 'The City at the Edge of the World', Keezarn seems to have reached a peak and collapsed with no mention of external influences, war or other catastrophe. Do you hold the view that civilisations will rise and fall as opposed to eventually progressing to a higher state of being?

I'd say the evidence so far is fairly compelling.

You again show the human face of the Federation in 'Rumours of Death' in the doomed and particularly well-drawn characters of Section-Leader Forres and Major Grenlee. By showing the audience that these men are 'real' not just faceless, nameless, unfeeling guards their deaths had more significance

than is customary in the series. Was this an attempt to show the very human suffering which is intertwined with any conflict?
It's possible but again I think it was probably just story-telling.

What is it about 'Death-Watch' that makes it your favourite Blake's 7 script?
It was the nearest I ever got to writing a western.

A quarter of a decade after you wrote 'Death-Watch' reality television has reached much greater levels of saturation and intensity. The voyeuristic nature of reality television is highlighted by the ability of, and the enjoyment derived by, the inhabitants of the confederacies of Teal and Vandor to mentally link with the combatants prior to and during each duel. What is your view on contemporary media in general and reality television in particular?
Reality TV is for the most part boring, unimaginative and unstimulating (unless you count embarrassment as stimulation) and some of it is plain nasty. There's a lot of airtime to fill these days and the stuff is cheap I suppose (in every sense of the word). The problem is that cheap crap doesn't just fill in the vast empty spaces round the occasionally decent stuff, it actually overwhelms every other possibility. I'm basically very lazy and I don't think I'm uncommon in that respect. Why bother with hard if you can have it easy? Cheap crap takes less effort, is less risky and in the short run is more profitable. In the long run of course audiences decline. The accepted wisdom is that it's because of new media and shorter attention spans and the need for audience involvement. No it's not. It's because of dull crap, and advertising which is even duller crap.

'Rescue', required a change in direction for the show following the events of 'Terminal' and the basic plot of the crew's apparent rescue by Dorian comes not from a science fiction source, but instead from Oscar Wilde's gothic horror novel The Picture of Dorian Gray. Do you have any particular interest in the works of Oscar Wilde or the gothic horror genre?
Not really. But if you are going to steal it's better to steal stuff that's out of copyright.

Amendments to the script were needed to accommodate the introduction of the new character of Soolin. Did an early draft of the script include Cally, as the original script for 'The Way Back' featured Arco?
Indeed it did. I'd written a script with her in it. Jan Chappell decided at the last minute she did not want to sign a new contract. That is one of the reasons you have a writer script editor rather than trainee producer script editor.

Blake's 7 whose final episode was first transmitted nearly 30 years ago is, to date, the last mainstream, primetime, ongoing political orientated British science fiction series. Its bleak depiction of the future, reinforced by the final episode, could make for uncomfortable viewing. Why, in your view, has no such other mainstream series been produced in the intervening years?
I blame cheap foreign imports. Where's the quota system when you need it? Actually I don't

know the answer to your question. It could be something to do with the personalities of the channel controllers and the commissioning editors. It could be that science fiction does not draw people who network well. Personally I have never been able to network at all. Indeed I find it difficult to talk to anyone I'm not actually related to. Terry was good at networking I think.

You wrote four books for the BBC's Past Doctors range of Doctor Who *novels:* Last Man Running, Corpse Marker, Psi-ence Fiction *and* Match of the Day, *all of which feature the fourth Doctor and Leela. Were you ever interested in writing for any other Doctor / Companion couplings?*
I would have been interested if writing for another pairing ('coupling' seems a rather loaded word given the recent trend for a more romantic link between Doctor and Companion) had it been an option. It wasn't; so I was happy to stay in the company of the characters with whom I was familiar. I have never seen the point of making life more difficult than it needs to be.

How different was it writing a novel as opposed to the television or radio script, and did you find the process more 'natural' over the course of the four books?
I am by trade (and by happenstance) a scriptwriter. I love doing it and I have always found it oddly easy to do. I'm not suggesting I have always done it well, but given the chance I have always done it easily. By 'given the chance' incidentally I mean someone has to pay me, otherwise not only can I not do it easily, I can't do it at all. Sad but there you go – we all have our quirks.

There were two reasons why I wanted to write the books – well book initially. First, I wanted to see if I could do it (and the jury's still out on that one). Yes I do realise there's a logical inconsistency here given my preference for not making life more difficult. Bear with me however because the second reason was that it was the only paid work I could find. And I needed paid work. And I kept on needing paid work hence more than one book. Over the course of four books it got slightly less daunting but I'm not sure it got more natural. If asked I would still say I am an unemployed scriptwriter (or, more probably, a retired scriptwriter) rather than an unemployed book writer.

Corpse Marker *is a direct sequel to your highly regarded* Doctor Who *story, 'Robots of Death'. Whose idea was it to write a sequel?*
Steve Cole, a fine young man of taste and discernment, blessings and peace be upon him, gave me the work and I think it was his idea that I should write a sequel. He never said as much but it could well have been that he was looking for a subject that I might make a better fist of than I had managed with the first book.

Your BBC Doctor Who *book* Corpse Marker *is actually a* Doctor Who / Blake's 7 *crossover, as it features Carnell. Whose idea was it to bring Carnell into the* Doctor Who *universe?*

Again, the editor Steve Cole, blessings be upon him, suggested the subject. If you like the crossover it was my idea: if you don't it was his. Actually I think it might have been his …

The character of Carnell is very much in the background in Corpse Marker. *Was that a deliberate decision?*
I think it may well have been. Crossovers like that are awkward. Unless you've got a good reason for them like a merchandising subtext – Terry fancied putting the Daleks into *Blake's 7* I remember – I don't think crossovers are a really good idea. My good reason was probably desperation...

Did you have a clear vision from the outset where the surviving characters from 'Robots of Death' would be twenty years later and how the events in that serial had affected them?
I honestly can't remember but I doubt it somehow. I have to tell myself these stories and I get bored if I know from the outset exactly what's going to happen and why. I expect I had to come up with an acceptable outline to get the commission but it was usually not until I settled down to write something that I could finally see what I was getting at. (First Rule of Outlines: The more effort you put into an outline the duller the end product. Second Rule of Outlines: A good outline almost never results in a good end product. Third Rule of Outlines: A strong outline is usually the sign of a weak writer). I do remember that as I worked I had to find explanations for some of the design embellishments that had been in the original serial. I do actually enjoy looking for ways to make existing characters and plot work in situations like that though. It's probably my god/script editor complex coming out. Give me the limitations and the rules (and the money) and I'll happily play for hours.

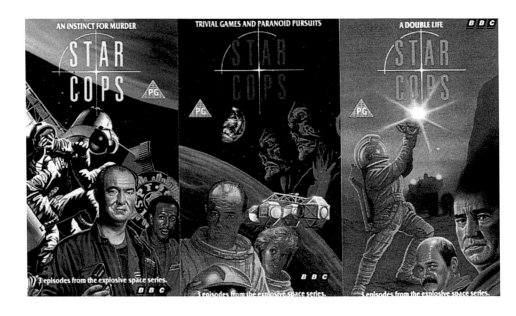

The first audio in the Kaldor City *audio series,* Occam's Razor, *was written by Alan Stevens and Jim Moore. Did you have discussions with them beforehand as to the direction the audio series should take?*
No. It was entirely their project.

You wrote the second Kaldor City *audio,* Death's Head. *What tempted you to write for these characters again and was there a particular story you wanted to tell?*
Alan, who is a friend, invited me to contribute a script (and offered me money). As I recall there was nothing I particularly wanted to get off my chest but as I said: give me the limitations and the rules and the money. And I do love radio.

Many of your works, including your Kaldor City *audio* Death's Head, *focus on the hidden manipulation of people. Would you say this is a conscious theme of your work, and what are your views on it?*
I think it was probably the cold war period I grew up in. Then there was the Kennedy assassination. Conspiracy theories are not the creation of the internet generation you realise. I suppose people are victims of systems and systems are occasionally created but mostly they just grow. It is a conceit of the story-teller to suggest that we can ever know how we are manipulated and to what purpose.

Could you foresee yourself writing for Carnell or any of the other Kaldor City *characters at some point?*

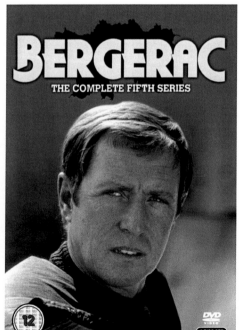

Anything is possible. Well not anything obviously. I suspect I'm a more likely candidate for the Terry Pratchett Memorial Abattoir for the Terminally Confused than I am for the England football squad. (Just to be clear by the way – that sounds as though I might not agree with him about the right to die when in fact I do. But I've never let good taste or reason get in the way of a smart-ass comment and I see no reason to start now).

You went on to script edit three crime dramas following Blake's 7; Shoestring, Juliet Bravo *and* Bergerac. *Was it a deliberate decision to move into crime drama on your part and do you have a favourite of these three?*
My favourite was *Bergerac*, for which I also wrote two scripts ('Fires in the Fall' –

the first feature length episode broadcast on Boxing Day 1986 and 'Memory Man', the first episode of season 5). And the residuals were better. My only deliberate decision was to keep working. Family to feed; bills to pay.

You devised Star Cops, *a hybrid science fiction and crime drama. Did this naturally follow your experience of writing both types of scripts?*
Yes. And it went against what I knew which is that hybrids are almost never successful. Let me rephrase that: hybrids are never successful.

You have stated in the past that Star Cops *was originally devised for radio. Was that concept much different from the television version?*
Not really. After all television is just radio with poorer pictures and less reliable dialogue.
There was talk a few years back that Big Finish would be doing a series of Star Cops *audio plays. What happened to the project?*
Nobody mentioned it to me. I would have loved to have done it. Still would…

Have you seen any of the new series of Doctor Who *and what is your opinion of it?*
It's a huge success and you can't knock that. I prefer longer plots which meant the two-parters were more to my taste. I like the scary stuff better. I found myself envying the CGI. Circumstances meant I didn't see all of them. I'll hold my hands up and say I was slightly discomfited by the Doctor's romantic leanings towards Rose and I could have done with less of her family and other families generally.

Have you seen any of the new Battlestar Galactica *series, which has been favourably compared to* Blake's 7? *If so, what do you think of it, and do you see the resemblance yourself?*
I loved it. I watched it on DVD. I was unhappy to realise I was putting even a small amount of money into Rupert Murdoch's coffers however. No I don't see any real resemblance. If you look hard enough you can see patterns and resemblances everywhere. You have to be careful because that way lays madness and death.

Do you have any final thoughts on Blake's 7?
At its worst it was awful; at its best it was as good as almost anything around. And from worst to best I loved every bloody minute of it. `

Trevor Hoyle Interview, April 2010

Trevor Hoyle worked as an actor, an advertising copywriter, a lecturer in creative writing and presented the arts and entertainments programme What's On *for Granada TV before becoming a full-time writer, mainly of novels and short stories. He won the* Radio Times *Drama Award with his first play* Gigo. *His published fiction includes* Relatively Constant Copywriter, Rule of Night, The Man Who Travelled On Motorways, Vail *and* Blind Needle. The Last Gasp, *which was a Doubleday Book Club Selection in the US, is now under option in Hollywood. He has written three* Blake's 7 *books and the season 3 episode 'Ultraworld'.*

Being a war baby, when you were growing up the war was very fresh in the minds of those around you. Do you think the closeness of the war and the impact of the Third Reich has had lasting influences on your writing?
No doubt it had an impact because where we're born and how we're brought up has a major effect on the rest of our lives, and hence, if you're a writer, on anything you might later write. Not sure about the 'Third Reich' reference. As a kid growing up in Lancashire just after the war we played war games of course, and the Germans and the Japanese were the baddies – naturally.

Almost impossible to know what direct impact or influence it had on my work. Maybe for others to judge.

At what point growing up did your family obtain a television? What was it like, as a child or young adult at the time, to suddenly have access to this new medium?
I was about 12 or 13 when we first had a telly – I can tell you now it was a Pye, 17" or so. Some of our neighbours had TVs before us and it was magical to go into their homes and watch films and quiz shows – in fact you'd watch anything, even the intermission with a kitten playing with a ball of wool or a man ploughing a field for 5 minutes because the whole thing was just so wonderful. My main lasting memory of early TV though is of watching *The Quatermass Experiment* on my auntie's TV which frightened the living daylights out of me (out of everyone – it was a massive TV 'event' – maybe the first ever in Britain.) And I have a vivid memory of watching Peter Cushing as Winston Smith in the live version of *1984*. I ran home at top speed through the darkened streets thinking Big Brother was after me.

Can you tell us a little bit about the first piece of writing you sold?
I had several stories in the local paper (*Rochdale Observer*) when I was about 13 but don't think they paid me anything. These were about a character called Tubby, inspired by the *Just William* stories, of which I was a huge fan – still am. My first proper paid work must have been several novels I did for NEL in the early seventies, just before I published *Rule of Night* about football and skinheads. It's really difficult to remember the actual first piece of paid

writing because I'd been a copywriter for 10 years and so was earning my living that way.

Prior to your first novel you had written several short stories. Was it always your desire to become a full time writer, or did the success of your short stories alter any other pre conceived notions you might have had?
I always wanted to write full-length novels and wrote three or four (one of them 900 MS pages long about the acting profession) which were rejected over several years before one was accepted. I'd been writing in my spare time since I was about nine years old (I even designed the jacket and title page) but for years it never occurred to me that I could make a living at it. Coming from my background, and not going to university, it simply wasn't an option – I didn't know anyone from my class who did such a thing. It was after I became a copywriter in a Manchester agency that it crept over me that people made careers as writers, and from them on I got the message – but I had been writing full-length work since I was about 16 – my first novel was called *Mark of the Beast* – but I did it simply because I was driven to it and had no choice.

Your first novel, Relatively Constant Copywriter *(1972) was turned down by eighteen publishers before you eventually published it under your own imprint. Why do you think it had suffered such a tortuous path towards publication?*
Copywriter was actually written in 1967 but not published until 1972. Even though I think it's okay for a 'first' novel (I'd written the ones I mention above before it) it was very experimental and I think publishers were very conservative in those days (they still are actually). I'm fond of it because in *Copywriter* I discovered my own voice for the very first time – the previous ones had imitated the styles of others writers but here I felt that no one else in the entire world could have written this particular book (whether it was good or bad) except me, and the first important step for any writer is to discover and recognise their own distinctive voice. Some writers never find it and go on writing copies and pastiches of other people's work.

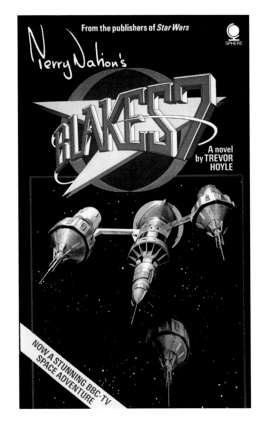

I should mention a couple of thing about *Copywriter*. First off, it picked up some excellent reviews in the *Sunday Times, Guardian, Penthouse* and other media. After it came out (published under my own imprint as you say) a publisher I'd submitted it to who'd rejected it rang me and said he'd been seriously thinking of doing it and would have taken it on if I hadn't done it myself – which was a fat lot of good then, wasn't it?

When did you switch to writing full time and was it a difficult transition?
I moved to Mallorca in 1969 and worked on a spy novel which wasn't published for another 5 or 6 years (*The Sexless Spy*). I was able to do this because I sold my share in an advertising creative group and this was enough cash to last about a year, but after that the money ran out. Then I did a stint with Granada TV, writing and presenting a weekly arts show, which kept me going while I wrote *Rule of Night*. The money on the early novels was not fantastic but was just enough to live on (I was married with two kids at the time) and the Granada money helped of course.

In the second novel of your Q series trilogy, Through the Eye of Time, *a group of scientists attempt to duplicate a human brain and chose to duplicate Adolf Hitler's. Of all of historical characters available to you, why did you select him?*
Don't think there was a specific reason (this was over 30 years ago remember) except that Hitler was and is a fascinating historical character with obvious dramatic potential. There was no

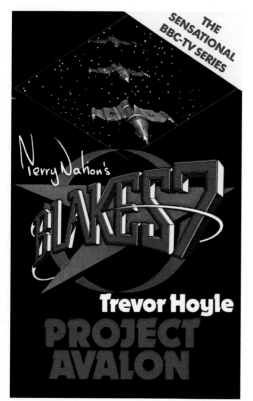

political or ulterior motive to the choice; it was simply what would make a good story.

How did your involvement with Blake's 7 *come about?*
My fiction editor, Nick Austin, who commissioned me to write the Q series, asked me if I'd like to do a novelisation of a new BBC science fiction series created by Terry Nation. Nick was editor at Sphere Books at the time, and as the money was good I said yes.

Your first Blake's 7 *novel was a novelisation of the first four episodes of the show. At the time you came to write it, were these episodes 'in the can' so that you could watch them, or were you reliant on the scripts for reference?*
After I'd agreed to do the book, Terry Nation rang me to discuss the early episodes which he was still writing (he'd finished the first two as I recall) and as I'd by then published

several SF novels he asked for some advice on the scientific/technical background to the show which he wasn't confident about. In particular he didn't know what type of spaceship and propulsion unit Blake and his crew should have. I suggested a couple of things and we discussed ion-drives and plasma thrusters and so on, but in the end I said it was probably better either not to specify the hardware at all or to keep it fairly vague, which is what he did.

In the novels most of the 'scientific' jargon in exposition (not dialogue) is my invention because that wasn't Terry's strong suit, which he freely admitted. In fact he made one or two howlers which I had to correct – in one episode when someone is ejected into space he had them screaming, until I pointed out that space is a vacuum and sound waves don't travel.

Terry fed the scripts through to me in first draft so I could get on with the book, but they'd only just started casting it (I think Gareth Thomas had been cast but none of the others) and so it made describing the characters difficult because no one knew which actors would play them. I had to add descriptive touches later on as I was sent photographs of the cast. Television production often works right up to the week (or even the day) before transmission whereas publishing schedules work months in advance. This was in the days before computers so the final edited manuscript had to be delivered to the publisher before the episodes were recorded so the book could be printed, bound, etc and distributed. As you may know, changes are made in the studio on the day of recording by which time the actual book is sitting in a warehouse somewhere.

The first episode of Blake's 7, 'The Way Back', underwent considerable changes in the scripting process. Did this affect you and your novel in any way?
That all depends on whether the changes were made before or after the publishing deadline. If they were made afterwards it was too late to change anything because the book was with the printer.

Were you aware that the book was sold in secondary schools pupils as part of the regular monthly book club purchases and became the 'book of the month' in many of them?
No. This is news to me.

The novel was sufficiently popular that it led to an immediate follow up title Project Avalon *which novelised five more scripts 'Seek-Locate-Destroy', 'Duel', 'Project Avalon', 'Deliverance' (in a heavily truncated form) and 'Orac'. Why did you decide to significantly excise much of the script of 'Deliverance'?*

I can't remember doing so. If it happened it was for one of two reasons. Either the script was heavily altered after the publishing deadline (see above) or the publisher decided to make the book shorter due to cost factors (publishers are wont to do this on occasion) but I personally wouldn't have made cuts to the original script – I never deviated by a single word from any script I was working on.

How did you come to write the third season script 'Ultraworld?'
I'd worked with script editor Chris Boucher on some aspects of the novels and he asked me to contribute to the series.

Were you aware that the opening episode of season two 'Redemption' had a similar premise?
No idea. If it had been that similar I think Chris would have pointed it out.

The production of your script seemed to have been afforded a higher effects budget than was customary. Can you shed any light on this?
Not sure the budget was any different actually. I did ask for a dozen or so 'Ultra' aliens but they could afford only three. Small planet, Ultraworld.

Were you happy with how your script translated from script to screen?
Within the confines and restrictions of television, yes. You have to make huge compromises between the writer's vision and what appears on screen. I know they decided to dumb down the various riddles that Vila is feeding Orac to make them suitable to a popular audience – they were taken from a child's joke book I believe.

Were you aware that on its first showing in the US, the death throes of the Brain were deemed to be too gruesome and they were cut prior to transmission?
No, really! Doesn't surprise me though. American mainstream TV is a joke.

The first book was published by Sphere Books, Project Avalon *by Arrow and* Scorpio Attack *by BBC Books. Why the changes in publisher?*
Presumably Sphere didn't pick up the option or Arrow made a better offer – outside my influence or expertise. BBC Books contacted me to write *Scorpio Attack* a few years later and I wasn't party to the publishing decisions that led to the gap. I was always asked to write the *Blake's 7* novelisations; I novelised the scripts I was asked to, I had no say in what was selected. Writers aren't in the loop on these matters. Publishing executives work in their own mysterious way.

In 1983 you wrote The Last Gasp *and seven years later a revised edition was published in the*

UK. Can you tell us the basic premise of the book?
The Last Gasp was published both in the US and the UK in 1983 and a revised version in the UK in 1990. Nick Austin, who had commissioned the book originally, thought it deserved to be re-published in 1990 and asked me to update it, which I did. The idea behind the book was that due to man-made pollution of the oceans and forests the oxygen in the air would become depleted, leading to catastrophic results for humankind. I spent 3 years researching and writing the novel, which was hailed as a 'landmark' in eco fiction by the *Washington Post* – but in early eighties America the media weren't interested in stories about the environment and global warming etc. I know this to be a fact because I went to the States to publicise it and didn't get a single TV or radio interview in three weeks from New York to Los Angeles. (Incidentally Terry Nation was living in LA at the time and asked me to send him a copy of *The Last Gasp* which of course I was pleased to do.)

The Last Gasp *is currently under option by a Hollywood Production Company. What can you tell us about this?*
The novel has been optioned three times by Hollywood production companies and I've been told that filming could begin later this year – though I won't hold my breath waiting for it to begin. Movies are like that.

Your next novel was the critically acclaimed black comedy Vail *set in a futuristic Britain. In the cold war atmosphere that prevailed in Thatcherite Britain at the time, future scenarios tended not to be upbeat, but in many ways yours was particularly doom laden. Was your novel a reaction to the political climate at the time?*
Absolutely. I hated Thatcher and everything she stood for. I think she destroyed the soul and spirit of this country and I will never forgive her for it. Yes the book was doom laden, as you say, but many readers found it wonderfully funny too – black humour taken to the extreme. I like *Vail* very much (and I am very critical of other novels I've written) and it comes as near as dammit to the novel I had in mind when I planned it, which is not often the case.

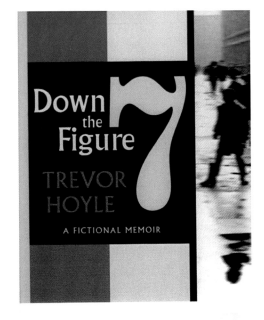

In 2003, your reissued your 1975 classic Rule of Night *which centres on a 16 year old violent hooligan, Kenny, who despite his acts of violence, sexism, racism and*

callousness you still care about what happens to him as you discover the person within. What drove you to write the story and then republish it when you did?
I've written about this myself; have a read of *Return of the Skinhead*.

Of your many radio plays, Gigo, *a comedy drama where the hero becomes increasing 'obsessed' with acausal connections in life, won the* Radio Times *drama award for best play. How did such an original concept for the play come to you?*
To be honest I haven't a clue. It must have stemmed from my fascination with quantum mechanics, which I've studied in a lay fashion for over 30 years – in fact the Q trilogy in the seventies was inspired by this too. The fact about GIGO (stands for Garbage In Garbage Out, by the way) is that radio is the perfect medium to present such ideas in a dramatic fashion – you can suggest so much that excites the visual imagination on radio which wouldn't work at all on TV or film. I don't think the cast (which included the excellent Alun Armstrong) had a clue what it was about, but that didn't matter, they didn't need to.

You have recently published a fictional memoir Down the Figure 7. *What is the book about and what inspired you to write it?*
It's set just after the Second World War in Rochdale, a hard-luck cotton town struggling to emerge from wartime rationing and the aftermath of loss and separation that many families experienced. The story is told through the eyes of 11-year old Terry Webb, who hero worships his Uncle Jack, who though still a young man is traumatised after serving with Monty's Desert Rats in North Africa.

I was principally inspired to write it because I felt then (and still do) that books dealing with childhood never told the whole truth – they always give us a sanitised version of growing up. In particular I'd never read a novel dealing with sexuality in quite young kids – 9, 10, 11 year olds. We're all from a very early age intensely curious about ourselves and the opposite sex – it's quite normal and healthy and perfectly natural, yet it's never dealt with or even mentioned in fiction about childhood. That's what I set out to do in *Down the Figure 7*.

What can you tell us about what you writing right now?
I have a contribution in a new Best SF Films anthology, *Cinema Futura*, where Sci-Fi and Fantasy writers were invited to write about their favourite SF movies – I have written the entry on *Solaris* (the Andrei Tarkovsky 1972 version).

I have a novel I'm working on about a neo-fascist takeover of Britain in the not-too-distant future (*Kingdom of Darkness*) using the internet as Goebbels used the press. This has been causing me all sorts of problems and I should buckle down to it and write the damn thing before the reality comes to pass, which it will do all too quickly.

There are other ideas floating around – a film screenplay about a girl stalking a French movie star, and there's a collection of short stories I'd like to publish. And there's a trilogy of novels set in the fifties (*The Rock n' Roll Diaries*) which is my era.

CURRENT MERCHANDISERS

Michael Stevens Interview, Commissioning Editor, BBC Audiobooks, May 2010

How long have you been working for BBC Audiobooks?
I've been with the company for ten years. When I joined it was BBC Radio Collection, based in London. We became BBC Audiobooks, in Bath, in 2003.

BBC Audiobooks has a healthy line of science fiction products, from Doctor Who *to your Classic Radio Sci-Fi strand. Is there a healthy appetite from your customers for science fiction related product?*
Yes – *Doctor Who* and *The Hitchhiker's Guide to the Galaxy* are two of our most successful ranges, and we find that there's an appetite for science fiction generally.

BBC Audiobooks released in January 1998 the full cast Blake's 7 *radio play* The Sevenfold Crown. *Did the healthy sales of this tape contribute to the commissioning of the follow-up adventure?*
I'm afraid this was before my time, so I'm not sure which way round it worked. Normally the commercial potential of a title doesn't influence commissioning decisions within the broadcasting departments.

The following Blake's 7 *play* The Syndeton Experiment *was released in April 1999. Both radio plays were re-released on CD in 1994 as 'The Radio Adventures' in packaging similar to the DVD releases. How did this come about?*
We wanted to make both stories available together, along with some bonus material which originated with BBC7. I was aware of the DVD range beginning, and thought it would be a good idea to tie in to that artwork. Our colleagues at 2entertain kindly supplied their templates, and we adapted them with our own photographs and copy.

Whose idea was it to commence the highly successful talking book range of Doctor Who Target *novelisations?*
That was my idea. I grew up being an avid reader and collector of the books, and knew what they represented to fans of my age. The idea of having them read by some of the actors we all love from the TV series was immensely appealing, and I felt sure there was a market for such a range. Happily, that has been the case.

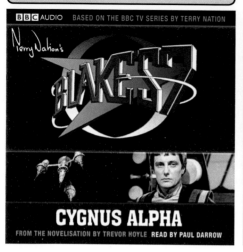

Did the idea for the Blake's 7 *talking books spring directly from there?*

Yes. I was also aware of the *Blake's 7* novelisations, and for all the same reasons I thought it would be great to make audio versions.

Was the length of Trevor Hoyle's initial book Blake's 7 *the sole reason for it being split over two distinct audio books;* The Way Back *and* Cygnus Alpha?

Yes, that's right. We always have to keep an eye on logistics, and the need to keep the price as low as possible but also have a viable project. Splitting the book into two affordable units seemed like a good idea, and actually the two halves operate very well on their own.

As both talking books derive from the same novel, what was the reasoning behind having Gareth Thomas narrate the first and Paul Darrow the second?

Simply to enjoy some variation between the two. They were both voices I knew would be good for the range, and so rather than have to choose one or the other, we went for both!

What was the critical and public response to The Way Back *and* Cygnus Alpha?

The critical response has been very good. I've heard nothing but good feedback about the readers, and about the music and sound effects which, as on the *Doctor Who* range, enhance the readings a great deal.

*With two more novels by Trevor Hoyle (*Project Avalon *and* Scorpio Attack*) available for adaptation there seems to be scope for this range to continue.*

Sales of the first two titles have been lower than we had hoped for, and indeed lower than on the *Doctor Who* range. But never-say-never – I'd love to be able to do more, one day.

Wakefield Carter Interview, Termight Replicas, October 2010

Did you read comics as a child and if so, were 2000AD *and* The Eagle, *particular favourites?*
I started reading comics in the mid '70s, choosing whatever looked interesting or had an appealing free gift. The first comic I remember reading regularly was *Warlord*, as were a lot of my school friends. However, in 1977 a friend of mine was getting picked on by other members of the '*Warlord* gang' and after his mother 'phoned round I was banned from reading it for a year. I was allowed to choose a replacement, and I picked *2000AD* which I knew had started not long before. My first issue was Prog 16, dated 16 June, 1977. A year later I was asked if I wanted to go back to *Warlord* but there was no contest. *2000AD* was far superior and apart from a brief gap as a young adult I've been reading it regularly ever since.

My interest in 'Dan Dare' predated *2000AD*. My family used to spend Christmas and Easter at my grandmother's house. There, she had a trunk of the first 12 volumes of *Eagle* comics belonging to my father and uncle. I remember that to start with I used to read them cover to cover but after the first volume or so I stuck to just reading 'Dan Dare'. Reading the 1950s version just before the *2000AD* version meant that I ended up actually liking both. When the *Eagle* relaunched in 1982 I started buying it, but soon gave up again. I was only reading it for 'Dan Dare', and those early 'Dan Dare' stories weren't good enough to justify a whole comic. *2000AD* was where the thrills were.

Do you have an interest in science fiction in general?
Absolutely. I have been a science fiction fan for as long as I can remember. At the age of 7, I was excited about the Viking Mars landers in 1975. *Star Wars* had a huge impact on my imagination in 1977 of course, along with *2000AD* itself. I think I started watching *Doctor Who* (with Jon Pertwee) as early as 1972.
My early TV favourites were mostly sci-fi: *Thunderbirds, Space: 1999, Logan's Run, Star Trek* (including the animated series), *Survivors* and *The Tomorrow People*. Saturday morning used to be *Buck Rogers* or Fl*ash Gordon* in black and white, along with *Tarzan*. I first came across *The Hitchhiker's Guide to the Galaxy* when the second radio series aired in 1980.

What led to the creation of Termight Replicas?
In December, 2003, a *2000AD* fan called Graham posted on the *2000AD* Online message board asking if anyone would be interested in buying a licensed replica Judge Dredd Lawgiver Mk II. He had worked with a Chinese factory on a previous project and thought they would be able to produce a run of solid resin guns which would appeal to fans. At the time I was webmaster for *2000AD* Online and I asked him if he would like me to help with the licensing,

sales and marketing. However, his idea was shelved a few months later. Graham was no longer in a position to invest and wasn't sure his factory would produce the quality he wanted.

Skip forward to 2005. I found a British prop making company and, with Graham's permission, resurrected the idea. While I was in the middle of working on the prototype, Jason Willbourn advertised a scratch-built Strontium Dog Westinghouse blaster on eBay. I contacted him and asked if he could make more, if I could secure a licence. On 1 October 2005 we met up at DreddCon in Oxford discussed the Westinghouse with Jason Kingsley from Rebellion who own the rights to *2000AD*, and also talked about vibrating electonuxes. Now with three products in the pipeline, Termight Replicas was born, and the website launched on 3 October 2005

The prop company I had been working with didn't manage to produce a satisfactory lawgiver, so Jason started working on that item too. Meanwhile I started talking to Charlie Towers and Jon Bayliss, who had been selling unlicensed resin badges and got permission to sell their products through Termight Replicas. My idea here was to give good quality fan made products some respectability, and ensure that Rebellion got licensing money from them as well.

This changed at the end of 2006, when I produced the first gold-plated metal Dredd badge. I used the same badge company as I had for small metal eagles for the lawgivers, and the quality was stunning. After that I started phasing out the fan made products and concentrating on high quality badges and buckles.

What are the origins of the company's name?
Termight is the name for Earth in Nemesis the Warlock, created by Pat Mills and Kevin O'Neill. It's a world where the population lives underground and the cities are connected by vast travel tubes. It was also the name of my existing *2000AD* fan page, which had been running since 1998, so was already associated with me.

The beauty of Termight as a name is that a *2000AD* fan will recognise it and as an unusual spelling of a single word is excellent for search engines too.

Termight Replicas is a slight misnomer though, since the name implies replicas of three-dimensional objects, like film props. Since most of my products are comic replicas, and I specifically did not have a licence to produce prop replicas based on the 1995 Stallone film, I produce items in 3D for the first time, based on original 2D artwork.

What were the first products that Termight Replicas released?
Although the lawgiver Mk II was the first item planned, the electronux and then the Westinghouse were the first ones produced. Neither sold very well, which was a shame. I can understand that the electronux seemed very expensive for a fairly simple piece of vibrating plastic, but Jason's Westinghouse looks fantastic, thanks to his painting skills, which is why I still have it listed on my website today.

Did you watch Blake's 7 *upon its original transmission?*
Blake's 7 showing between 1978 and 1981 was perfectly timed for me. Post *Star Wars*, pre secondary school, *Doctor Who* still riding high with Tom Baker at the TARDIS controls. I probably watched almost every episode and loved the fact that the heroes were so fallible, spending much of their time arguing with each other.

What led you to seek a licence to produce a Federation Badge, some thirty years after the show's original television broadcast?
Jason Willbourn's website shows a *Blake's 7* teleport bracelet he once made for himself. I asked him about whether he could produce a run of them, if I could secure the licence, but he told me that the copyright for the teleport bracelets was held by Martin Bower, who occasionally produced runs of replicas himself which he sold through the *Blake's 7* fan club, Horizon. Early in 2010 I contacted Martin, whose website I had already visited many times because of the Dan Dare replica space ships he had once made. He told me that he could produce a run of bracelets but I would need to commission 19, since that was the number he could make from a length of EMA tubing. They weren't going to be cheap, either, and I started looking for *Blake's 7* fans willing to buy a bracelet for £140. I spent about £30 in advertising on Facebook in addition to asking the existing fans of Termight Replicas, but I only managed to find a handful of people ready to buy a bracelet. I cancelled the project, but by then my Termight Replicas Facebook page had nearly 300 extra fans, most of whom I assumed were there because of *Blake's 7*. I wanted to come up with a product that would appeal to them, but also fit their budgets and badges are what I do best. Although *Blake's 7* isn't a comic, I think it does still fit in with Termight Replicas as British science fiction, with a cult following but not so much appeal that it has already attracted the larger merchandising companies.

From whom did you obtain the licence?
I approached Andrew Mark Sewell, Executive Producer at B7 Productions Limited, who put me in touch with their licensing agent at Metrostar Media. I believe that they had to get permission for me to use the Federation logo from BBC Worldwide.

Is Termight Replicas planning a range of Blake's 7 *products if the Federation Badge sells well?*
Unfortunately the badge has not sold in large quantities, but if sales do pick up then my current licence does cover Federation logo key rings, so that would be the obvious choice. I'm not entirely happy about the size and orientation of the black rectangle for use as a key fob, so I will probably need to redesign the background to make it work better.

In addition to your website (www.termight.co.uk) are your products available to buy in any stores?
At the moment, my products are only available on my website, plus they are usually displayed on the FutureQuake small press table at the Bristol and Birmingham comic conventions. I have had some interest from Forbidden Planet in the past, and I am hoping that the Federation badge may help me with selling to retail. I am also now talking to board game stores and distributors.

John Archdeacon Interview, October 2010

John Archdeacon is the proprietor of Titan Find Models (www.titanfind.com) a specialist model making company that has produced highly detailed models of the Liberator, *the* Chase Craft, *a Federation Pursuit Ship and the* Scorpio.

Tell me a little about your background and how you got in model making.
My life in less than 30 words! I was born 1969 in Cork, Ireland where I lived for 26 years, having had a pretty normal childhood. My Dad made RC airplanes and I was always pestering him to let me 'help'. That's probably where the initial interest in models developed. I was always fascinated by Sci-Fi and like many people *Star Wars* was a defining moment in my life. I hunted down every scrap of info on how the effects were done and I was totally hooked. *Blake's 7* and *Space: 1999* were on TV and again I was amazed. I saved every penny I could and bought the Airfix Eagle and the *Star Wars* kits. There was nothing around at that time for *Blake's 7*. And I've been hooked ever since.

Did you make models as a child?
Yes, but mostly all I could get my hands on (and afford) were the cheapest of the Airfix kits, mostly military kits. I do remember initially building them as fast as I could and getting glue everywhere. I gradually took more care as I got older and ended up with reasonable buildups.

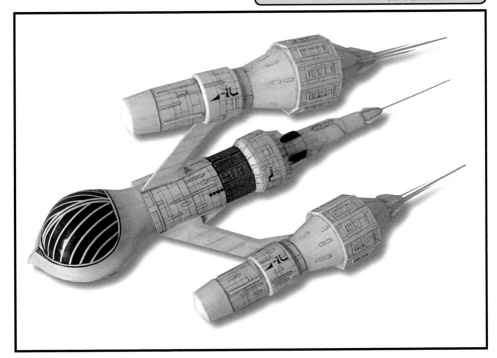

Looking at some of the models you have made in the past (Batman, Aliens, The X Files to name but a few) it seems that you may lean towards science fiction/fantasy models? If so, what draws you to these as opposed to say, boats or planes?
I love the design and the imagination that was poured into the films you mentioned and a lot of others too. *Aliens* was a serious hardware movie and all of it was very believable. The Batwing in the first two *Batman* movies was a masterpiece in design. Compared to those most boats and planes are boring, to me anyway.

Excluding your own, do you have a favourite model in your collection? And if so why?
That's a really hard one. I have a lot of models and I really do mean a lot! I just got Randy Cooper's 3 ft Imperial Star Destroyer. I have not built it yet but it's a beauty. I have a really nice *Nebukenezer* from the *Matrix* done by a really talented guy from Argentina. Really, there are too many to pick out just one.

Are you a science fiction fan in general? If so, what type (TV, fiction, anime, movies)?
Yes, definitely a Sci-Fi fan. I generally like the movies, TV and novels. Not a huge interest in Anime, although there is some really cool stuff there too.

Did you initially watch Blake's 7 *when it was shown? And if so were you a regular viewer?*
I watched *Blake's 7* when it first aired in Ireland in the late '70s and early '80's. I have been a fan since the beginning!

When did you establish Titan Find Models (TFM)?
It was 2006 I think.

Are you the sole creative force behind TFM?
Yes. It's just me, although 'creative force' might be stretching it a bit.

The first model that you produced through TFM was the Liberator. Can you talk us through how this came about?
It was kind of on a whim really if I think about it. I was/am going through a nostalgic phase (read mid-life crisis!) and it just happened to coincide with the release of the *Blake's 7* DVDs. Watching the DVDs kind of piqued my interest. I had built the Comet *Liberator* years before and left it in Ireland. So with the help of my pal eBay I picked up another. It's a really well done model but I was never happy with the size of the Comet kit. I wanted a bigger *Liberator* to do her justice. So I figured why not make it happen. Through the modelling circles I knew people that could help me realise the idea and the rest is history.

Roger Murray-Leach's design of the Liberator is very innovative. Is there something about this particular design that drew you to her?
I simply loved the design. It was simple but different, graceful but exuding power. I was totally hooked and not expecting it at all. The *London* transport is the first ship you see in B7 and its pretty utilitarian and low budget stuff. Then along comes the *Liberator* and blows it away.

Your model is extremely accurate. How did you find all of the necessary detail to design the model?
Thanks, but it's not as accurate as I would like it to be. I should also point out that I did not do the masters for it. An amazing modeller called Alfred Wong did them. He was working from reference I sources and provided to him. We were also working to a budget so some compromises had to be made. The one thing I did not want to compromise on was the ability to light the engine. I would have liked to have photo-etched parts like the Comet kit did, especially for the gold panes around the main body. Anyway it turned out pretty OK and a

good paint job can help with certain issues.

Did you have access to any detailed plans other than schematic that was printed in Space Voyager *magazine?*
I did have the Horizon Technical manual drawings. The *Space Voyager* drawing is not really that close to the studio model. I also scrounged up any reference I could.

Did you have many high quality photographic references of the full scale Liberator *model?*
Unfortunately no. I did have some pictures from some specialty books that were put out by the guys behind the now defunct *Sci-Fi and Fantasy Models* (Mike Reccia and others). Also Martin Bower's site had a few photos.

How long did the project take from inception to your prototype being finalised?
About two weeks, if you can believe that! Alfred Wong works fast!

Can you tell us the size of the completed model
It's about 14 inches and the weapons antennae add another couple of inches.

What is the best way to display the completed model in your opinion?
Really good question and one I have been pondering for several years. When I set out to do the *Liberator* first I neglected to include any kind of base. Fast forward several years and I finally plan to remedy that. I am working with Alfred Wong to develop a suitable base and I intend to make it available as an accessory product. But again it's driven by my desire to have a proper way to display it.

Are you happy with the finalised product?
Yes and no. Mostly yes! It was a great experience being that it was the first kit. It could be better and more accurate but it was a balance between time and money.

What skill level do you think is required to build the Liberator*?*
It's definitely not a kit for a novice. I would say intermediate to skilled. Getting the weapons pods mounted correctly on the main body is tricky.

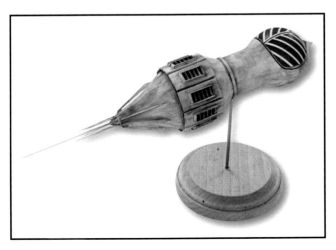

Detailed instructions on how to build the Liberator *are supplied with each kit and are available to download from the Internet. Did you write these?*
Yes, I built a prototype casting first to figure it all out and took pictures as I went. Then I did the instructions. There are many ways to build it but that was how I went about it.

How would that compare to say, building out the Comet version of the Liberator *that was released in 1989?*
They both have their challenges. The Comet one is so small that it's really difficult just to manipulate the pieces. I remember struggling mightily with some of the small photo-etched parts. The TFM *Liberator* is big and that has issues with weight and the danger of the support arms for the weapons pods sagging. We tried to address this by casting a brass rod into the actual support arms.

The initial run of kits sold out very quickly. How could someone obtain a kit now?
The *Liberator* was very popular, especially for a garage kit. I did several runs before I retired it to move onto other kits. I kept getting requests for it so recently ran a survey to see if there was sufficient interest to warrant a reissue. A lot of people want to see the kit made available again but it's all down to economics. There are a minimum number of orders required to make the project viable.

At the start of the second season of Blake's 7, *the* Liberator's *builders were revealed together with their 'Chase Craft'. Was it the design similarities with the* Liberator *that resulted in this craft being the next one that you produced?*
Yes, it was. As you probably guessed it is essentially a weapons pod from the *Liberator*. Having said that there was a lot of work to do to make it as accurate as possible. It really diverges from the *Liberator* pod in many ways. I did the masters for that myself

but it took me somewhat longer than two weeks and gave me a whole new respect for what Alfred Wong does.

Did you modify your Liberator *design or did you start the Chase Craft from scratch?*
I took some *Liberator* weapons pod castings and cut them up. To get the tapering angle correct I used the front part from two pods and stuck them together. The collar for the red engine domes was tricky as it was hand sculpted. It took lots of sanding to get that right. The detail panelling around the pod is different as are the vanes near the nose. It was different enough to be a pain to get it right. But I think it actually turned out well. It did not sell anywhere near as well as the Liberator however!

Is the Chase Craft in scale to your Liberator *model?*
Yes it is or at least as close as I am aware.

If someone had both kits and was of limited model making experience, would you suggest they build out the Chase Craft first?
Yes, definitely it's the easier of the two to build. It will also help with the *Liberator* as the engine design was approached in the same way.

You have also released kits for the Federation Pursuit Ship and for the Scorpio. *Is there a pattern developing here?*
Possibly …

What was the process from inception to creation?
It was pretty much the same as the *Liberator* but with one major difference. By the time I got around to the Pursuit Ship I had been trawling the Internet for reference material. I had also managed to track down some of the people involved with the show. In this case it was Matt Irvine and he just happened to have one of the original Pursuit Ships. The *Scorpio* was a completely different matter as there just is not a lot of reference material out there.

Did you already have a strong library of images, the measurements of the Pursuit Ship, etc. or did you have to collate them?
Matt Irvine graciously provided me with pictures from all angles and I was able to furbish Alfred Wong with those. About three weeks later I had the masters for the Pursuit Ship done! I did also have the Horizon Technical Manuals to work from as basic plans. But in general reference material for the show is not great and is hard to come by.

While a kit had previously been released of the Liberator, *in the thirty years since its television debut, no other craft from Blake's 7 has been released until now. Why do you think that is?*
It is a mystery to me. We have Gerry Anderson material coming from all directions. *Doctor Who* is huge again. Don't get me wrong. I love all those shows too but for some reason *Blake's*

7 got the short end of the merchandising stick. If it was not for the fan base there would be precious little. Being a model nut I always like the ships and it's my desire to have models of the ships that resulted in Titan Find. That these models are also garage kits is secondary but it does help pay for the masters and fund the next project.

Your latest model is the Scorpio. *What can you tell us about this model?*
Ah, the *Scorpio*. I really like the *Scorpio*. I think it's underrated but the *Liberator* is a tough act to follow. It's pretty much the last of what I would call the *Blake's 7* signatures ships. There are a few other marginal ones but the *Scorpio* is major. Until now, it's never been done as a model kit which I thought was a shame. Again I was very lucky to get in contact with very generous people who were willing to share their reference material. And there is precious little for the *Scorpio*. Or at least there wasn't when I started looking. Again I was lucky enough to get in contact and ultimately meet with Ron Thornton who made the original *Scorpio*. Ron had some great pictures of the studio model. He is probably better known for his CG work on *Babylon 5*.
The ironic thing about the *Scorpio* is that in many ways it's the best Titan Find kit that has been produced. That and the fact that it has never been available led me to predict that it would be popular. To my surprise it has not been as popular as I would have hoped. It's a much more complex kit than the *Liberator* and its cost way more to produce resulting in a more expensive kit. That and the economy have probably contributed to the lacklustre sales.

Have you thought about what you might come next from TFM?
I have branched out into a new little project doing *Lost* caricatures. The first two out are Hurley and Sawyer and Locke will follow these. They are fun little kits and not too expensive. Regarding more *Blake's 7*, I am currently working with a colleague on the masters for a new, larger, *Liberator* model. I was also playing with the idea of *Liberator* and *Scorpio* bridge dioramas with Zen and Slave. Those probably will not happen but it's fun to speculate.

Any final thoughts?
I want to thank you for the opportunity to talk about TFM and *Blake's 7*. I hope that maybe we can keep enough interest alive in the show that it could get a reimagining on TV. What if it was done to the same calibre as *Battlestar Galactica* (love that show)? Now wouldn't that be something.

WWW.HOWESTOYBOX.CO.UK

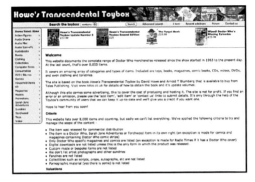

THE NEW ONGOING ONLINE RESOURCE FOR ALL INFORMATION ON THE VAST AND AMAZING UNIVERSE OF DOCTOR WHO MERCHANDISE!

OTHER TOYBOX TITLES FROM TELOS PUBLISHING

HOWE'S TRANSCENDENTAL TOYBOX: SECOND EDITION by DAVID J HOWE & ARNOLD T BLUMBERG

Complete guide to Doctor Who Merchandise 1963–2002.

£25.00 (+ £5.00 UK p&p) Standard p/b ISBN: 1-903889-56-1

EXCLUSIVE TOYBOX COLLECTIBLE!

All orders for Howe's Transcendental Toybox: Second Edition will receive, while stocks last, a free Chromed Gunner Dalek Rolykin. This variant is not available anywhere else and has been produced for Telos in a limited edition of 600 units by Product Enterprise.

HOWE'S TRANSCENDENTAL TOYBOX: UPDATE No 2: 2004-2005 by DAVID J HOWE & ARNOLD T BLUMBERG

Complete guide to Doctor Who Merchandise 2004-2005. Now in full colour.

£12.99 (+ £2.50 UK p&p) Standard p/b ISBN: 1-84583-012-1

HOWE'S TRANSCENDENTAL TOYBOX: UPDATE No 3: 2006-2009 by DAVID J HOWE & ARNOLD T BLUMBERG

Complete guide to Doctor Who Merchandise 2006-2009. Now in full colour. 448 pages.

£25.99 (+ £5.00 UK p&p) Standard p/b ISBN: 978-1-84583-033-5

THE HANDBOOK: THE UNOFFICIAL AND UNAUTHORISED GUIDE TO THE PRODUCTION OF DOCTOR WHO by DAVID J HOWE, STEPHEN JAMES WALKER and MARK STAMMERS
Complete guide to the making of *Doctor Who* (1963 – 1996).
£14.99 (+ £5.00 UK p&p) Standard p/b
ISBN: 1-903889-59-6
£30.00 (+ £5.00 UK p&p) Deluxe signed and numbered h/b ISBN: 1-903889-96-0

BACK TO THE VORTEX: THE UNOFFICIAL AND UNAUTHORISED GUIDE TO DOCTOR WHO 2005 by J SHAUN LYON
Complete guide to the 2005 series of *Doctor Who* starring Christopher Eccleston as the Doctor
£12.99 (+ £3.00 UK p&p) Standard p/b
ISBN: 1-903889-78-2
£30.00 (+ £3.00 UK p&p) Deluxe signed and numbered h/b ISBN: 1-903889-79-0

SECOND FLIGHT: THE UNOFFICIAL AND UNAUTHORISED GUIDE TO DOCTOR WHO 2006 by J SHAUN LYON
Complete guide to the 2006 series of *Doctor Who*, starring David Tennant as the Doctor
£12.99 (+ £3.00 UK p&p) Standard p/b
ISBN: 1-84583-008-3
£30.00 (+ £3.00 UK p&p) Deluxe signed and numbered h/b ISBN: 1-84583-009-1

THIRD DIMENSION: THE UNOFFICIAL AND UNAUTHORISED GUIDE TO DOCTOR WHO 2007 by STEPHEN JAMES WALKER
Complete guide to the 2007 series of *Doctor Who*, starring David Tennant as the Doctor
£12.99 (+ £3.00 UK p&p) Standard p/b
ISBN: 978-1-84583-016-8
£30.00 (+ £3.00 UK p&p) Deluxe signed and numbered h/b ISBN: 978-1-84583-017-5

MONSTERS WITHIN: THE UNOFFICIAL AND UNAUTHORISED GUIDE TO DOCTOR WHO 2008 by STEPHEN JAMES WALKER
Complete guide to the 2008 series of *Doctor Who*, starring David Tennant as the Doctor.
£12.99 (+ £3.00 UK p&p) Standard p/b
ISBN: 978-1-84583-027-4

END OF TEN: THE UNOFFICIAL AND UNAUTHORISED GUIDE TO DOCTOR WHO 2009 by STEPHEN JAMES WALKER
Complete guide to the 2009 specials of *Doctor Who*, starring David Tennant as the Doctor.
£14.99 (+ £3.00 UK p&p) Standard p/b
ISBN: 978-1-84583-035-9
£30.00 (+ £3.00 UK p&p) Signed h/b
ISBN: 978-1-84583-036-6

WHOGRAPHS: THEMED AUTOGRAPH BOOK
80 page autograph book with an SF theme
£4.50 (+ £2.50 UK p&p) Standard p/b
ISBN: 1-84583-110-1

WIPED! DOCTOR WHO'S MISSING EPISODES by RICHARD MOLESWORTH
The story behind the BBC's missing episodes of *Doctor Who.*
£15.99 (+ £3.00 UK p&p) Standard p/b ISBN: 978-1-84583-037-3

TIMELINK: THE UNOFFICIAL AND UNAUTHORISED GUIDE TO THE CONTINUITY OF DOCTOR WHO VOLUME 1 by JON PREDDLE
Discussion and articles about the continuity of *Doctor Who.*
£15.99 (+ £3.00 UK p&p) Standard p/b ISBN: 978-1-84583-004-5

TIMELINK: THE UNOFFICIAL AND UNAUTHORISED GUIDE TO THE CONTINUITY OF DOCTOR WHO VOLUME 2 by JON PREDDLE
Timeline of the continuity of *Doctor Who.*
£15.99 (+ £3.00 UK p&p) Standard p/b ISBN: 978-1-84583-005-2